The Shortage of Skilled and Technical Workers

Studies in the Social Implications of Science and Technology

under the general editorship of **Hugh Folk,** *Professor of Economics and of Labor and Industrial Relations, University of Illinois, Urbana-Champaign.*

There can no longer be any doubt that the uncontrolled proliferation of scientific and technological growth often produces unexpected and undesirable side effects. *Studies in the Social Implications of Science and Technology* will be devoted to investigating some of these effects, including urban growth and transportation systems, central city labor market information systems, scientific and technical manpower and information, population dynamics and control, work and automation, consumer protection, technological displacement of the rural poor, the politics of science and technology, and many other topics.

Other Books in the Series

The Shortage of Scientists and Engineers, by Hugh Folk, University of Illinois.
The Asian Engineering Brain Drain, by John R. Niland, Cornell University.

The Shortage of Skilled and Technical Workers

An Inquiry into Selected Occupations in Short Supply

Walter Franke

Institute of Labor and Industrial Relations
University of Illinois at Urbana-Champaign

Irvin Sobel

Department of Economics
Florida State University

Heath Lexington Books
D. C. Heath and Company
Lexington, Massachusetts

This project was prepared under Contract No. MDTA 5-64 for the Manpower Administration, U. S. Department of Labor, under the authority of the Manpower Development and Training Act. Researchers undertaking such projects under Government sponsorship are encouraged to express their own judgment. Interpretations or viewpoints stated in this document do not necessarily represent the official position or policy of the Department of Labor.

Printed in the United States of America

Library of Congress Number: 76-121395

Table of Contents

	Tables and Figures	xiii
	Foreword by Melvin Rothbaum	xix
	Acknowledgements	xxiii
Part I	**Introduction**	1
1	**Framework and Design of the Study**	3
	The Approach of the Study	3
	Procedures	8
	The Labor Markets	8
	Setting of the Study and the Occupations	9
	The Occupations	9
	Report Plan	11
2	**Occupational Characteristics and Trends**	14
	Licensed Practical Nurses	14
	Training and Licensing	15
	Employment Trends	17
	Wages, Hours, and Working Conditions	21
	The Current Demand and Supply Situation	22
	Medical Technologists	24
	Education and Training	26
	Employment Trends	27
	Salaries, Hours, and Working Conditions	27
	The Current Demand and Supply Situation	29

	Engineering Technicians	29
	The Technological Team	29
	Education and Patterns of Entry	31
	Employers and Earnings	36
	Trends in the Employment of Engineering Technicians	36
	The Current Demand and Supply Situation	37
	Tool and Die Makers	39
	Earnings, Hours, and Conditions of Employment	39
	Training	40
	Employment Trends	42
	The Current Demand and Supply Situation	42
Part II	**The Medical Occupations**	47
3	**Extent and Nature of the Shortage, Chicago and St. Louis**	49
	Employment Trends	49
	Vacancies	51
	Employer Views of the Market	53
	Worker Experience in the Market	54
	The Shortages and Pay Levels	59
	Other Evidence of Shortages	69
4	**Factors Affecting Supply: Information, Counseling, Guidance, and Recruitment**	72
	Sources of Occupational Information and Knowledge	72

Access to Information and Entry: Characteristics of Trainees and Workers 86

Recruitment – Efforts to Tap Potential Supply 98

Hospital Recruitment 99
Training School Recruitment 102
Worker Experience 105

5 **Factors Affecting Supply: Training and Placement** 110

The Nature of Training Schools 110

Training and the Supply of Labor 112

Training Capacity 112
The Costs and Financing of Training 115
Evaluation of Training 121

Placement 127

6 **Factors Affecting Supply: Internal Adjustments and Employee Benefits** 132

Utilization Patterns 132

Hiring Policies 132
Training 134
Job Redesign 136
Capital Substitution 141
Quality of Service 142

Employee Benefits and Employee Relations 144

Part III **The Industrial Occupations** 147

7 **Extent of the Shortage** 149

Employment Trends 150

Employer Views of the Market 151

Other Views and Market Experiences 161

Pay Levels and Trends 163

Worker Characteristics 177

8 **Factors Affecting Supply: Information, Counseling, Guidance, and Recruitment** 186

Sources of Information and Knowledge 186

Recruitment – Efforts to Tap Potential Supply 196

Minimum Hiring Standards 196
Employer Recruitment Efforts 201
Recruitment by Training Schools 206

9 **Factors Affecting Supply: Training and Placement** 214

The Nature of Training Schools 214

The Role of Employers in Training 225

Tool and Die Maker Programs 226
Tool and Die Designers 235
Engineering Technicians 237

	Training Capacity	238
	Costs and Financing of Training	239
	Evaluation of Training	244
	Placement	253
10	**Factors Affecting Supply: Internal Adjustments and Employee Benefits**	264
	Manpower Utilization	264
	Hiring and Training	264
	Job Redesign	271
	Capital Substitution	276
	Quality of Service	277
	Employee Benefits and Employee Relations	278
Part IV	**Summary and Conclusions**	287
11	**Summary and Conclusions**	289
	General Conclusions on the Adjustment Process	289
	Extent of the Shortages	289
	General Factors in Market Adjustment	291
	The Medical Occupations	291
	The Industrial Occupations	293
	Major Adjustment Considerations	297
	Policy Implications	299
	Entry into the Occupation	300
	Training and Training Institutions	302
	Placement	304
	Occupational Retention	305
	Manpower Utilization	306

	Appendixes	**309**
A	**General Tables**	**311**
B	**Occupations Selected for Study**	**315**
C	**The Design for Data Gathering**	**316**
D	**Definition of Technician Occupations**	**329**
E	**Tables Supplementing the Chapter 2 Discussion of the Medical Occupations**	**331**
F	**Tables Supplementing the Chapter 2 Discussion of the Industrial Occupations**	**343**
G	**Employer Interview Schedule: Topical Outline for Hospital Interviews**	**360**
H	**Employer Interview Schedule for Interviews with Industrial Firms**	**362**
I	**Worker Interview**	**368**
J	**Training School Administrator Questionnaire**	**374**

K Mail Questionnaire Survey of Recent Trainees for Those Completing Training Programs 377

L Mail Questionnaire Survey of Recent Trainees for Those Who Dropped Out of Training Programs 379

Notes 383

Index 389

Tables and Figures

2-1	Number and Rate of Admissions to Professional and Practical Nursing Programs, 1960-1961	18
2-2	Employed Practical and Registered Nurses, Number Employed, 1940-1960; Percentage Increase in Number Employed, 1950-1960	19
2-3	Practical and Professional Nurses in Practice in the United States, Illinois, and Missouri, 1957 and 1960	20
2-4	Percentage Increases in Employed Nursing Personnel in the United States, 1954-1959	20
2-5	Average Monthly Salaries for Licensed Practical Nurses and Select Group of Occupations, Chicago, 1965	23
2-6	Employed Medical and Dental Laboratory Technicians by Sex, 1940, 1950, 1960	28
2-7	Educational Level of Employed Engineering and Physical Science Technicians, 1960	33
2-8	Employment of Technicians in the United States by Sex, 1940 and 1950	37
2-9	Employment of Technicians in the United States, 1950 and 1960	38
2-10	Employment of Tool Makers, Die Makers, and Setters in the United States, Chicago, and St. Louis, Decennially, 1930-1960	43
2-11	Estimated Changes in Manpower Requirements in the Metalworking Industries, 1960-1980	44
3-1	Percentage of Hospitals with Staffing Difficulties and with Training Programs and Turnover Rates, by Size	55
3-2	Percent Working on First Job Less Than One Month After Completing Training	56
3-3	Percent of LPN's and Medical Technologists Rating Horizontal Mobility in Their Work as Excellent or Good	60

3-4	Various Salary and Wage Data for Licensed Practical Nurses, Medical Technologists, and Other Worker Groups	62
3-5	Racial Distribution of Licensed Practical Nurses and Medical Technologists, Chicago and St. Louis Sample Hospitals	66
3-6	Mean Starting Salaries for Licensed Practical Nurses and Medical Technologists, Chicago and St. Louis Sample Hospitals at the Time of the Survey (1964)	68
4-1	Factors Related to Entry into Training, Licensed Practical Nurses and Medical Technologists (Percent Distribution)	74
4-2	Training Qualifications of Sample Licensed Practical Nurses and Medical Technologists, Chicago and St. Louis (Percent Distributions)	88
4-3	Characteristics of Workers Employed as Licensed Practical Nurses and Medical Technologists, Chicago and St. Louis Samples (Percent Distributions)	90
4-4	Educational Attainment, by Race, Worker Samples (Percent Distributions)	96
4-5	Sources of Additional Employees for Chicago and St. Louis Hospitals (Percent Distributions)	100
5-1	Percent of Recent Chicago Trainees Who Received Financial Support from Various Sources, Practical Nurses and Medical Technologists	120
5-2	Length of Time to First Job Following Training, Practitioners and Recent Trainees (Percent Distributions)	128
6-1	Employment Ratios for Nursing Occupations, Selected Years	138
7-1	Employment in Sample Firms, Four Occupations, Chicago and St. Louis Labor Markets, 1959 and 1964	152
7-2	Reasons Employment in the Selected Occupations has Increased (Percent Distribution)	154

7-3	Factors Reflecting the Extent of the Shortage, Four Occupations, Chicago and St. Louis (In Percents)	156
7-4	Vacancy Rates, Four Occupations, Chicago and St. Louis	160
7-5	Time to First Job, Worker and Recent Trainee Samples (Percent Distributions)	164
7-6	Perceptions of Mobility Possibilities (In Percents)	166
7-7	Hourly Wage Levels and Trends, Four Occupations, Chicago and St. Louis, Sample Firms and Other Survey Data	168
7-8	Characteristics of Worker Samples, Four Occupations, Chicago and St. Louis (Percent Distributions)	178
7-9	Level of Educational Attainment, Workers in Four Occupations, Classified by Recent-Veteran Status (Percent Distributions)	183
8-1	Factors Related to Entry into Training, Four Occupations, Chicago and St. Louis (Percent Distributions)	188
8-2	Employer Hiring Requirements, Four Occupations, Chicago and St. Louis Combined (Percent Distributions)	197
8-3	Employer Recruitment Practices, Four Occupations, Chicago and St. Louis Combined (Percent Distributions)	202
8-4	First Post-Training Job, Four Occupations, Chicago and St. Louis Combined (Percent Distributions)	205
8-5	Training School Recruitment, Four Occupations, Chicago and St. Louis Combined (Percent Distributions)	208
8-6	Extent of Active Recruitment by Training Schools, Four Occupations, Chicago and St. Louis Combined (Percent Distributions)	212
9-1	Level of Education and Training of Workers, St. Louis and Chicago, Four Occupations	218

9-2	General Educational Factors in Practitioners' Backgrounds, Four Occupations, Chicago and St. Louis Combined (In Percents)	223
9-3	Aspects of Company Training Programs, Chicago and St. Louis Combined, Four Occupations (In Percents)	227
9-4	How Training Was Financed, Recent Trainees in Chicago (In Numbers)	243
9-5	Aspects of Workers' Training Programs, Four Occupations, Chicago and St. Louis Combined (In Percents)	246
9-6	Proportion of Practitioners Trained in Sample Training Schools, Chicago and St. Louis	252
9-7	Post-Training Employment Experiences of Recent Chicago Trainees and Drop-Outs (In Percents)	254
10-1	Aspects of Internal Adjustments to Occupational Shortages by Firms, Four Occupations, Chicago and St. Louis Combined (In Percents)	266
10-2	Worker Perceptions of Their Occupation, Four Occupations, Chicago and St. Louis Combined (In Percents)	272
10-3	Fringe Benefits in Sample Firms, Four Occupations, Chicago and St. Louis Combined (In Percents)	280
A-1	Nonagricultural Employment in the United States, Chicago, and St. Louis, by Industry, 1960	312
A-2	Total Employment in the Service Industries in the United States, Chicago, and St. Louis, 1960	314
C-1	Hospital Sample Design	318
C-2	Employer Sample Design, Metalworking and Electrical Machinery Industries	320
C-3	Worker Sample, Medical, Electronic, and Metalworking Industries	324
C-4	Result of Mail Survey of Chicago Recent Trainees	328

E-1	Trends in the Number of Professional Nurse Graduates	333
E-2	Trend in the Number of Practical Nurse Graduates from Accredited Nursing Programs	335
E-3	Sex Distribution of Employed Practical Nurses, 1950 and 1960	336
E-4	Age Distribution of Employed Female Practical Nurses in the United States, 1960	337
E-5	Average Monthly Starting Salaries and Monthly Going Salaries for Licensed Practical Nurses, Illinois Hospitals, 1955-1965, Metropolitan Chicago Hospitals, 1963 and 1965	338
E-6	Average Starting Salaries and Monthly Going Salaries for Medical Technologists (ASCP) Employed by Hospitals in the State of Illinois, 1955-1965, and in Metropolitan Chicago, 1963 and 1965	339
E-7	Median Salaries of Medical Technologists (ASCP) by State, 1959	340
F-1	Significant Types of Education and Training Acquired by Engineering and Physical Science Technicians in the Experienced Civilian Labor Force, 1962	345
F-2	Level of Education of Technicians by Occupation and Age, 1963 (Percent Distributions)	347
F-3	Technicians, by Industry, 1960 Employment and Projected 1970 Requirements	350
F-4	Technicians, by Occupational Specialty, 1963 Employment and Projected 1975 Requirements	356
F-5	High, Intermediate, and Low Projections of the Supply of Technicians from Pre-Employment and Technician-Related Training, 1963-1974	357
F-6	High, Intermediate, and Low Projections of Technician Requirements and Supply, 1963-1975	358

Figures

2-1 Type of Training from which New Technicians Entered Employment in 1963 34

E-1 Average Monthly Starting Salaries for Hospital Personnel in the State of Illinois and Metropolitan Chicago, 1955-1965 342

Foreword

The analysis of labor market problems associated with shortage occupations has suffered both from deficiencies in the resources devoted to the problem and from a failure to take a sufficiently comprehensive approach. Much of the effort to date has been expended on the identification of shortages. At one end of the spectrum, economists have designed and carried out studies to test various economic definitions of shortages. In general, these studies have attempted to define shortages in terms of certain types of wage behavior and then carried out empirical analyses to determine whether the particular labor markets in question exhibit such behavior. At the other end of the spectrum, labor market agencies have proceeded pragmatically to try and identify occupations with substantial potential demand for such purposes as counseling and training programs. They have utilized job vacancy information, employer surveys and forecasts of industrial and occupational change.

Both types of studies have provided useful information and policy guidance but not the depth of information desirable for private and public manpower policies. They lack the richness of detail about institutional decision making, the effectiveness of linkages and consistency of programs among the relevant institutions, and the variety of alternatives available for solving particular shortages that are needed for a sophisticated policy. Flexible wage behavior is a necessary but often not a sufficient requirement for adaptation of the labor force. Where wages and labor supply do not adapt quickly enough, we need to know more about the institutional blockages that bring about this result. Perhaps more important, we need to know more about the alternative courses of action that would reduce the burden on the wage-equilibrating mechanism and that might bring about the desired results in a faster, more effective, and less costly way. Similarly, studies identifying areas of high demand for purposes of supplying additional training and related funds tend to concentrate on marginal increments to the flow of workers in particular occupations within a given structure of education and training. While theoretically it is recognized that there is an interdependent system with dozens of alternative or complementary intervention points from school counseling to job redesign, the pressures of practical implementation concentrate on a few such points where financial leverage is likely to produce quick results. And, in fact, information ordinarily is not available on the effectiveness with which a variety of institutions are performing in regard to specific occupations in specific areas. Thus it would be difficult to array and choose among the various intervention points and to establish a coordinated set of policies likely to achieve the best result.

This study by Professors Walter Franke and Irvin Sobel is an attempt to deal with some of these problems through an in-depth analysis of several occupations in the Chicago and St. Louis labor market areas which allegedly had serious problems of shortages. Utilizing extensive interviews and statistical analyses, they have explored a wide range of factors affecting education and training, recruitment, placement, utilization, and retention of workers in six technical occupations. Their interest focuses on the effectiveness of labor market processes and the various institutions that are involved. They have identified both a large number of adjustments designed to alleviate the occupational shortages as well as the bottlenecks that have prevented adjustments. The complexity of the problems involved is readily apparent. Each of the occupations poses some special problems of its own, and the problems for a specific occupation may differ between geographic areas.

This intensive type of analysis has permitted Professors Franke and Sobel to provide much more illuminating answers even to traditional questions. Thus in regard to whether a shortage actually exists, they find that there is a serious shortage of the two medical occupations (licensed practical nurses and medical technologists) but not of the four industrial occupations (tool and die maker, tool and die designer, engineering technician-electronics, and engineering technician-metalworking). This shows up in the relative wage rise for the medical as against the industrial occupations. The result is validated by nonwage aspects – both the existence of large numbers of vacancies in the medical occupations and only minor inconvenience in the industrial occupations (occasional stretching out of production schedules or subcontracting) and a surprising amount of unemployment. In addition, the analysis shows that too little wage adjustment probably took place in the medical occupations because of the wage restraint policies practiced by hospitals, a policy that would have been more difficult to pursue in a more competitive sector.

The data collected also permit an exploration of the more serious shortage of licensed practical nurses in St. Louis than in Chicago. This partly flows from relative wage differences in the two labor market areas. However, the authors also are able to analyze the failure to expand the number of training slots in St. Louis and how this relates to discrimination against the large number of black applicants. Clearly the problems in the St. Louis market require a different emphasis than in Chicago.

Similarly, the in-depth analysis of education and training spotlights the difficulty of a hospital easily affecting the supply of medical technologists when training is basically done in colleges. In turn, the problem is aggravated by the perverse labor market effects of raising academic requirements at a time when a shortage exists. The excessive costs and lack of coordination in education and specialized training for this occupation lead the authors to suggest the coordination of both parts of occupational preparation under one institution. To facilitate this, they propose a reorganization of the occupation to provide more job levels than currently exist.

The more satisfactory labor market adjustments among the industrial occupations reflects not only the more competitive milieu in which they operate but also the lesser degree of formality of the skill acquisition process. Among these occupations, the closest approach to a shortage problem has arisen in the tool and die maker classification in which a large proportion of workers are trained under a formal apprenticeship program. For the other occupations, a much greater variety of paths to occupational competency exists than for the tool and die maker or for the licensed medical occupations. While there are obviously some constraints, this suggests that adaptation to shortages would be facilitated by breaking down stereotypes about skill acquisition that unduly narrow the range of potential candidates.

These few examples indicate some of the many ways in which the study by Professors Franke and Sobel provides grist for the manpower policy mill. Fortunately the study is being published at a particularly opportune moment. The high costs associated with the rapidly increasing demand for health services has generated an increasing interest in reorganizing the occupational structure in order to produce these services more efficiently. The need to integrate disadvantaged groups into the work force has similarly created new interest in developing entry jobs that articulate with satisfying career ladders in expanding industries. Concern with the quality of work life has resulted in new ideas about job redesign. And the rapid changes that take place in knowledge and technology has forced us to explore ways by which individuals may achieve maximum flexibility through occasional "retooling" to adjust either to market shifts or changing individual tastes.

The approach taken in this study is useful for all of these problems. While it focuses on problems of occupational shortages, its major strength is its emphasis both on the interaction of market and institutional forces and the need for tailoring policy to the specific context in which manpower problems arise. In a period when increasing authority for manpower decisions is being delegated to states and cities for precisely this purpose, this study should prove especially useful.

Melvin Rothbaum
Director, Institute of Labor and Industrial Relations
University of Illinois

Acknowledgements

Professor Richard C. Wilcock was the original principal investigator for the research investigation reported herein. His untimely death in December, 1963, a few months after the research was begun, left its completion to us, but we owe a very large debt to him for the initiation and basic formulation of the investigation.

It is not possible to acknowledge the specific contribution of the many persons who participated in the study. We are particularly grateful for the work of James Bavis, Allan Harrison, and Michael Van de Kerckhove in supervising much of the field work, and to Michael Marmo and Mary (Shebesta) Carmichael who prepared the original draft of Chapter 2. Other graduate students who participated in the interviewing and data processing included William Hermann, Charles Mooney, E. Ray Canterberry, and Kenneth Bopp from Washington University in St. Louis, and John Altenburg, Dale Bennett, Paul Gaertner, Fred Heeney, Bert Levan, Gary Marrs, Lauren Miller, John Nelson, Bruce Rafey, Allan Spritzer, Gerald Swartz, and Glenn Zipp from the University of Illinois.

At the U. S. Department of Labor, Howard Rosen, Director of the Office of Manpower Research of the Manpower Administration, and William Paschell, Chief, Special Manpower Problems Research Group, gave advice and encouragement during the research phases. They also, together with Mrs. Mary Bedell, Chief, Clearing House and Utilization Service, offered valuable suggestions for improving the draft manuscript.

At the University of Illinois, we were greatly assisted by the work of Anice Duncan and Dorothy Wetzel. Preparation of the various versions of the manuscript was very capably supervised by Miss Duncan, and the editorial work of Mrs. Wetzel and her preparation of the Index contributed significantly to the final result. Finally, our thanks go to Mrs. Marian Brinkerhoff, who typed the final manuscript.

We alone are responsible for the accuracy of our information and the conclusions drawn from it.

Walter Franke
Irvin Sobel

I: Introduction

1 Framework and Design of the Study

The general objectives of the study upon which this book is based were summarized in the original research prospectus as follows:

A major and continuing manpower problem is that severe occupational shortages have been coexistent with high levels of unemployment and the displacement of many workers from their long-standing occupations. These shortages in recent years have been concentrated in technical occupations that require a considerable amount of training. In order to obtain insights and understanding that will help permit more rational adjustments to occupational changes, we propose to study six key technical occupations in which there are critical shortages of workers. In the study,both the causes of critical occupational shortages and the effectiveness of current labor market processes and institutions in removing shortages will be examined.

The research was conceived in 1963 at a time when the United States was in the midst of a long period of relatively high unemployment. At the same time there was much discussion and literature, both popular and professional, about the problem of serious shortages of skilled and technical manpower. In passing the Manpower Development and Training Act of 1962, Congress explained that this act was addressed to at least two aspects of the manpower situation; namely (1) that even in periods of high unemployment, many jobs remain unfilled because of shortages of qualified workers, and (2) there is a critical need for more and better trained workers in many vital job classifications.

This study was stimulated, in part, by the above types of observations and the questions they raised about appropriate public and private policies to meet the perceived problem. The general question raised is: Why, amidst a general abundance of unutilized labor, does there appear to prevail an insufficient number of workers available to fill certain jobs?

The Approach of the Study

The first requisite for systematic analysis is an operative definition of an occupational shortage. Some confusion has arisen from unstated definitions which involve a variety of concepts and approaches, some of which are devoid of meaning in standard economic terms.[1] However, the conventional economic definitions can be encompassed within the analytical framework used by economists. Thus, David Blank and George Stigler propose that "a shortage exists when the number of workers available (the supply) increases less rapidly than the number demanded at the salaries paid in the recent past."[2] The result of such a disequilibrium situation is that wages for the occupation will rise relative to wages paid in other occupations through the competition of employers for workers. The solution to a shortage situation, therefore, is to allow the market to adjust relative wage rates among occupations in much the same fashion that prices in a competitive product market are supposed to adjust supply to demand and vice versa for particular goods.

Kenneth Arrow and William Capron have modified this conceptual framework in an attempt to develop a more viable analytical tool for the explanation of persistent shortages of engineers and scientists.[3] The shortages are explained as resulting primarily from two causes: time lags involved in the adjustment of wages to an increase in demand for labor, and continuous expansions in demand which make it impossible for wage adjustments to reach equilibrium levels and thus eliminate the shortages. Time lags result from the time required for firms to recognize the need for more workers, to recognize the need for higher wages or salaries to obtain the workers, to calculate (or estimate) what the wage offers should be, to obtain approval from management to raise wages and hire additional workers, and to put into operation the recruitment and hiring process. Arrow and Capron label the time involved to complete the wage adjustment process "the reaction time." Following the initiation of this process additional time is required for the higher wage rates to bring forth an increased supply of workers. Similar time lags on the supply side of the market for recognition of opportunities and response by potential entrants to the field and by training institutions are equally important. Finally, as the market approaches an equilibrium position, demand for labor expands further, with the result that the process begins again, equilibrium is never reached, and shortages persist. This final factor of continually expanding demand produces what Arrow and Capron call a "dynamic shortage."

The symptoms of a dynamic shortage in an occupation are: (1) a rapid and steady rise in demand, (2) a low elasticity of supply, especially for short periods, and (3) a slow reaction speed on the market. Although the authors recognize nonwage factors as part of the difficulties involved in eliminating shortages, the emphasis in the analysis is on the dominant role of relative wage movements. They conclude:

> While the relative rigidity of supply in the short run is unpleasant (from the buyer's standpoint), and the price rise required to restore the market to equilibrium may seem to be very great, it is only by permitting the market to react to the rising demand that, in our view, it can allocate engineer-scientists in the short run and call forth the desired increase in supply in the long run.[4]

The Arrow-Capron analysis of the engineer-scientist case would appear to present an accurate picture of the general market forces operating to produce persistent occupational shortages in cases where demand is expanded and where supply is either relatively inelastic or cannot expand with sufficient speed in the short run.

One plausible interpretation of the Arrow-Capron model is that as the market actors acquire experience in learning, adjustment speed increases, especially if the increases in demand are continuous. Employers acclimate themselves to the continuing increases in demand by adjusting wages more rapidly while the number of training vacancies as well as number of trainees should also respond more rapidly over time as the changes continue to take place. Certainly if one postulates rational response on the part of employers, training entities, and potential recruits, the period of adjustment to continuous upward changes in demand should grow shorter and shorter.

The analysis, however, and the conclusions which grow out of it, largely ignore or take as given the labor market mechanisms and institutions through which adjustments (increases) in supply are expected to take place. The shape of the supply curve and the position of the demand curve are essentially viewed as independent variables which result in price adjustments and movement toward equilibrium in the market. Arrow and Capron specifically state, in fact, that "over short periods of time . . ., the shift of the short-run demand or supply functions can be taken as *exogenous* trends, and will be so treated in this paper."[5] And in arguing for their view of how shortages develop they further emphasize that "it should be made clear that we are not arguing that the market is subject to unusual imperfections. Rather, the very way in which the market performs its functions leads to the shortage in this particular period."[6]

To review, Blank and Stigler argue that in the engineer-scientist case there had in fact been no shortage at all because over the long run relative wages in the occupations had not risen. Noting an increase in relative salaries following the beginning of the Korean War they dismiss it as "hardly more than a minor cross-current in a tide."[7] Arrow and Capron, more interested in shorter-run phenomena, conclude there was a shortage during the 1950's and explain it as resulting from the inability of the normal functioning of the labor market to keep pace with a constantly expanding demand.

Both of these approaches to the problem of occupational shortages rest on the assumption that the behavior of wages and the relationship among wages in different occupations can be taken as evidence (proof) of the state of the labor market and that adjustments to changed labor market conditions, particularly in the short run, are primarily or exclusively made through changes in the wage rate. This is clear in the Blank and Stigler definition of occupational shortage, which recognizes a shortage only when relative wages have risen in the long run and in the Arrow and Capron insistence that shortage in the case they studied was due not to any malfunctioning of the labor market but to time lags which do not enable wage rates to rise with sufficient rapidity to eliminate shortages.

Viewing shortages in these ways rules out the possibility that an important cause of occupational shortage might be unnecessary limitations and rigidities in labor market institutions, and the possibility that there might be important causes of shortages other than relative wage imbalances, or that adjustment to shortages might occur in forms other than shifts in relative wage rates. The two models assume that the major, if not the only, means for drawing an increased supply of labor to an occupation is rising wage rates.

Without minimizing the important, and even key, role of wage rate adjustments in equating demand and supply and thus eliminating occupational shortages, it is possible to view the labor market as involving a more complex adjustment process. In the first place, it is obvious that the labor market adjustments, whatever their form, take place through a diverse number of labor market institutions. For each occupation the nature and functioning of labor market institutions differ. It is not necessarily the case that these institutions always operate in directions that serve to eliminate shortages when they occur. For example, to eliminate occupational shortages, it might be necessary that the capacity of training institutions be expanded. Whether the expansion takes place or not may not be exclusively a function of demand-supply relationships in that given occupation. Capacity may not be responsive to changes in relative wages. The organization of training opportunities, the sources of funds for training institutions, political pressures, and other factors can be important considerations in the response and adjustment of training institutions to shortage situations. Or, to cite another example, if entry to an occupation is subject to standards set by professional societies or associations, it is quite possible that entry standards might be pushed up at the same time that shortages are increasing. Although there might be limits to the extent to which such practices can be carried before counter-pressures are developed by other institutions representing users of that given skill, so long as these limits are not exceeded shortages might be perpetuated over very long periods of time. Because institutional practices might resist or even run counter to the policies which adjustment seemingly requires, it seems necessary to study these facets of behavior rather than to limit analysis of shortage situations exclusively to wage adjustments and demand-supply responses.

Secondly, it is also possible that adjustment to shortages takes place not only through changes in relative wages but also through changes in the practices of the labor market institutions themselves. For example, the supply of workers in a particular occupation might be increased, without increasing relative wages in the occupation, by increasing the quantity and quality of information or improving the dissemination of information about job opportunities in the occupation. Or the available supply might be increased, again without adjustment of wages, by the removal of barriers of discrimination that previously had prevented entry for large groups of potential workers.[a] The adjustment to shortages could also take the form of job redesign; that is, through a process of job dilution in which the simpler tasks of the occupation are broken out and reassigned to other occupational groups in greater supply. In this case again, equilibrium of supply and demand might be brought about without adjustment in relative wage rates.

These and other possibilities suggest that in analyzing the causes of occupational shortages it is appropriate to focus investigation on labor market

[a]It could be argued that these wages which may not be attractive to members of the dominant racial or ethnic group might appear relatively higher for a minority group and thus in reality amounts to that which the Arrow–Capron model could designate as relative wage increase.

institutions through which both wage and nonwage adjustments to market imbalances must take place. This study is directed at two key aspects of labor market institutions as they relate to the problem of occupational shortages. First, the study examines the institutional arrangements through which workers are prepared for and employed in jobs in selected occupations to determine whether there are in these arrangements barriers to entry and employment that are susceptible to elimination or reduction. Second, the study attempts to determine the extent to which labor market institutions are themselves modified or changed in response to shortage situations. In other words, to what extent do modifications in market institutions represent a force in bringing about equilibrium between demand and supply, and do adjustments by labor market institutions differ in various occupations.

The focus of the study, then, is the relationship between occupational shortages and the operational effectiveness of labor market processes and institutions. The concern is with the entire labor market process for selected technical and skilled occupations, ranging from the way in which demand in manifested through entry into training and ultimate placement on the job. Thus, factors affecting occupational choice, qualifications for entry into training, the content and length of training programs, the financing of training, the organization of training, labor market information, employer hiring and utilization practices, as well as wage trends, are examined with reference to their effect on labor supply and on demand-supply relationships.

The concept of occupational shortage is a difficult one to deal with operationally. The concept can be made very concrete if it is viewed in the Blank and Stigler sense as related to relative wage trends. It has already been shown, however, that their view assumes as given the very factors that are the subject matter of this investigation; namely, the labor market institutions and processes through which adjustments to demand and supply changes take place. Arrow and Capron put more emphasis on these factors as related to the problem of shortages, but they also treat them as given. In their analysis, occupational shortages are identified through the symptoms of dynamic shortage; that is, rapidly rising demand, low elasticity of supply, and sufficiently slow reaction speed in the market so that before a given level of adjustment has been reached demand has risen again. As will be indicated later, these are factors that were considered in the selection of occupations for study, but they are not factors that can be readily quantified for purposes of identifying the extent of labor shortage in an occupation.

For the purposes of this study, a shortage was defined as a situation existing over an extended period of time in which employers were unable to hire at going wages or salaries sufficient numbers of qualified persons to fill positions for which there were budgeted funds and for which personnel were required to meet existing demands for services. The definition is neither altogether concrete and precise nor is it susceptible to precise measurements. Viewed in the context of a study whose purpose is to examine the degree to which labor market institutions respond to and facilitate adjustment to varying degrees of labor market tightness, the definition is, however, meaningful and operational. Interviews with employers and others were designed to obtain information that provided a variety of indexes of the extent to which shortages existed in the selected occupations.

It should be pointed out that this criterion is used solely as a starting point and that other indirect indexes such as the ease of horizontal mobility, time between jobs, reasons for apparent joblessness, effects upon either quantity or quality of services and output, along with relative rises in wage rates, were also utilized as evaluatory criteria in determining not only whether shortages existed but their apparent severity. These indirect criteria constitute key determinants of whether the labor market participants themselves behave as though a shortage existed.

Using this concept of occupational shortage, the study examined the entire labor market process involved in the attraction, training, placement, and retention of workers in the selected occupations.

Procedures

The study was conducted in two large metropolitan labor markets, Chicago and St. Louis. Six skilled and technical occupations were chosen for study. This section summarizes the procedures followed in conducting the investigation in the two labor markets.

The Labor Markets

The Chicago and St. Louis labor market areas[b] were chosen as the sites for the study not only because of their accessibility, but also because of the extent of their size and diversification. Each of these labor markets utilized sufficiently large numbers in the occupations to enable generalization about labor market processes. These two large labor markets, in short, were ones in which not only did the research teams enjoy relatively easy access, but also the two areas are reasonably representative of larger labor markets in the United States.

[b]The Chicago labor market area was defined as Chicago and suburbs. This area, which comprises nearly all of Cook and DuPage Counties, is defined by the boundaries established for the Chicago Office of the Illinois State Employment Service. See any issue of Bureau of Employment Security, *Illinois Statewide Summary of the Employment and Unemployment Situation*. The St. Louis labor market area was defined as the city of St. Louis and St. Charles County.

Appendix A depicts the industrial distribution of employment in the two areas and in the United States in 1960. For the purposes of this study, whose main interest is evaluation of labor market institutions in modern, complex labor markets, the choice of the two cities appears appropriate. This is not to say, however, that findings of a similar study in other specific labor markets would be precisely the same. However, while the precise magnitudes might differ in some types of labor markets, namely an area concentrating in research and development in space production, it is believed that any generalizations derived from the data and subsequent analysis are qualitatively valid.

Setting of the Study and the Occupations

In mid-1963, at the time the study was initiated, the unemployment rate was reported as about 4.6 percent in both the Chicago and St. Louis labor market areas. In both areas, therefore, moderate labor surpluses existed at the time the study began. Most of the data for the two medical occupations (see Appendix C) were collected between mid-1963 and mid-1964, during which time the unemployment rate averaged 4.1 percent in Chicago and 4.3 percent in St. Louis. Between mid-1964 and mid-1965, when most of the data for the four industrial occupations were gathered, the unemployment rate averaged 3.4 percent in Chicago and 3.6 percent in St. Louis. Field work for the study was concluded for all six occupations between mid-1965 and early 1966, during which period the unemployment rates in Chicago and St. Louis averaged 3.0 and 3.4 percent respectively.

The period during which the study was conducted could be characterized as one in which the labor market in both cities was in transition from moderate labor surplus to a situation approximating a full employment balance. The medical occupations were studied during a period when there was moderate labor surplus; the industrial occupations were investigated during a period when the labor markets in both cities appeared to be close to demand-supply balance and moving toward a tight labor market situation.[c]

The Occupations

Six skilled and technical occupations were selected for study. Two of them, licensed practical nurse and medical technologist, were chosen from the medical services industry. The other four – tool and die maker, tool and die designer, engineering technician-electronics, and engineering technician-metalworking – were studied in the metalworking and electrical machinery industries.

[c]The unemployment figures are for the Chicago and St. Louis Standard Metropolitan Statistical Areas. They are based on the bi-monthly estimates published in the Bureau of Employment Security publication *Area Trends in Employment and Unemployment*. Unemployment rates are not available for the specific areas used for this study, which are substantially smaller in size than the SMSA's.

The nature of the six occupations is described in detail in Chapter 2, which is introductory to the presentation of the results of the field work.[d] At this point a few comments concerning the general nature of the six occupations will be helpful in relating their selection to the purposes of the study. More specific information about the occupational samples and the design for data gathering appear in Appendixes B and C.

The two medical occupations are of particular interest for a number of reasons. They are, first of all, part of an industry that does not fit the competitive model very well. Most persons in the occupations are employed by hospitals, and for most hospitals profits are not the primary motivating force. It is, therefore, of considerable interest to look at the operation of labor markets in this particular nonprofit sector of the economy. Second, employment in both occupations has been expanding rapidly in recent years. This aspect of the situation fits well an important part of the Arrow-Capron model of a dynamic shortage. Again, it is of particular interest to assess the relevant labor market institutions and their ability to adjust to a situation of rapidly expanding demand. Third, the two occupations represent two quite different points in the range of paramedical occupations. The licensed practical nurse occupation requires a rather brief period of specialized training, usually about a year; a high school education, and often less, qualifies one for entry into training. The medical technologist, on the other hand, is required to pursue a rather lengthy preparatory course, usually involving at least three years of college level education and a year of laboratory training. Finally, qualification standards and licensing in both occupations are either set or greatly influenced by professional associations in the industry, and the two occupations provide good cases for examination of that particular labor market influence.

The tool and die maker trade is a highly traditional one characterized by long-established channels of entry and training. Unlike the two medical occupations, demand for workers in this occupation has not been expanding rapidly. In spite of this and the fact that entry to the occupation has apparently long been formalized through apprenticeship, there appears to be a chronic shortage of qualified tradesmen. This is a case of shortage that cannot be readily explained by the dynamic-shortage model as it has been explicitly formulated. It, therefore, offers a shortage situation of a different type to examine and explain.

Tool and die designer is an example of a specialized technician. In at least one way, the occupation does not fit well the general criteria used in selecting the occupations for study. It is not and has never been an occupation in which large numbers of people are employed. Even a large metal machinery firm may employ only a few tool or die designers. Many firms employ none at all. Nonetheless, it was selected for study because it was an occupation in which there could seemingly be established a severe shortage of qualified persons. Unlike the tool and die maker case, the route to entry to the occupation is not well defined or formalized; nor is the occupation itself as well defined as that of

[d]The specific definitions used for the two engineering technician occupations are in Appendix D. These two occupations were the most difficult to define, and their descriptions were spelled out in detail to assure that employers and other interviewees would respond in the proper context.

tool and die maker. A firm which claims to have no tool designers may have a graduate engineer with some other title doing the same work as a tool designer in another firm with no college education. This obvious contrast with the tool and die maker case made it a tempting case to look at; the above cited characteristics, however, made it a difficult case to analyze.

The two engineering technician occupations were selected to represent the large group of technical workers in the subengineering category in industry. The job title used here is meant to indicate that the position is one in which the technician, in effect, works as an assistant to the graduate engineer.[e] The actual incumbents in such positions are called by scores of different job titles. The two job titles used in this study differentiate the two occupations mainly with reference to the industries, and, therefore, the type of product, in which they are employed. The two occupations are on exactly the same level in the job hierarchy.

Employment of technicians expanded rapidly during the 1950's and, although published figures are not available for employment of engineering technicians as defined for this study, it can be assumed that these two cases also represent cases in which demand expanded rapidly. It might be expected, therefore, that these would be cases which fit the dynamic shortage model. They were therefore viewed as an interesting contrast with the medical occupations, because in addition to representing a case of rapidly expanding demand for an occupation, they also are found in industries whose characteristics come much closer to the competitive model traditionally used for analyzing shortage situations than the hospital industry.[f] These differing labor market and product market circumstances thus not only presented interesting contrasts, but, it was hypothesized, would yield insights regarding the over-all utility of shortage models under varying circumstances. These same contrasts are crucial elements for establishing more generalized propositions regarding both market theory and policy.

Report Plan

The results of the field work are discussed separately for the two medical

[e]See Appendix D for the detailed job description used.

[f]One further comment regarding the selection of the occupations is of some significance. The four industrial occupations were selected only with some difficulty. It proved to be rather difficult to identify occupations in the two industry groups that were clearly in short supply and also met the general criteria set forth for selection. A number of occupations were identified, but they were too insignificant in size to consider (e.g., technical writer). Consideration was given to going to other industry groups, but investigation turned up no promising leads that fit into the general study plans. It is of interest, however, particularly in view of the very widespread feeling of the time that much of our unemployment could be attributed to structural factors (i.e., a shortage of adequately skilled and prepared workers), that it proved so difficult to identify significant occupations of the type sought for this study.

occupations on the one hand and the four industrial occupations on the other. In following the report of the results of the field work it is necessary to keep in mind the various sources of data that are used. To this end, a summary of the terminology used in reference to these sources of data might be helpful. Data collected from officials of employing establishments are referred to as employer or company interviews or as hospital interviews. Respondents to the worker interviews are referred to as workers or practitioners. They are sometimes referred to as recent entrants or veterans to designate how long they had been practitioners of the occupation. Data from the training school administrator survey are referred to as training school or trade school data. Respondents to the mail questionnaire are referred to as Chicago recent trainees or drop-outs.[g]

[g]See Appendix C for the description of the various parts of the study design.

2 Occupational Characteristics and Trends

Each of the occupations under scrutiny have distinct characteristics which influence the nature and institutional structure of their labor markets and condition worker behavior within them. This chapter describes the functional characteristics of the occupations in the context of the technology indigenous to performance of occupational activities, the training and education requirements leading to entry into the field, salary trends, and working conditions in the occupation. These are related to the current and emergent demand and supply situation applicable to each field. Where statistical data relevant to these considerations are used they are generally brought up to the mid-1960's, the time at which the field work was being conducted.

Licensed Practical Nurses

Licensed practical nurses (LPN) constitute a growing segment of an occupational family devoted to rendering nursing care. The family consists of registered nurses (RN), licensed practical nurses, and nurse aides, attendants, and orderlies.

An LPN is employed chiefly in the capacity of an assistant to more technically proficient personnel in the medical and health profession. By virtue of educational background and nursing skill, the hierarchical position of the LPN is subordinate to the position of the RN. However, under certain conditions, such as work-load fluctuations and rapidly expanding nursing care needs, the RN and the LPN may be used interchangeably. This interchangeability is occurring with increasing frequency. Minimal educational and training requirements consist of two years of high school education (six states require a high school diploma) plus one year of training in an accredited school of practical nursing. In order to become eligible for a license a practical nurse must also pass an examination administered by a state licensing agency.

Under the direct supervision of a physician or an RN, an LPN ordinarily performs the following nursing functions: taking and recording temperature, blood pressure, pulse and respiration rate; dressing wounds and giving enemas, alcohol rubs, and massages; applying compresses, icebags, and hot water bottles; administering certain kinds of medication; sterilizing equipment and supplies; recording fluid and food intake; and dressing and assisting patients.[1]

Employment opportunities for LPN's encompass the major fields of nursing and include: general and psychiatric hospital nursing, public health nursing, industrial nursing, private duty nursing, nursing education, and nursing in the private office of a physician or dentist.

According to the Surgeon General's report, *Toward Quality in Nursing,* older practical nurses are disproportionately engaged in private home-patient care, and young graduate LPN's are employed largely in hospitals. In 1962, 127,000 practical nurses were employed in hospitals, approximately 40 percent more than in 1950. The employment distribution of recent graduate LPN's among the various fields of nursing has been estimated at 75 percent or more in general hospital nursing, 10 to 15 percent in private practice and patients' homes, and 10 to 15 percent in nursing homes, public health agencies, and offices of physicians.[2]

Nursing in the United States is primarily a female occupation. The proportion of employed male practical nurses was 4.3 percent of the total number of employed practical nurses in 1950. Between 1950 and 1960, the relative number of employed male practical nurses increased more rapidly than female practical nurses in Illinois, metropolitan Chicago, and St. Louis, as well as in the nation as a whole. Despite this relatively greater increase of practicing male practical nurses, men are still grossly under-represented in the field of practical nursing (Appendix E, Table E-3). The public image of nursing as a woman's occupation, and inadequate economic rewards act as deterrents to men who might otherwise consider a career in the field of nursing.

From a labor market perspective, the most important developments in the nursing services field include a tremendous increase in the demand for health and medical care, resulting in an increase in the number of persons engaged in institutionalized nursing, quantitative and qualitative changes in the educational preparation of nursing personnel, and the development of legal control of nursing education and practice through state accredited training programs and licensing.

Training and Licensing

In 1941, the National Association for Practical Nurse Education was organized to set up an accredited program for practical nursing training. In addition to establishing practical nursing training school standards, the Association published an annual list of approved schools. Within a single decade, the number of practical nursing training schools increased from 10 to 144. Between 1950 and 1963, the number of such schools increased five-fold, from 144 to 737.[3] In the state of Illinois, the number of approved practical nursing schools increased from

11 in 1957 to 19 by 1961.[4] (Analogous information for the state of Missouri is not available.)

In order for a nursing training school to receive accreditation, the school must meet certain faculty and curriculum educational standards set by state boards of nursing. Most practical nurses today receive their training in a public vocational course or a hospital nursing training program.

The number of states providing for licensing of practical nurses also increased substantially during the postwar period. From 20 states issuing licenses to practical nurses in 1950, state licensing had become universal by 1961.[5] Between 1950 and 1959, the number of licenses issued to practical nurses increased from 64,800 to 236,900.[6]

Licensing of practical nurses is a prerogative of each individual state; however, there is reciprocity among a few states. Compliance with state laws, which require the completion of an approved formal training program plus acceptable performance on a state administered examination, legally entitles a practical nurse to employ the initials, "LPN."

Admission into and graduation from practical nursing programs grew apace with the expansion of training facilities, and the growth was much greater than for professional nursing training (RN's). During the period from 1950 to 1963, the annual number of professional nurse graduates increased by 25.6 percent, somewhat less than the increase in the female labor force (Appendix E, Table E-1). The relatively small increase in the number of graduates of professional nursing schools within the past decade or so contrasts with the trend in the number of graduates of practical nursing schools. Whereas the rate of admissions to professional nursing programs per every 1,000 girls 17 years of age declined between 1951 and 1961 from 43 to 34, the rate of admissions to practical nursing programs increased from 5 to 17.[7] Numerically, graduates of accredited practical nursing programs rose from 2,828 in 1950 to 16,635 in 1961. (Appendix E, Table E-2), an increase of nearly 500 percent. In comparison, the increase in the number of graduates of professional nursing programs during the same period was only 17 percent. In 1963, approximately 20,000 nurses received certificates of practical nursing.[8]

In Illinois, the rate of admissions per every 1,000 girls 17 years of age to professional nursing programs is above the national average and the corresponding rate for practical nursing programs is below the national average. In Missouri, admission rates for both types of programs are above the national average (Table 2-1).[a]

Practical nursing training schools generally accept students up to the age of 55 years. Prior to World War II married women were rarely accepted in nursing training programs. Today, neither age nor marital status is a barrier to obtaining practical nursing training, and many older married women, whose families no longer need their full-time services, embark upon a delayed career in the field of practical nursing. In the academic year 1959-1960, one-third of the students who entered practical nursing programs were under 20 years of age, one-third

[a]Information on the number of graduating nurses would give a more accurate picture of the supply of nursing personnel in the states of Illinois and Missouri because admission and enrollment rates overstate the number of nurses actually completing training. Presently, however, information of this nature is not available.

were between the ages of 20 and 35 years, and one-third were over 35 years of age.[9]

Slightly more than two-thirds of all practical nursing students today are high school graduates. Approximately 75 percent of the students are white and 25 percent are black. The proportion of blacks relative to whites is significantly greater in the field of practical nursing than professional nursing, with respect to both training-school enrollments and employment.

In the academic year 1959-1960, 23,060 potential students were admitted to programs of practical nursing, but only 16,491 students graduated that year. In 1960-1961, 24,955 potential students were granted admissions and 16,635 students were graduated.[10] A three-year study conducted by the National League for Nursing Education revealed that among 159 schools of practical nursing, 31 percent of the students enrolled therein did not complete the training course. Failure in class work, dislike for nursing, and disappointment in the nursing curriculum accounted for 46 percent of the withdrawals during the first year of study. Marriage, personal reasons, and health were additional important factors responsible for trainee separations.[11]

Employment Trends

One of the most significant developments in the field of nursing has been a rapid growth in the demand for and utilization of nursing personnel, especially in hospitals and homes for the aged. Between 1940 and 1960, the number of employed professional nurses increased from 352,486 to 582,379 and the number of employed practical nurses increased from 91,107 to 205,974. The states of Illinois and Missouri and the metropolitan areas of Chicago and St. Louis likewise experienced a substantial growth in the number of practicing professional and practical nurses during the past two decades. Percentage increases in the number of employed practical nurses between 1950 and 1960, however, strikingly reveal that the state of Illinois has not kept pace with employment trends for the nation as a whole (Table 2-2). This does not hold true for the state of Missouri as the figures in Table 2-2 indicate. In Illinois and Missouri the number of employed practical nurses increased by 36.7 percent and 50.5 percent, respectively, compared to an increase of 50.9 percent for the entire United States. Similar figures show that metropolitan Chicago falls far short of the national increase during this period, whereas the growth in the number of practicing practical nurses in metropolitan St. Louis exceeds national employment trends. In terms of the number of practical nurses in practice as a proportion of the population, Illinois is below the national average and Missouri is above the national average (Table 2-3).

The increased employment of practical nurses is, in part, the result of a persistent shortage of RN's. Unable to obtain a desired supply of RN's, many hospitals have been forced to rely more heavily on the services of auxiliary

Table 2-1

Number and Rate of Admissions to Professional and Practical Nursing Programs, 1960–1961

	Professional Nursing				
	Total	*Baccalaureate Program*	*Associate Program*	*Diploma Program*	*Rate per 1,000 Girls 17 Years Old*
United States & Puerto Rico	49,487	8,700	2,085	38,702	34.2
Illinois	2,981	256	22	2,703	39.2
Missouri	1,358	162	25	1,171	41.7

	Practical Nursing	
	Total	*Rate per 1,000 Girls 17 Years Old*
United States & Puerto Rico	24,955	17.3
Illinois	847	11.1
Missouri	573	17.6

Source: U. S. Department of Health, Education and Welfare, Public Health Service, *Toward Quality in Nursing*, report of the Surgeon General's Consultant Group on Nursing (Washington, D. C.: U. S. Government Printing Office, February, 1963), Appendix Tables 10 and 11, pp. 66–69.

Table 2-2

Employed Practical and Registered Nurses, Number Employed, 1940–1960; Percentage Increase in Number Employed, 1950–1960

Practical Nurses

	1940[1]	*1950*	*1960*	*Percent Increase 1950–1960*
United States	91,107	136,541	205,974	50.9%
Illinois				
State	4,157	6,174	8,440	36.7
Chicago[2]	1,617	3,191	4,001	25.3
Missouri				
State	2,515	3,895	5,862	50.5
St. Louis	570	1,400	2,620	87.1

Registered Nurses

	1940[3]	*1950*	*1960*	*Percent Increase 1950–1960*
United States	352,486	400,221	582,379	45.5%
Illinois				
State	22,854	23,268	32,117	38.0
Chicago[2]	11,230	15,629	19,611	25.5
Missouri				
State	8,168	8,334	12,224	44.9
St. Louis	3,344	4,698	6,331	34.8

[1]Includes midwives.

[2]Standard Metropolitan Statistical Area.

[3]Includes employed professional student nurses.

Source: U. S. Census of Population Reports, "Detailed Characteristics of the Population," (Washington, D. C.: U. S. Government Printing Office, 1940, 1950, and 1960).

Table 2-3

Practical and Professional Nurses in Practice in the United States, Illinois, and Missouri, 1957 and 1960

	Professional Nurses 1957		Practical Nurses 1960	
State	*Number*	*Rate Per 100,000 Population*	*Number*	*Rate Per 100,000 Population*
United States	464,138	271	205,974	115
Illinois	24,024	251	8,440	84
Missouri	8,841	208	5,862	136

Source: U. S. Department of Health, Education, and Welfare, Public Health Service, *Toward Quality in Nursing*, report of the Surgeon General's Consultant Group on Nursing (Washington, D. C.: U. S. Government Printing Office, February, 1963), Appendix Table 2, pp. 59–60.

Table 2-4

Percentage Increases in Employed Nursing Personnel in the United States, 1954–1959

Type of Personnel	Percentage Increase
Registered Nurses	25%
Licensed Practical Nurses	57
Nurse Aides and Attendants	29
Orderlies	49

Source: *Facts About Nursing: A Statistical Summary* (New York: American Nurses' Association, 1960), p. 185.

nursing personnel. A decline in the number of employed student professional nurses from 76,426 in 1950 to 57,340 in 1960 has probably also led to the more intensified use of LPN's.[12] As a consequence, between 1954 and 1959 the proportion of practicing practical nurses in the U. S. increased more rapidly than for any other nursing group (Table 2-4).

Wages, Hours, and Working Conditions

Practical nurses employed by hospitals are periodically required to work on holidays, in the evening, and at night because hospitals operate 24 hours a day the year round. Most hospitals function on a three-shift basis. Hospital nurses generally work 40 hours a week and receive their regular rate for overtime work or are permitted equal time off from employment. Wage differentials are usually paid for the 3:00 p.m. to 11:00 p.m. and the 11:00 p.m. to 7:00 a.m. shifts.

Some hospitals in recent years have adjusted their work schedules to meet the needs of female nurses with family responsibilities. Convenient hours and half-time shifts draw some women who are unable to work a 40-hour week back into practice. Between 1948 and 1962 the number of general duty professional nurses employed part time in nonfederal hospitals increased from 17,000 to more than 77,000 (350 percent).[13] Whether a similar increase in part-time employment has occurred among practical nurses is not known, but there is probably a greater percentage of practical nurses working part time today than a decade ago.

Nurses, regardless of their place of employment, spend a considerable proportion of their working hours on their feet and occasionally encounter unpleasant sights and experiences. According to a study of 34 hospitals in 1956, 76 percent of the practical nurse's employment time is spent performing duties for which she was specifically trained, 7 percent of her time is relegated to lower or higher skill level nursing functions, and 17 percent of her time is devoted to clerical and other non-nursing chores.[14]

Nurses employed by hospitals usually receive some sick leave allowance and hospital and medical benefits. Retirement pension plans of some type are generally provided by employing institutions. Social Security programs are voluntary for hospitals owned by nonprofit organizations or government units; however, 60 percent of all state and local government hospital employees and approximately 95 percent of the employees in nonprofit hospitals are covered. Employees of nonprofit hospitals are covered by unemployment insurance in only a few states; state and local government hospitals are covered in less than half the states. Also, hospital nurses are covered by workmen compensation laws in less than 25 states. Vacation time varies among employing institutions, but the length of vacation granted nurses is generally calculated on the basis of length of service.[15]

State nursing associations and the American Nurses Association depend largely on conference techniques and public opinion for securing acceptable wages, hours, and working conditions. In 1950, the American Nurses Association voluntarily relinquished its right to strike, but it continues to represent nurses in all matters affecting their employment. Nonprofit and state and local government-owned hospitals are exempted from the National Labor Relations Act and, therefore, are not required to engage in collective bargaining with their employees over conditions of employment, except in states where state law requires it.

The chief characteristic of employment conditions in the nursing profession is that of low wages relative to other occupations requiring comparable skill and training. Hospitals were not covered by the Federal Fair Labor Standards Act until 1967, and of the 24 jurisdictions in which state minimum wage laws apply, only nine provide a minimum of $1.25 or more.

Although information on national average salaries for LPN's is not available, salary data for the state of Illinois and metropolitan Chicago, compiled by the Illinois Hospital Association, give some indication of wage trends in the field of practical nursing and a fairly accurate picture of the current economic status of LPN's. Between 1955 and 1965, the average monthly starting salary for LPN's employed in Illinois hospitals increased from $178 to $267. The average monthly going salary during this same period increased from $192 to $289. In 1963 and 1965, the LPN's employed in metropolitan Chicago received a higher monthly salary than did the LPN's practicing in the state of Illinois as a whole (Appendix E, Table E-5).

Salaries for LPN's employed in Illinois and metropolitan Chicago, as well as for LPN's in general, do not compare favorably with salaries in other occupations requiring similar education and skills. Although some problem of comparability exists for the data incorporated in Table 2-5, they furnish ample evidence of substantial disparity between LPN salaries and salaries for a select group of similar occupations.

The Current Demand and Supply Situation

Despite the tremendous increase which has occurred over the past couple of decades in the number enrolled in professional and practical nursing programs and the increase in the number of practicing nursing personnel, the demand for trained nurses apparently still exceeds the available supply. A list of occupations in demand recently compiled by the U. S. Employment Services indicates a serious shortage of RN's, LPN's and auxiliary nursing personnel. A study by the American Nurses Association (1961) revealed 20 percent of the budgeted positions for professional nurses and 18 percent of the positions for practical nurses, in the hospitals included in the sample, were vacant.[16] In 1962, there were 1,200 faculty vacancies in professional nursing schools and 225 vacancies in practical nursing programs.[17]

In an effort to alleviate the existing shortage of nursing personnel in the U. S., federal funds have been allocated in increasing amounts to expand and improve

Table 2-5

Average Monthly Salaries for Licensed Practical Nurses and Select Group of Occupations, Chicago, 1965

Occupation[1]	*Monthly Salary*[2] *Chicago*
Licensed Practical Nurse	$331
General Stenographer	$381
Keypunch Operator – Class A	$394
Switchboard Operators – Class A	$403
Switchboard Operators – Class B	$331
Typists – Class A	$366

[1]Women comprise 90 percent of the occupation or more.

[2]Except for Licensed Practical Nurse the salary figures are based on average weekly straight-time earnings and have been multiplied by 4.33 to convert to monthly form.

Source: Illinois Hospital Association, "Hospital Salaries in Illinois," report no. 26 (September, 1963), pp. 17–18; and report no. 33 (December, 1965), pp. 17–18; Bureau of Labor Statistics, *Occupational Wage Survey, Chicago, Illinois, April, 1965,* Bulletin No. 1430-72, U. S. Department of Labor (Washington, D. C.: U. S. Government Printing Office).

professional and practical nursing educational programs. Federal expenditures for public vocational practical nursing programs, for example, were increased from $800,000 in 1957 to $5 million in 1963.[18]

In the fall of 1962, additional funds for expanding practical nursing training were made available under the Manpower Development and Training Act. By 1964, when the hospital interviews were being conducted for this study, LPN's, nurse aides, and orderlies were among the 10 occupations, out of a total of 700, with the highest enrollment under the institutional program.[19] In mid-1964, approximately 5 percent (4,100) of all trainees in the entire MDTA program were enrolled in LPN projects. The majority of LPN trainees under MDTA received their training in projects operating in New York, California, Illinois, and Michigan.[20]

Nevertheless, listings by the U. S. Employment Service of shortage occupations continued to show LPN's on the list throughout the 1960's. And occupational projections continued to show the demand for nursing personnel increasing substantially in the years ahead. Although the mix among registered nurses, licensed practical nurses, and auxiliary personnel is not precisely predictable, projections indicate an anticipated growth in employment of all nursing personnel from about 1.2 million to 1.7 million between 1965 and 1975.[21]

Medical Technologists

Medical technology is a distinct branch of medical activity concerned with the performance of laboratory tests for the purpose of detecting, analyzing, and diagnosing human diseases and physical disorders. Many different types of personnel, however, are engaged in medical testing procedures and a fine line often separates the medical technologists from other workers in the laboratory.

Medical laboratories typically operate under the direction and general supervision of a pathologist, a physician trained to employ laboratory methods to aid in the diagnosis and treatment of disease through scientific testing of body tissues, fluids, and excretions. The pathologist or laboratory director reports and interprets these findings to the patient's physician. Certification by the American Board of Pathology requires three or four years of college premedical training, four years of medical school training, one year of internship, and four years of pathology residency.

The medical technologist is the top level laboratory worker who, under the direction of the pathologist, engages in supervision, testing, teaching, and research in a wide range of complex diagnostic and treatment procedures. The American Medical Association has undertaken a strong effort to standardize the educational and experience requirements for gaining recognition as a medical technologist through a registration procedure. To become a registered medical technologist the candidate must complete at least three years of college work, including minimum course requirements in chemistry, biology, and mathematics, and one year of specialized training in a school of medical technology approved by the American Medical Association. Following this training and the passing of an examination administered by the Board of Registry of Medical Technologists of the American Society of Clinical Pathologists, the technologist is certified as a professional medical technologist and may use the designation MT (ASCP) after his name.

Many technologists, however, engage in high level laboratory work without having met the formal requirements for registration by the ASCP. Frequently, for example, persons who have earned bachelor or higher college degrees in one of the sciences (mainly biology or chemistry) are employed by laboratories as medical technologists and do the same work as registered technologists, without taking the year of specialized training in medical technology. There would seem to be no question but that these persons, as well as those with ASCP registration, should appropriately be designated as medical technologists.

There are other technical workers often loosely referred to as medical technologists for whom the appropriateness of the designation is not so clear. Three organizations, none of which is recognized by organized medical groups, conduct registries for medical laboratory personnel. The American Medical Technologists (MT), the International Registry of Independent Medical Technologists (IMT), and the Registry of Medical Technologists of the International Society of Clinical Laboratory Technologists (RMT), each grant registration to high school graduates on the basis of various combinations of experience and/or commercial school or other training and the passing of an examination. Having met, for example, the minimum requirements established by the American Medical Technologists, a person is authorized by that organization to use the designation "MT" after his name. None of the designations authorized by these organizations are recognized by organized medical groups as representing any particular level of professional competence.

In an effort to clarify and to standardize the levels of laboratory work, the American Society of Clinical Pathologists and the American Society of Medical Technologists initiated a new program for the training and recognition of laboratory workers in 1963. Under this program, high school graduates are given one year of practical and technical training in routine laboratory work. Accreditation of hospital and laboratory schools offering this program is given by the Board of Laboratory Assistants. Graduates of these schools who pass an examination given under the Board's direction may use the letters "CLA" after their names to indicate their certification as qualified laboratory assistants. The certified laboratory assistant (CLA), whose status is obtained under the auspices of organized medicine, works under the direction of the medical technologist and a pathologist or other qualified physician, and performs routine laboratory procedures in bacteriology, blood banking chemistry, hematology, parasitology, serology, and urinalysis.

The certified laboratory assistant, as well as other technical workers who do not have the requisite scientific training provided by college level work in the sciences, are not included in the designation of medical technologist used in this study.[22] There are other specialty fields in medical technology, however, for which the level of education and training required is comparable to that of the medical technologist (ASCP) which do fall within the definition. Examples of these are cytotechnologists, CT (ASCP), and nuclear medical technologists, NMT (ASCP).

Medical technologists, in general, work in the capacity of assistants to pathologists who interpret and prepare reports on the results of laboratory tests which have been conducted by them. Laboratory procedures carried out by the medical technologist include: conducting chemical, microscopic, and bacteriological tests to provide data for use in the treatment and diagnosis of diseases; making quantitative and qualitative chemical analysis of body substances such as urine, blood, and tissue; cultivating and identifying bacteria, parasites, and other microorganisms; cutting, staining, and mounting tissue sections for study by a pathologist; performing blood tests and transfusions, and preparing vaccines and serums.[23] Medical technologists may be found performing these laboratory procedures in hospitals, physician's offices and clinics, public health laboratories, university and medical school research laboratories, industrial companies which manufacture and develop drugs, serums, vaccines, and antibiotics, and in the armed services.

The origins of the Medical Technologist (ASCP) can be traced back to 1928, the year in which the American Society of Clinical Pathologists established a registry to examine and certify educated medical technicians. Prior to the latter 1920's there were few clinical and diagnostic laboratories in the country and to a large degree physicians based their diagnosis on a patient's medical history and/or physical examination.

About 90 percent of all ASCP registered technologists are women. In this respect, the field of medical technology resembles the field of nursing. In both fields, custom and relatively low salaries have prevented the entrance of men to any notable degree. Although a lack of comparative data precludes validation of this hypothesis, turnover rates are probably high among practicing medical technologists. According to a U. S. Department of Labor report, an estimated 7,000 trained and registered medical technologists have left the laboratory in recent years.[24] Marriage and family responsibilities are probably largely responsible for this exodus.

Education and Training

Prior to the establishment of the Board of Registry of the American Society of Clinical Pathologists in 1928, there were few schools which provided higher education for medical technologists. The first collegiate medical technology training programs in the country were instituted by the University of Minnesota and the University of Tennessee in the mid-1920's. The University of Minnesota has been credited with establishing the first Bachelor of Science degree program in Medical Technology. During the 1920's, 1930's and 1940's, the large majority of medical technologists received their training in hospital-affiliated medical schools. There was strong opposition to any suggestion that medical technologists should have at least two years of college or university training.

By 1936, 96 schools offering training in medical technology had received ASCP approval.[25] In 1957, there were 656 ASCP-American Medical Association approved schools with a total capacity of nearly 5,000 students. The state of Illinois claimed 37 of the 656 schools.[26] Between 1953 and 1959 the number of accredited schools increased 28 percent and the number of students enrolled increased 56 percent.[27] By 1960, there were 749 ASCP-AMA approved schools for medical technologists, three-fourths of which were affiliated with accreditated colleges or universities that offered degrees in medical technology.[28] By 1965 about 800 accredited schools located in a variety of hospitals, medical schools, and state boards of health were in operation.[29]

The expansion in collegiate training programs for medical technologists which has occurred during the past two decades is largely a response to a progressive upward trend in educational requirements for certification by the ASCP. No formal educational requirements for certification existed prior to 1933; by 1962 three years of college were required. Very recently, the minimum requirement for admission to an approved school of medical technology has been increased to 120 semester hours of college; that is, four years of college training.

In the academic year 1959-1960, 209 accredited higher educational institutions conferred a total of 996 Bachelor of Science degrees in Medical Technology, an increase of 38 percent over the 728 degrees awarded in 1955-1956. Although, according to Board of Registry (ASCP) statistics, the number of medical technologists holding postgraduate degrees in the medical sciences is still small, a remarkable increase has occurred in the educational training of medical technologists in general. In 1930 there were no ASCP registered medical technologists with a college degree, but today more than 85 percent of ASCP registered technologists are college graduates.[30] Between 1928 and 1960 a total of nearly 37,000 medical technologists had been registered by the ASCP. Illinois and Missouri ranked fifth and ninth respectively in numbers of registered technologists.[31]

Employment Trends

Trends in the employment of medical technologists (ASCP) per se cannot be discerned because available statistical data do not differentiate between the main categories of laboratory personnel. The demand for laboratory personnel in general has been increasing since the 1940's. Between 1940 and 1960 the numbers of employed medical and dental technicians increased from 62,998 to 138,162, the greatest increase occurring between 1950 and 1960.[b] During this same period, 1940 to 1960, the proportion of males relative to females declined from approximately 66 percent to 38 percent (Table 2-6). A survey of 5,633 hospitals conducted by the American Hospital Association in 1955 showed that these hospitals employed a total of 30,585 medical laboratory workers. Some 25,952 were employed on a full-time basis and 4,361 on a part-time basis. A similar survey in 1958 indicated that 6,108 hospitals employed 31,995 full-time and 6,216 part-time medical laboratory workers. As of mid-1960, about 28,000 of the 37,000 technologists who had ever been registered by the ASCP were employed.[32]

Salaries, Hours, and Working Conditions

Hours of work among medical technologists vary considerably. Medical technologists employed by hospitals in the state of Illinois work an average 40-hour week. Medical technologists employed by hospitals are required at times to work weekends, odd hours, and serve night duty. Medical technologists who

[b]The census employs the all-inclusive category medical technician for all laboratory workers, technicians, and technologists.

Table 2-6

Employed Medical and Dental Laboratory Technicians by Sex, 1940, 1950, 1960

Year	*Total*	*Percent Increase*	*Male*	*Female*	*Percent Male*
1940	62,998		41,487	21,511	65.9
1950	76,662	21.7	33,219	43,443	43.3
1960	138,162	80.2	51,891	86,271	37.6

Source: U. S. Census of Population Reports, "The Labor Force," vol. 3 (1940), p. 75; "Characteristics of the Population," pt. 1, U. S. Summary (Washington, D. C.: U. S. Government Printing Office), p. 528.

work in doctors' offices, industrial and academic medical laboratories, and biological companies generally work regular daytime hours.

Hospitals frequently employ medical technologists part time to supplement the regular staff in order to handle peak loads, evening, and weekend work. Two hospital surveys conducted by the American Medical Association in the later 1950's show that the proportion of medical technologists employed part time is in the vicinity of 16 percent to 20 percent.[33]

Considerable variation exists with regard to fringe benefit policies and practices of employing institutions. Generally, medical technologists receive retirement provisions, vacations with pay, and sick leave with pay.

Salary data for medical technologists are very limited but the indications are that salaries have increased substantially over the past two decades, partially in response to an increase in the level of education of medical technologists. The median annual salary for medical technologists (ASCP), including postgraduate degree holders, in 1963 was $5,190 ($433 monthly), 50 percent higher than in 1953.[34]

Salaries for medical technologists (ASCP) employed in Illinois and metropolitan Chicago hospitals have also risen substantially since the mid-1950's. Between 1955 and 1965 the average monthly starting salary for hospital-employed medical technologists (ASCP) in Illinois increased by approximately 42 percent. A 1959 survey ranked Illinois fourth and Missouri twentieth among 35 states responding to a survey questionnaire (Appendix E, Tables E-6 and E-7).

A comparison of monthly starting salaries for medical technologists (ASCP) employed in Illinois and Chicago hospitals with other personnel indicates that medical technologists' salaries are higher than salaries for registered nurses and licensed practical nurses (Appendix E, Figure E-1). The salary differential among registered nurses, licensed practical nurses, and medical technologists (ASCP) reflects the higher level of education and training of medical technologists.

The Current Demand and Supply Situation

According to a recent report of the U. S. Department of Labor, the supply of ASCP registered medical technologists has not kept pace with an increasing demand. In response to personnel shortages, some hospitals have reduced laboratory services rendered to private physicians and also have found it necessary to employ college graduates who have degrees in biology and chemistry but no specialized training in laboratory procedures.[35]

The demand for highly skilled medical technologists will continue to rise in the future; in fact, the Manpower Administration suggests that clinical laboratory jobs will probably expand twice as fast as jobs in the health service field in general during the period 1965 to 1975.[36]

Engineering Technicians

The Technological Team

The scientist and engineer are, and for many years have been, a part of what has sometimes been referred to as the technological team. Although the technological team has been in existence for some time, the kinds of people who comprise this team have been in a constant state of flux.

Thirty years ago the team consisted of two groups of men: engineers and skilled craftsmen. Then, practical applications were based on well-known theories and these two groups worked closely together in solving the problems that arose as they developed new, and in comparison with today, relatively simple, technical products.[37] However, as the rapid pace of technological progress of the past 25 years forced engineering work to higher and higher scientific levels, a gap appeared between the engineer and the skilled craftsman.[38] Science and engineering have, in the past quarter of a century, developed complicated procedures, equipment, and products that cannot be thoroughly understood by men trained only as skilled craftsmen. A new member of the technical team was needed to bridge the gap between the scientist and the engineer and the skilled manual worker. This man was the engineering technician.

Technicians are, at present, gradually taking over work that used to require the professional knowledge of engineers. Years of experience in industry have routinized much engineering work, and its procedures can now be taught to students in a technology course.

Perhaps the most important fact to note about the technological team is that there are no clear-cut lines of demarcation among the kinds of work performed by the engineer, the technician, or the skilled craftsman. The line between professional and technical work is often blurred as is the line between technical workers and craftsmen. In the classification of technological jobs:

> You don't find two straight lines that cut across all industries. In some the work of the technician may be quite routine. In others he does work almost as complex as most engineers do. Sometimes work that could be done as well by a technician is done by an engineer. Or work is assigned to a technician that really belongs to a skilled craftsman.[39]

The term technician as commonly used in industry and in government comprises a large number of vaguely defined occupational groups. It is used by different employers to refer to workers in a great variety of jobs requiring a wide range of education and training. The classification "is applied to employees doing relatively routine work, to persons performing work requiring skills within a limited sphere, and to persons doing highly technical work, among them assistants to engineers and scientists."[40]

Our research concern is restricted to semiprofessional technicians who assist and/or support professional engineers and scientists in electronics and metalworking industries. For purposes of analysis the term *engineering technician-electronics* has been chosen to designate engineering technicians employed in electronic industries, and the term *engineering technician-metal working* has been chosen to designate engineering technicians employed in metalworking industries. Engineering technicians may be defined as those persons having a knowledge of engineering and mathematical science equivalent to one to three years of formal post-high school training and some practical skill, or comparable on-the-job training and experience, and engaged in engineering work at a skill level lower than that of a professional engineer or professional scientist. In other words, an engineering technician has greater knowledge of scientific and engineering theory and methods than a craftsman but less extensive training than a professional engineer.[c] This definition of an engineering technician excludes traditional skilled craftsman occupations such as those held by electricians, engineers with college degrees, and semiskilled workers engaged in engineering tasks that require only a brief period of on-the-job instruction.

The type of work performed by the engineering technician varies greatly, depending upon the functional area within which he works. In research, development, and design work, which is one of the largest areas of employment, technicians conduct experiments or tests, set up, calibrate, and operate instruments, and make calculations. They also assist scientists and engineers in the development of experimental equipment and models by making drawings and sketches and, under the direction of the engineer, often do some design

[c]In this study the definition of engineering technician is similar to the definition adopted by the American Society of Engineer Education in *Characteristics of Excellence in Engineering Technology Education*, 1962.

work.[41] Technicians also work in jobs having a production orientation. Here they usually follow the general direction of the engineer but often without close supervision. They may work in the various phases of production operations, such as working out specifications for materials and methods of manufacture, devising tests to insure quality control of products, or making time-and-motion studies. They may also act as intermediaries and perform liaison work between engineering and production or other departments.

One of the better known specialties grouped within the classification of engineering technicians and also one of the occupations chosen for examination in this study, is that of the tool designer.[42] After an engineer has designed a new product, the next job is to develop the means of producing it. Sometimes a model of the new product is built in a model shop, with skilled or technical workers translating the drawings of the engineer into what is called a prototype. The newly designed product must also be described exactly in drawings. Using the drawings and the prototype as a basis, the tool designer must work out the tools to be used in making the new product.[43]

The remaining member of the technological team is the skilled craftsman, the tool and die maker. Tool and die makers frequently are highly skilled, creative workers. Tool makers specialize in producing jigs and fixtures; the latter is a device required to hold metal while it is being shaved, stamped or drilled. They also make gauges and other measuring devices that are utilized in the manufacture of precision metal parts. Die makers, as the name indicates, construct dies, which are metal forms used in die casting and in molding plastics. Tool and die makers can also be found repairing dies, gauges, jigs, and fixtures. At the price of further obscuring the already rather nebulous classification of tool designers as technicians, it must be noted that some tool and die makers help design tools and dies.

"In comparison with most other machine workers, tool and die makers have a broader knowledge of machine operations, shop practices, mathematics, and blueprint reading, and can work to closer tolerances and do more precise handwork."[44] Tool and die makers must be able to use almost every type of machine tool and precision-measuring instrument.

Although these attempts to define and delimit the technician and skilled occupations provide insight of major importance, they cannot provide precise and necessary distinctions which differentiate the specific occupational labor markets being studied. More precise formulation of the specific nature of the labor markets and the channels of entry and recruitment are necessary before any generalization about either the extent or nature of shortages and their amelioration can be attempted.

Education and Patterns of Entry

Engineering technicians may receive their occupational training in a variety of ways. Training may be obtained in formal training programs offered in technical institutes, junior and community colleges, area vocational technical schools, extension divisions of colleges and universities, technical and technical-vocational high schools, as well as through upgrading. Persons can also become qualified for technician jobs by completing an on-the-job training program, through work experience and formal courses taken on a part-time basis in postsecondary or correspondence schools, or through training and experience obtained in the armed forces. It is also possible for engineering and science students who have not completed all requirements for their bachelor's degree to qualify for technician jobs after they obtain some additional technical training and experience.

A recent study revealed that slightly less than a majority of employed engineering technicians have some college education but do not hold a bachelor of science degree (Table 2-7). The same study revealed that engineering technicians currently employed received their training largely through special training provided by employers, college and technical institute training programs, on-the-job experience, and military service (Appendix F, Table F-1).

The educational attainment of technicians is continually increasing. This is illustrated by the fact that younger technicians have completed more schooling than older technicians (Appendix F, Table F-2). About two-thirds (65 percent) of those 24 years of age or less have completed at least some college work, as contrasted with only about 45 percent of those age 55 or older. Less than 6 percent under 25 years of age have not completed high school, as compared with about 43 percent 55 years of age or older.[45]

In 1963, about 450 schools offered postsecondary technician training; about 100,000 full-time students were enrolled. About 25,000 students were graduated in 1963. Follow-up studies indicate that about 16,000 of these graduates entered technician jobs and the largest proportion of the remainder continued their schooling in bachelor's degree programs.[46]

An estimated 6,000 persons with two or more years of college training in engineering or science curriculums entered technician occupations in 1963. Of this total, about half entered technician jobs after receiving the bachelor's degree.[47]

Some large corporations conduct their own training programs designed to meet their need for technically trained personnel. Instruction is given both through formal classes and training on the job; the training is predominantly technical and rarely includes any general studies.

Those workers who acquire all of their training on the job usually receive only a minimal theoretical background. Many corporations without training programs reimburse their employees for tuition after they have satisfactorily completed evening courses at local schools or correspondence courses. The workers usually are expected to take courses directly related to their work assignment and on occasion are permitted to attend classes on the employer's time. Training for some occupations in the technician category, such as tool designer and electronic technician, may be obtained through completion of a formal apprenticeship. In addition to on-the-job training, supplementary

Table 2-7

Educational Level of Employed Engineering and Physical Science Technicians, 1960

		Percent Distribution
Total	270,985	
Less Than a High School Graduate		14.5
High School Graduate		25.8
At Least Two Years of College but Less Than Four Years		2.6
Some College but no Degree		48.3
Bachelor's Degree or More		8.7

Source: Howard V. Stambler and Annie Lefkowitz, "Education and Training of Technicians," *Monthly Labor Review*, vol. 87, no. 11 (November, 1964), p. 1279.

education in mathematics and science is provided. Industry technician training programs prepared an estimated 21,600 workers for entrance to technician occupations in 1963.[48]

Although most engineering technician jobs require education beyond the high school level, or the equivalent in experience, a few technical and technical-vocational high schools, principally in large urban areas, offer programs which qualify their graduates for some technician entry jobs. In 1963, an estimated 13,000 students were receiving secondary school technician training in approximately 300 schools.[49] Few advanced technical courses are offered in these schools, so graduates generally cannot enter technician jobs directly. However, follow-up studies indicate that about two-fifths of these graduates continue their education in postsecondary schools.[50] For this reason, secondary school technician training plays a much more important role in the overall picture of technician education than is indicated by the number of graduates going directly into technician occupations.

Technician training is also offered by all branches of the armed forces. Technician training programs given in the armed forces generally last from three to eighteen months, and training usually includes little theory. Since military electrical and electronic equipment usually is unlike equipment used in civilian

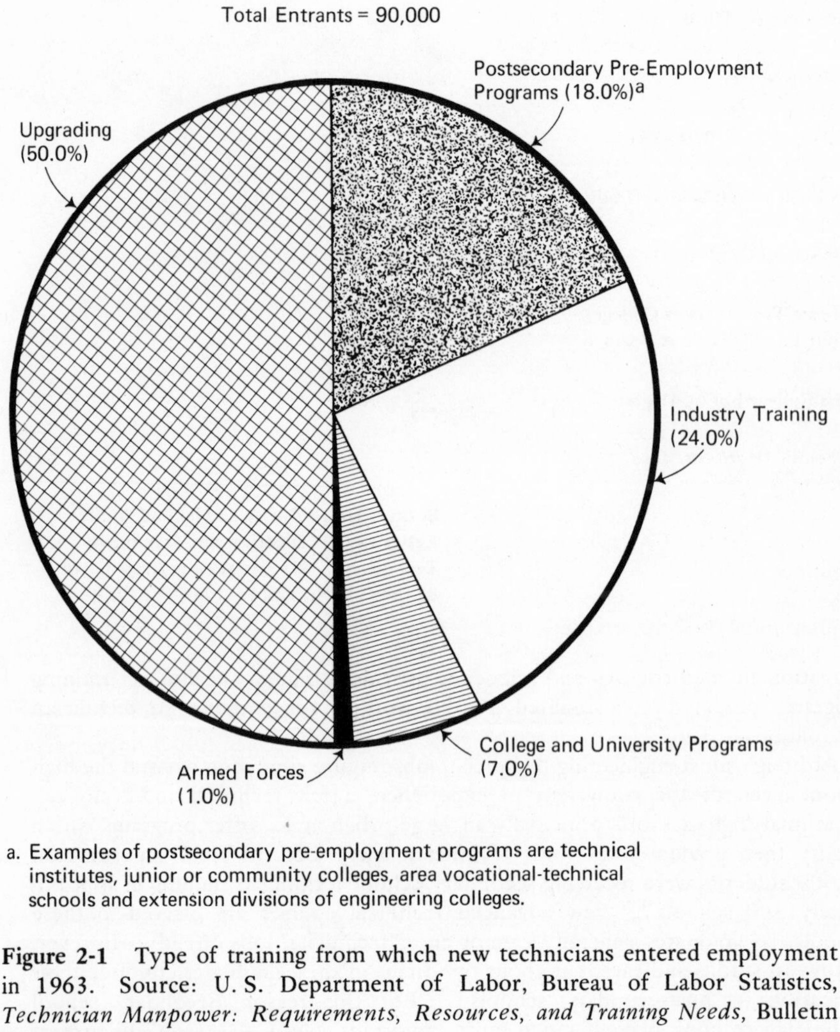

a. Examples of postsecondary pre-employment programs are technical institutes, junior or community colleges, area vocational-technical schools and extension divisions of engineering colleges.

Figure 2-1 Type of training from which new technicians entered employment in 1963. Source: U. S. Department of Labor, Bureau of Labor Statistics, *Technician Manpower: Requirements, Resources, and Training Needs,* Bulletin No. 1512, June, 1966, p. 39.

industry, the vast majority of military technicians must undergo additional training before they can enter civilian technician jobs. Although the number of technicians separated from the armed forces in any given year is large, the proportion of these who enter civilian technician jobs directly after separation is believed to be small.

The Manpower Development and Training Act has provided training for technicians in programs generally lasting about a year. MDTA programs have tended to stress applied technical courses rather than theory or general education. As a result, graduates of these programs are well grounded in the practical aspects of the particular occupations but tend to be less flexible than graduates of programs offering more instruction in theory.

Upgrading is usually conducted by employers when they cannot recruit workers with pre-employment or technician-related training and when it is not economically feasible to initiate their own training program. Many company officials believe that the costs of initiating a training program would be higher in the long run than having a relatively unproductive worker on the job until he gains the training to perform his work adequately through his job experience. Workers who are upgraded usually have had several years experience working in positions where they gain at least some familiarity with the technician job which they ultimately fill. It has been estimated that in 1963 upgrading was the largest single source of new technician supply.[51]

Figure 2-1 illustrates the type of training new technicians received in 1963.

Current trends in technician education indicate that formal channels of training are becoming increasingly significant. Although it is estimated that more technicians learned to perform their jobs through company training than through any other means, the relatively large number of young technicians who have recently entered technician work with some college training indicates that this latter source is growing in importance. It, therefore, appears likely that technicians trained in junior colleges and other types of schools offering postsecondary pre-employment technician training will constitute an increasing proportion of all new technicians during the years ahead.[52] This trend, if continued, will undoubtedly mean greater standardization of qualifications and training and will facilitate greater delineation of each specific technician labor market.

These vast varieties of programs of on-the-job instruction related to different processes and equipment and featured by varying proportions of general theoretical versus specific training, imply that a given broad technician category, such as electronic technician, may be subdivided into a large number of specific industry or process oriented technician subspecialties with different job titles. Frequently these specialties have limited transferability between job categories. These job characteristics imply considerable feudalization or balkanization of technician labor markets with consequent difficulty in generalizing about the magnitude of shortages within a given general technical classification. These distinctions within broad categories make precise pinpointing very difficult and suggest the desirability of a general, uniform, theoretical package for each broad technician group before specialization is attempted.

Employers and Earnings

An estimated 620,000 engineering and science technicians,[d] not including draftsmen and surveyors, were employed in mid-1964.[53] Of this total, about 12 percent were women. Nearly 475,000 of these technicians were employed by private industry, the largest employers being companies in the electrical equipment, machinery, chemicals, and aerospace industries. In mid-1964, approximately 130,000 technicians were employed by various government agencies. This group included 75,000 engineering and science technicians employed by the Federal government, 40,000 employed by state government, and about 15,000 working for local governments. The rest of the employed technicians worked for either colleges and universities or nonprofit organizations.

A wide variance exists in salaries paid to technicians. One of the main reasons for this is the tremendous skill differential existing among technicians. Existing classification systems do not properly delineate the specific labor markets where differential patterns involving skill and other important supply-demand conditions may prevail. The large differences in salaries is indicated by two recent studies undertaken by the Bureau of Labor Statistics which showed that depending on skill level, the average salary of a technician may vary by almost $4,000.[54] In federal government agencies in early 1965, the starting salary for beginning engineering and science technicians was $4,005, $4,480, or $5,000, depending upon the type of job vacancy and the applicant's education and other qualifications.

Trends in the Employment of Engineering Technicians

All available evidence indicates that within the past decade semiprofessional technicians have been one of the most rapidly growing occupational groups in

[d]A basic difficulty in any study of technicians is the fact, already alluded to, that there is no general consensus of who should be included within the category of technician. Statistical comparisons and the attempted indication of trends are particularly handicapped by this shortcoming. We shall attempt to make the best of this difficult situation by indicating, when we use the term, exactly who we are referring to as engineering technicians.

Table 2-8

Employment of Technicians in the United States, by Sex, 1940 and 1950

	Male		Female	
Total, 14 Years and Over	*1950*	*1940*	*1950*	*1940*
Technicians, Medical and Dental; Technicians, Testing	91,759	43,517	60,071	23,791
Technicians (Not Elsewhere Classified)	22,639	8,947	4,243	901

Source: U. S. Census of Population Report, "Detailed Occupation of Employed Persons, by Sex, For the United States: 1950 and 1940," vol. 2, pt. 1 (Washington, D. C.: U. S. Government Printing Office, 1953), Table 125.

the nation. Although methodological problems which relate to definitions and the continuity of various time-trend data make it impossible to accurately portray trends in the employment of technicians over an extended period of time, an examination of those statistics which are available gives a reasonably clear picture. Census data (Table 2-8) indicate that in all of the categories surveyed, the number of technicians at least doubled between 1940 and 1950. The tremendous increases in the employment of technicians continued through the 1950's (Table 2-9). The most striking aspect of these data is that while the labor force as a whole was increasing by 14.5 percent, increases in the various technician categories ranged from about 80 percent for medical and dental technicians to nearly 700 percent for electrical and electronic technicians. Total employment of technicians increased almost two and one-half times between 1950 and 1960, from less than 200,000 to nearly 500,000. By 1963 employed technicians numbered in excess of 600,000.[e] The conclusion is quite clear: Employment of technicians in the past 20 to 25 years has increased rapidly and at a much faster rate than the labor force as a whole.

The Current Demand and Supply Situation

There appears to be a general consensus among employers and government officials that our country is presently experiencing a shortage of qualified

[e]The figures exclude draftsmen. (See Appendix F, Table F-4.)

Table 2-9

Employment of Technicians in the United States, 1950 and 1960

	1960	*1950*	*Percent Increase 1950–1960*
Total Employed: All Occupations	64,639,256	56,435,273	14.5
Technicians: Medical and Dental	138,162	76,662	80.2
Technicians: Electrical and Electronic	91,463	11,738	679.2
Technicians: Other Engineering and Physical Sciences	183,609	90,995	101.8
Technicians (Not Elsewhere Classified)	65,723	18,606	253.2

Source: U. S. Census of Population Report, "Detailed Occupation of the Employed by Sex, For the United States: 1960 and 1950," vol. 1, pt. 1 (Washington, D. C.: U. S. Government Printing Office, 1963), Table 202.

engineering technicians. In recent years, technicians have been one of the fastest growing occupational groups, and it is estimated that this rapid growth will continue. In general, it has been anticipated that demand will be strongest for graduates of postsecondary school technician training programs to fill high level engineering technician jobs. Secretary of Labor, W. Willard Wirtz, in presenting testimony in 1962 on the Technical Education Bill, stated that semiprofessional "engineering and scientific occupations have been among the fastest growing occupational fields in recent decades, and at present, we do not have enough persons with the requisite education. There is every indication that these occupations will continue to grow rapidly . . . and that if future requirements in this field are to be met, a considerable increase in the number of persons who receive the essential education will be necessary."[55] The National Science Foundation in a recent report likewise suggests that in recent years the supply of semiprofessional technicians has lagged behind industrial, government, and academic demand for such personnel.[56] In 1962 some 1,100 employers interviewed by the New York State Department of Labor reported 4,500 vacancies in technical occupations.[57] Assuming relatively high levels of economic activity and employment, the National Science Foundation estimated a 67 percent increase in technician employment would occur between 1960 and 1970. Projected growth in technician requirements for various categories is shown in Appendix F, Table F-3.

The Bureau of Labor Statistics has estimated both requirements and anticipated supply for technicians in 1975 under varying assumptions.[58] These global data indicate continuing tightness of the over-all labor market for technicians and imply the need for expansion of all channels for recruitment and entry into technician positions.

Tool and Die Makers

Since World War II, continuous shortages of tool and die makers have been well publicized. This occupation, the so-called aristocrat of the craft field, is sufficiently different in channels of entry and recruitment, type of training, structure of employment, and even pay trends to differentiate its labor markets from those classified as engineering technician. This despite the fact that the lines of demarcation between the tool and die designer and maker are frequently blurred and substantial proportions of those in the so-designated higher category actually have only tool and die maker training. Thus, at the risk of some repetition, a delineation of broad labor market trends for members of this occupation will be attempted.

Earnings, Hours, and Conditions of Employment

Tool and die makers are among the highest paid skilled workers. A 1963

Department of Labor survey estimated that average lifetime earnings of tool and die makers were higher than any of the other selected skilled trade occupations listed.[59]

In April through June, 1965, average straight-time hourly earnings of tool and die makers in machinery manufacturing shops (those producing tools, die sets, and fixtures as the end product) in 13 areas were as follows.

Boston	$3.23
Buffalo	3.25
Chicago	3.99
Cleveland	3.35
Detroit	3.95
Hartford–New Britain–Bristol	3.05
Los Angeles–Long Beach	3.63
Milwaukee	3.66
Minneapolis–St. Paul	3.43
Newark–Jersey City	3.25
New York City	3.38
Philadelphia	3.42
St. Louis	3.38

Tool and die makers in various manufacturing industries in 58 areas surveyed in 1963-1964 were paid average straight-time hourly earnings ranging from $2.74 in Miami, Florida, to $3.98 in San Francisco-Oakland, California.[60]

Straight-time hourly earnings data are somewhat misleading in that overtime is the norm for tool and die makers. Hours of work have been increased and maintained to levels far above the national average. For example, in May 1966, the average workweek was almost 49 hours in the tool and die industry as compared with an average for all manufacturing of 41.5 hours.

Most tool and die makers are members of such unions as the International Association of Machinists; the International Union of Electrical, Radio and Machine Workers; the United Automobile, Aerospace, and Agricultural Implement Workers of America; the United Steelworkers of America; and the Mechanics Educational Society of America.[61] Technicians, in the main, are not unionized, although some efforts at organization have resulted in groupings in some plants.

Training

Tool and die making requires several years of varied training and experience which can be obtained either through formal apprenticeship or equivalent on-the-job training. Since this work is highly skilled, "persons planning to enter the trade should have a good working knowledge of mathematics and physics as well as considerable mechanical ability, finger dexterity, and a liking for painstaking work."[62] In selecting apprentices, most employers require a high school or trade school education. Some employers test apprentice applicants to determine their mechanical and mathematical ability. Certain basic temperaments are deemed essential to apprentices, including: the ability to perform a variety of tasks often characterized by frequent change, the ability to work from blueprints and work orders, and the ability to work to the precise attainment of prescribed tolerances and standards.[63]

The specifics of apprenticeship programs for tool and die makers vary in their details but formal programs ordinarily last four or five years. Most of the time is devoted to practical shop training, but some related classroom work also is included as part of the training program. During shop training, the apprentice learns to operate major machine tools, such as lathes and milling machines, and the use of handtools for fitting and assembling tools, gauges, and other mechanical equipment. The study of heat treating and other metalworking processes are included in the apprenticeship program. Classroom training in shop mathematics, shop theory, mechanical drawing, tool designing, and blueprint reading also is given. After apprenticeship, several years experience often is necessary to qualify for more difficult tool and die work.

Many metal machine workers have become tool and die makers without completing formal apprenticeship. After acquiring years of experience as machine tool operators or as machinists plus vocational or correspondence school training, these men have developed into all-around workers who can skillfully perform almost any metal machining operation, including tool and die making.[64]

A 1959 study by the Bureau of Apprenticeship and Training found that at that time industry was training only about 60 percent of the tool and die apprentices necessary to replace journeymen lost from death and retirement.[65] In more recent years some efforts have been made to stimulate increased training of tool and die makers through preapprenticeship and other programs under the Manpower Development and Training Act.[66]

A training program which predates the passage of the Manpower Development and Training Act by many years is one conducted by Chicago's Tool and Die Institute (TDI), an organization made up of several hundred area firms. Training is at present taking place without MDTA funds. Classes, which are held in conjunction with the Chicago Board of Education's Vocational Training Department, began in 1934. Instructors are recruited from industry by TDI and their pay is shared by the city and TDI. About 100 students are graduated each year. Classes are open to students from TDI member companies and must be bona fide apprentices. The member registers the student in the school, and TDI sets up the curriculum for each pupil.[67]

Employment Trends

An examination of employment data on tool and die makers indicates that the greatest increase in tool and die employment in the U. S. occurred in the decade of the 1940's when employment increased by 62 percent. At the same time, employment increased by 125 percent in Chicago. Comparable figures for St. Louis are not available. However, in the 1950's both Chicago and St. Louis lagged behind the national rate of increase in the employment of tool and die makers, as well as behind the 14.5 percent increase in the labor force as a whole (Table 2-10).

More recent figures show that from 1963 through 1966, the tool and die industry expanded its workforce by an estimated 15 percent. The increase for the 12 months ending May, 1966, alone was 8 percent. This new surge in employment appeared to be the result of Vietnam requirements.[68]

The Current Demand and Supply Situation

The labor market situation for tool and die makers is tight in virtually all areas of the nation. According to a recent manpower survey of the machine tool industry conducted by the U. S. Employment Service,[69] recruitment of workers with metalworking skills has become increasingly difficult in most metalworking centers. Because of contributing local stringencies, employers have been requesting the Employment Service, through its interarea recruitment system, to find workers for them in other areas of the country. Among the largest numbers of job openings placed in interarea recruitment in June, 1966, were those for machinists and tool and die makers. This shortage of skilled tool and die makers had been in effect for at least seven years.[70] A 1959 study conducted by the Bureau of Apprenticeship and Training of the Department of Labor indicated that firms were encountering difficulties in hiring journeymen in local labor markets.[71] On an industry-wide basis, over 43 percent of the companies were unable to hire sufficient numbers of craftsmen who could meet their hiring standards.

Although employers often tend to exaggerate labor shortages, according to *Steel,* a publication of the metalworking industry, practically all tool and die shops report that the shortage of competent, skilled workers is causing a tremendous loss of production and income. According to many of the industry's managers, "about 20 percent more business could be handled if competent workers were available."[72]

In the Chicago area, George Straub, Secretary of the Tool and Die Institute of Chicago, noted in 1962, "We get about three calls per week for journeyman machinists, tool and die makers, and molders. For the past couple of years we've

Table 2-10

Employment of Tool Makers, Die Makers, and Setters in the United States, Chicago, and St. Louis, Decennially, 1930–1960

Years	*United States*	*Chicago*	*St. Louis*
1960	182,345	12,883	2,413
Percent Increase From 1950	19%	6%	11%
1950	152,658	12,161	2,170
Percent Increase From 1940	62%	125%	-
1940	94,145	5,399	-
Percent Increase From 1930	19%	34%	-
1930	78,794	4,330	-

Percent increase reflects increase occurring in decade bracketed by years.

Source: Census data.

had to turn down 80 to 90 percent of the requests. If anything, the shortage is getting tighter. . . ."[73]

Manpower projections are always difficult to make because of the large number of interrelated variables involved in making these forecasts. Alternate sets of assumptions may produce strikingly different estimates of manpower requirements. These difficulties are nowhere more evident than in the projections made for tool and die makers.

The Bureau of Labor Statistics, in its *Occupational Outlook Handbook* indicates that employment of tool and die makers is expected to "increase moderately during the 1965-1975 decade as a result of the anticipated expansion of metalworking activity."[74] The bureau believes that long-range expansion in the machinery, electrical equipment, and other metalworking industries will result in a continued increase in the employment of tool and die makers. Their skills will be needed to make the tools and dies used to produce the large numbers of metal parts required in these industries and to help put many technological developments into effect. The bureau, of course, recognizes that numerically controlled machine operations require fewer of the special tools and jigs and fixtures that are now made by tool and die makers. It is also aware that numerically controlled machines could replace many of the conventional machines now used in manufacturing tools, jigs, and fixtures, thus increasing

Table 2-11

Estimated Changes in Manpower Requirements in the Metalworking Industries, 1960–1980

	Number of Workers	
Machining Occupations	*1960*	*1980*
Machine Operators	600,000	800,000
Machinists	200,000	100,000
Tool and Die Makers	150,000	100,000
Setup and Layout Men	50,000	50,000
Total Production Workers	1,000,000	1,050,000
Part–Programmers	-----	200,000
Total	1,000,000	1,250,000

Source: Corplan Associates, *Technological Change – Its Impact on Industry in Metropolitan Chicago – The Metalworking Industries* (Illinois Institute of Technology Research Institute, 1964), p. 49.

output per tool and die maker. However, since the "specific effects of numerical control on the employment of these workers cannot be foreseen at this time," the bureau did not allow for them in its projection of trends.

Corplan Associates of the Illinois Institute of Technology Research Institute, in a review of expected developments in the metalworking industry, made employment projections which included what they believed to be the probable results of the introduction of numerically controlled machines and arrived at totally different projections.[75] Assuming a rate of economic growth of three to three and one half percent per year between 1960 and 1980, Corplan Associates expect that the introduction of numerically controlled machines will cause employment of tool and die makers to decrease from 150,000 to 100,000 during this 20 year period (see Table 2-11).

Although these two sets of projections show extremely different results, we should not allow their differences to obscure their points of agreement. First, there appears to be general agreement that there will be an expansion of the metalworking industries in the next 10 to 20 years. Secondly, many openings will become available as experienced tool and die makers transfer to other fields of work, retire, or die.

It is, of course, extremely difficult to determine the effects of the introduction of numerically controlled machines over the next 15 or 20 years. The number of craftsmen who will be employed is, in addition, not independent of price changes in machine tools as a result of new technology. The utilization of this new technology will affect not only the number of tool and die makers required, but will also determine the job content of those craftsmen employed. It is likely that as numerically controlled machines replace conventional machines in the manufacture of tools, jigs, and fixtures, "many of the decisions, judgments, shop practices, and precision machinery functions presently required of these highly skilled craftsmen will also be transferred to the planning and programming operations to be coded as instructions on a control tape."[76]

The extent of labor displacement or expansion in metalworking industries depends greatly on the economic circumstances of the change and the speed with which numerical control is introduced. If production is relatively constant or increasing only slowly, the increased output per man-hour resulting from numerical control could result in reduced employment. While these possible future trends loom large, and the evolution of this technology over the next few years may even follow these predictions, the current level of demand seems sufficiently higher than the supply of new entrants through conventional channels to warrant continued concern about the supply of craftsmen.

II: The Medical Occupations

3 Extent and Nature of the Shortage, Chicago and St. Louis

The investigation of shortages of personnel in the licensed practical nurse and medical technology occupations took place during a period of relatively loose labor market conditions in the metropolitan areas of Chicago and St. Louis. To ascertain the nature and extent of the shortages it was necessary to relate labor market behavior to supply-demand relationships for these occupations. Such analysis is basic to establishing whether a shortage is a meaningful one in dynamic economic terms and is helpful in appraising possible factors slowing or impeding market adjustment.

In this study, a shortage was defined as a situation in which employers were unable to hire at existing salaries qualified persons to fill positions for which there were budgeted funds and for which personnel were required in order to meet existing demands for services. It follows from this definition that a shortage exists either when budgeted positions are unoccupied (i.e., for more than a brief period) or when positions are filled by persons who are clearly inadequately qualified to give services in the quantity and quality generally regarded as standard (e.g., when unqualified nurse aides are used in place of licensed practical nurses). In addition to the budgeted vacancy criterion other less specific but nonetheless possibly more valid criteria must be considered. These relate to whether the labor market parties could be inferred to have acted as though a shortage actually existed.

Factors discussed below which indicate both the existence and extent of labor shortages include trends in employment and earnings, employer experience and perceptions with staffing problems, number of vacancies in the occupations, worker experiences in obtaining employment, perceptions of mobility, certain characteristics of employees and trainees in the occupations, and the nature of administrative problems associated with the utilization of available manpower.

Employment Trends

Although the records of the sampled hospitals were not adequate to obtain a precise measurement of employment changes for LPN's and medical technologists in recent years, it is clear that trends in these hospitals have been qualitatively compatible with regional and national patterns in two basic respects. Not only has employment in these occupations increased rapidly but it also has represented a relatively larger share of total employment in the nursing and laboratory service areas. The figures indicate that in the five years preceding the hospital interviews, increases in employment of LPN's were in the magnitude of 80 to 90 percent; for medical technologists the increase was 40 to 45 percent. The relative increase in both occupations was greater for the medium and large hospitals than for the smaller ones. Furthermore, as the following tabulation indicates, a large majority of the hospitals in both cities, but particularly the larger ones, were utilizing growing proportions of LPN's in nursing and medical technologists in the laboratories.

Percent of Sample Hospitals Using Relatively More LPN's and/or Medical Technologists

	LPN'S	*Medical Technologists*
Number of hospitals responding	34	28
Small hospitals	46%	38%
Medium hospitals	80%	67%
Large hospitals	86%	83%
Total	71%	63%

To the extent that there is a shortage of personnel in these occupations, it should be noted that it is related to both an absolute and relative increase in the utilization of these categories of workers. The reasons for the relative increase in utilization, however, differ substantially for the two occupations. Nearly half of the hospitals using relatively more LPN's (49 percent) attribute this to the shortage of higher level personnel (registered nurses). Most of the other hospitals cite as reasons the desire to improve the quality of patient care via the substitution of LPN's for nurse aides or orderlies (24 percent). A third important consideration is the attempt to lower costs by substituting LPN's for registered nurses (19 percent).

Increasing technical complexity of diagnostic tests constitutes the overwhelming reason for increased utilization of medical technologists. Over 80 percent of the hospitals employed relatively more of them because of increased use of laboratory tests as a diagnostic technique. A heightened need for testing for research purposes in the laboratory could also be cited. Greater over-all complexity of tests and a higher research component, despite some offsetting mechanization and routinization of standard tests, increased the relative desirability of highly trained professional ASCP personnel.

The possible mechanization and routinization of standard tests offer substantial long-run possibilities for the use of lesser trained and qualified personnel with no impairment in testing accuracy. In the interim, however, such possibilities are not being completely exploited and thus the greater complexity of some tests plus growing research needs seem to overbalance the job dilution potentials.

For the minority of hospitals which had not increased the proportion of LPN's and medical technologists in their employ, the reasons again differed for the two occupations. While over half the hospitals (58 percent) said they hadn't increased the proportion of LPN's utilized because of the shortage of qualified candidates, only 18 percent gave the same reason for medical technologists. For the latter occupation, most hospitals were either satisfied with the present ratio of medical technologists to other laboratory personnel or were bound by a hospital policy not to hire more.

In evaluating these differing reactions and experiences among the sampled hospitals, it should be noted that considerable variation exists in their perceived employment needs. Some laboratories hire only ASCP registered technologists, for example, while others use large numbers of technicians whom they train on the job. Similarly, some hospitals have been using LPN's for a considerable period of time while others are only beginning to use them for some of the tasks previously performed by registered nurses or nurse aides. The staffing experience at a particular time in a hospital or laboratory is also related to the quality it would like to achieve, as well as whether it is a training institution and can, therefore, obtain some services from trainees.

Vacancies

The variation in approaches to staffing problems also affects any attempt to measure very precisely the extent of shortages in the occupations under study. As an example, the attempt to determine the extent of shortages by estimating the number of vacant positions at the time of the study was complicated by the fact that some of the hospitals did not budget specifically for LPN's. Rather, they budgeted for nonprofessional nursing services – registered nurses, LPN's, aides and orderlies – as a group and hired those deemed the best from among these substitutable categories. Similarly, some hospitals, because they had been unable to fill vacancies for LPN's or medical technologists, had hired lower level nurse aides or medical technicians instead and thus were unable to report any budgeted vacancies at the time of the interview. Another measurement difficulty resulted from the practice of some hospitals to hire LPN's in groups a couple of times a year, with the result that the number of vacancies was greatly affected by whether they had just hired a group or were about to hire.

Nevertheless, an attempt was made to get at least a rough idea of how many persons the hospitals were short of at the time of the interview. The results indicate, first of all, that the number of hospitals with unfilled openings for LPN's and medical technologists was as follows.

Number of Hospitals with Unfilled Openings

	For LPN	*For Medical Technologist*
Chicago	11 of 22 = 50%	14 of 23 = 60%
St. Louis	13 of 15 = 86%	7 of 13 = 53%
Total	24 of 37 = 64%	21 of 36 = 58%

The figures suggest that slightly more hospitals had vacancies for LPN's than for medical technologists, that the demand-supply situation was about the same in the two cities for medical technologists, and that the market was much tighter in St. Louis than in Chicago for LPN's. All of the large hospitals in both cities, with the exception of one Chicago hospital which had no openings for medical technologists, had unfilled openings for both LPN's and medical technologists.

Vacancy rates for the two occupations were determined by comparing the total number of unfilled openings in the sample hospitals with the numbers employed by the hospitals in the two occupations. The indicated percentage of unfilled openings was as follows.

Rate of Unfilled Openings

	LPN	*Medical Technologist*
Chicago	10%	13%
St. Louis	25%	25%
Total—both cities	17%	16%

The vacancy data alter the demand-supply picture somewhat in that a more serious imbalance in St. Louis for both occupations is suggested.[a]

The vacancy rate, in addition to being difficult to measure, is a questionable

[a]The vacancy data for Chicago compare closely with those shown for the Chicago metropolitan area in a June, 1963, survey by the Illinois Hospital Association. The vacancy rate shown in that survey was nine percent for LPN's and ten percent for medical technologists with ASCP registration. The percent of hospitals with full-time vacancies, however, was somewhat lower than in our survey—40 percent for LPN's and 29 percent for medical technologists. The Association survey data, however, are collected differently than our data. The survey covers all hospitals in the Chicago metropolitan area (and therefore includes a higher proportion of small hospitals), and the data are collected through mail questionnaires (and are thus subject to nonresponse errors). See Illinois Hospital Association, *The Shortage of Professional and Technical Hospital Personnel*, report no. 27, October, 1963, pp. 4 and 6.

index of the extent of the shortage of personnel in the two occupations. A number of the hospital administrators interviewed indicated that the number of positions budgeted each year is not so much a matter of requirements as it is an estimate of how many people they think they will be able to hire. In other words, the estimated supply determines the number of positions that are budgeted. Consequently, the vacancy rate, to the extent that the supply is accurately estimated, at any given time is likely to reflect mainly the turnover rate in the occupation. In the sampled hospitals turnover rates for LPN's were reported as about 22 percent and for medical technologists about 16 percent, both relatively close to the vacancy rates. The hard vacancy data, therefore, although indicating shortages, leave much to be desired as specific indicators either of the degree of labor shortage or even of its real existence, and it is necessary to turn to more indirect indexes for any final appraisal of shortages.

Employer Views of the Market

One such index is the response of hospital officials to a question asking them to indicate the degree of difficulty in hiring personnel in the two occupations. The open-ended question was coded to reflect whether obtaining personnel was easy or difficult and, if difficult, whether hiring standards had to be reduced in order to obtain sufficient help. The percentage of responses was distributed as follows.

	LPN			Medical Technologist		
	Chicago	*St. Louis*	*Total*	*Chicago*	*St. Louis*	*Total*
Number of hospital officials interviewed	19	15	34	20	13	33
No difficulty	63%	13%	40%	25%	15%	23%
Difficulty	37	87	60	75	85	77
Necessary to lower standards	0	26	11	25	23	24

Except for the case of Chicago LPN's a large majority of the sample hospitals indicated difficulty in staffing for these occupations. With the same exception, one-fourth of the hospitals volunteered the information that hiring standards had to be lowered. From these responses it is clear that the shortage of LPN's was much more severe in St. Louis than in Chicago, and considering the two cities together, that the shortage of medical technologists was somewhat greater than the shortage of LPN's. Table 3-1 shows the same data classified by size of hospital as related to data on the participation of hospitals in training programs and hospital turnover rates. The data indicate that the staffing of LPN's tends to be more of a problem in the larger hospitals while smaller hospitals have more difficulty obtaining technologists. The data on training programs and turnover rates offer no persuasive explanation for these relationships. The relatively small sample size makes it questionable to attach too much importance to these data breakdowns. However, factors related to difficulties in obtaining personnel will be discussed later in relation to the recruiting efforts of hospitals.

In addition to the experiences of the hospitals in attempting to secure staff, the judgments of officials of training institutions offer evidence of the extent of the shortages. These officials were asked whether they thought enough qualified persons were being trained to fill the available openings in the two occupations. Four of the six directors of LPN training schools replied in the negative as did all 16 of the directors of medical technology programs. In addition, four schools offering training for laboratory assistants were interviewed and three of them indicated that insufficient numbers were being trained for that occupation. The two training directors of LPN schools who thought enough were being trained were among the four LPN schools interviewed in Chicago; the latter supports the conclusion reached earlier that the shortage of LPN's in Chicago was less severe than in St. Louis.

Worker Experience in the Market

Most persons working as LPN's and medical technologists had little difficulty finding jobs after the completion of their training, indicating there was a favorable job market if not a shortage situation. About 90 percent of the LPN's and 85 percent of the medical technologists in the worker sample indicated they were working on their first job within a month of completing their training (Table 3-2). The percentage of recent trainees finding work within a month was somewhat less, but it is probable that many of those who didn't find work immediately were not looking for a job. This is suggested by the labor force status of those not working at the time of the mail survey of recent trainees in Chicago. About 20 percent of the recent trainees in both occupations were not working at the time of the survey. Of these, only 21 percent of the LPN's and 15 percent of the medical technologists were looking for jobs. The remainder were in school or training, doing housework at home, or for other reasons were out of the labor force. It is hard to ascertain whether those not working and in school were training for a different occupation or merely obtaining additional and more modern training in their jobs. No specific cases of training for other fields were found. The group breakdowns shown in Table 3-2 indicate that only nonwhite medical technologists in the two cities and white LPN's in Chicago were much below the norm in the length of time to the first job. Age, not shown in the

Table 3-1

Percentage of Hospitals with Staffing Difficulties and with Training Programs and Turnover Rates, by Size

		Small	*Medium*	*Large*	*Total*
LPN	N=	14	15	8	37
Difficult to Staff		46	69	62	60
Have Training Program:[1]					
Formal, Accredited		6	39	45	30
Total, Formal & OJT		12	52	81	48
Turnover Rates (Median)		27	14	25	22
Medical Technologist	N=	13	15	8	36
Difficult to Staff		82	86	63	77
Have Training Program:[1]					
Formal, Accredited		33	50	27	37
Total, Formal & OJT		53	72	90	76
Turnover Rates (Median)		7	25	20	16

[1]Percentages computed on the basis of number of training programs mentioned. A hospital with a formal training program leading to ASCP accreditation plus an on-the-job training program for lower level laboratory jobs was counted in both categories.

Source: Hospital interviews.

Table 3-2

Percent Working on First Job Less Than One Month After Completing Training

		Licensed Practical Nurse		
	N=	*Two Cities* *144* *Percent*	*Chicago* *73* *Percent*	*St. Louis* *71* *Percent*
Total Worker Sample	144	90	89	90
Recent Entrants	90	88	84	91
Veterans	54	93	97	88
White	39	82	77	92
Nonwhite	103	93	96	89
Primary Earners	73	90	88	93
Secondary Earners	69	89	90	87
Trainee Sample	307	--	79[1]	--

	Medical Technologist		
	Two Cities	*Chicago*	*St. Louis*
N=	*144*	*72*	*72*
	Percent	*Percent*	*Percent*
144	85	89	82
68	88	97	79
76	83	82	84
89	89	91	86
52	75	79	72
103	84	87	82
41	88	95	82
69	--	76[2]	--

[1]Includes one percent with jobs before training began.

[2]Includes nine percent with jobs before training began.

Source: Worker interviews and mail questionnaire for recent trainees.

table, was not a factor among medical technologists and was of only slight importance for LPN's.

Another test of the market used in the study was a measure of the workers' perception of the degree of horizontal mobility, or access to similar jobs in other hospitals, they possessed. They were asked, "What do you think of your chances of finding a similar or better job as a (LPN or medical technologist) in other hospitals? Explain." Large majorities in both occupations and in both cities indicated that their chances were excellent or good, as indicated in Table 3-3.[b] Presumably they would not view their chances optimistically if they did not perceive the job market as one in which there were ample job opportunities. In fact, in explaining why they thought their mobility was good, a majority in both occupations, 80 percent of the LPN's and 54 percent of the medical technologists, cited the shortage of people trained in the occupation. A large number of the medical technologists (32 percent) also cited their own training and experience as the main factor which made them occupationally mobile.

The difference in perception of opportunity for horizontal mobility between LPN's and technologists cannot be explained by the available data. It is possible that the lesser degree of optimism displayed by technologists in this regard can be attributed to the greater importance of experience within a given hospital plus some greater degree of specialization which could not necessarily be transferred easily. In addition the number of job openings were fewer.

The somewhat higher mobility perceptions of the Chicago workers in both occupations should be noted. Our earlier conclusion that the shortage, particularly for LPN's, seemed to be more severe in St. Louis than in Chicago would lead one to expect the St. Louis workers to view themselves as more mobile. The lower mobility perceptions of LPN's in St. Louis appears to be due mainly to the more pessimistic view of the market by the blacks in the sample. The same percentage of whites in the two cities rated their mobility as excellent or good, but substantially fewer blacks did so in St. Louis than in Chicago.[c] The lower mobility ratings in St. Louis for medical technologists, on the other hand, seems to cut more generally across categories and probably reflects a smaller number of hospitals active in the technologists' labor market.

At a later point in the interview, the workers in the two occupations were asked whether they agreed with the statement that not enough people were

[b] The responses to the open-ended question were coded into the following five categories: excellent, good, fair, poor, and doesn't know.

[c] Substantial differences between the two cities also occur in the category of veterans and in the 35-44 age category. However, 93 percent of the veteran category in St. Louis were blacks as were 78 percent of the 35-44 age group.

being trained in their occupation. Large majorities in both cities agreed, as the following tabulation indicates.

	LPN's	Medical Technologists
	Percent	*Percent*
Both cities	78	86
Chicago	76	86
St. Louis	80	87

On the basis of the workers' perceptions of the market situation and their favorable experiences in finding employment, therefore, one could conclude that shortages of LPN's and medical technologists existed in both cities.

There is no evidence, given the nature of our samples, that employers other than hospitals experienced any lesser degree of shortages when hiring the same type of personnel. There is some considerable evidence from other studies that LPN's in private home care are considerably older and if accredited more likely to have obtained their accreditation before standards were imposed. Thus the two labor markets are not comparable.

The Shortages and Pay Levels

A common index used to identify the existence of shortages in particular occupations is the movement of relative wages over time. In the case of salaries of LPN's amd medical technologists, the available data are not satisfactory for a precise analysis of the behavior of salary trends relative to those of other occupations. The data in Table 3-4 however, give a rough indication of salary changes for these occupations in the five years preceding the hospital survey and show changes for the same period in wages in other sectors of the economy. The five-year period is used for comparison because the sample hospitals were asked to indicate what changes had occurred in salaries over that period of time. The data, although very limited, suggest that salary increases have been rather modest during this time period. While salaries have possibly increased somewhat more rapidly than have wages in general in the economy, particularly for LPN's, they do not reflect a very substantial response to the shortage situation. Nor do the going salary levels in 1963 reflect what one might expect in an Arrow-Capron type of shortage situation.[d]

The study did not attempt to gather detailed information that would be helpful in explaining why salaries in the two occupations have not been more responsive to the shortage of personnel. Some of the comments of hospital administrators, however, suggested that cooperation of varying degrees of formality among hospitals operates to keep salaries of hospital personnel out of

[d]The average going salaries in Illinois as shown by the Illinois Hospital Association survey convert to hourly rates of $1.53 for LPN's and $2.63 for medical technologists with ASCP registration, which may be compared with the production worker rates shown in Table 2-4.

Table 3-3

Percent of LPN's and Medical Technologists Rating Horizontal Mobility in Their Work as Excellent or Good

		Licensed Practical Nurse		
	N	*Two Cities Percent*	*Chicago Percent*	*St. Louis Percent*
Total	158	90	95	83
Tenure Status				
Recent Entrants	101	94	98	90
Veterans	57	81	90	71
Race				
White	41	93	93	93
Black	112	87	96	81
Other Nonwhites	1	100	100	--
Age				
Under 25	44	94	100	85
25 - 34	45	96	100	93
35 - 44	41	81	90	70
45 - 54	20	85	90	82
55 - 64	8	88	86	100

Medical Technologist

N	Two Cities Percent	Chicago Percent	St. Louis Percent
177	79	83	76
83	88	92	84
94	73	77	68
114	81	87	74
50	76	78	74
10	90	83	100
51	84	94	78
77	84	90	79
28	75	65	86
14	57	66	40
7	57	75	33

Source: Worker interview.

Table 3-4

Various Salary and Wage Data for Licensed Practical Nurses, Medical Technologists, and Other Worker Groups

Worker Category	*1958*	*1963*	*Percent Change 1958–1963*
Licensed Practical Nurse			
Illinois (Ill. Hospital Association)[2]			
Average Monthly Starting Salary	$200	$244	22%
Average Monthly Going Salary	219	265	21%
Chicago–St. Louis Hospital Sample[3]			
Chicago–Mean Starting Salary	237	304	28%
St. Louis–Mean Starting Salary	205	250	22%
Medical Technologist			
Illinois (Ill. Hospital Association)[2]			
Average Monthly Starting Salary (ASCP)	350	411	17%
Average Monthly Going Salary (ASCP)	389	456	17%
Chicago–St. Louis Hospital Sample[3]			
Chicago–Mean Starting Salary	290	365	26%
St. Louis–Mean Starting Salary	276	346	25%
Some U. S. Wage Trends:[1] (Average Gross Hourly Earnings of Production Workers)			
All Manufacturing			
Total	2.11	2.46	17%
Excluding Overtime	2.05	2.37	16%
Nonmanufacturing–Total	2.47	2.76	12%
Wholesale and Retail Trade	1.70	2.01	18%

Table 3-4 (*continued*)

Worker Category	*1958*	*1963*	*Percent Change 1958–1963*
Service Industries			
Hotels, Motels, Etc.	1.03	1.22	18%
Laundries and Cleaning Estab.	1.17	1.33	14%

[1]From U. S. Department of Commerce, Office of Business Economics, *Business Statistics,* 1965 Biennial Edition, Bureau of Labor Statistics Data, pp. 81–84.

[2]Illinois Hospital Association, *Hospital Salaries in Illinois*, report no. 26, September, 1963.

[3]Hospital interviews.

competition. In fact, some recent studies have indicated substantial degrees of cartelization in the hospital labor market.[e] More directly, the hospital administrators were asked whether they attempt to meet the shortage problem by offering higher pay. Most of the respondents replied in the negative to this question for LPN's (83 percent) and a majority (57 percent) did so for medical technologists. Proportionally, more than twice as many Chicago hospitals said they attempted to adjust to the shortages by increasing pay than did the St. Louis hospitals. The percentages of hospitals replying affirmatively to the question for LPN's and medical technologists were 25 percent and 55 percent respectively in Chicago and 14 percent and 23 percent in St. Louis. The failure of St. Louis LPN salaries to move more positively than in the Chicago labor market area where the extent and magnitude of the shortage was substantially less serious would support the proposition that St. Louis hospitals have attempted to exercise more restraint in the administration of salary increases.

The relatively depressed salary rates in the face of a shortage of labor is also related to some of the personal characteristics of employees in the two occupations. Almost all of the LPN's and a large majority of the medical technologists (80 percent) in the interview samples were women and therefore suffer the fate of relatively low pay characteristics of most occupations that are primarily female occupations. Due to the large female contingent represented in the occupations, substantial proportions of the workers, 49 percent of the LPN's and 29 percent of the medical technologists, were secondary earners. The availability of relatively large parts of the labor supply from categories of workers not primarily responsible for the support of themselves or their families undoubtedly takes some pressure off wages. Also, as Table 3-5 shows, the hospitals were making use of large numbers of workers who were members of minority groups. Since these are workers whose alternative employment opportunities of equal attractiveness and status were relatively more limited, they could probably be attracted into the occupation and to the work place at wages which averaged below the standard for which their skill and training would seemingly qualify them.

Jobs which are of lower status in terms of pay and prestige among white workers may have relatively high net advantages for black workers. In fact, it is probably correct to say that the hospitals in the face of labor shortages, turned to the minority groups as a source of labor which could be tapped without raising wages drastically. As indicated in Table 3-5, by the fact that both veterans and recent entrants to the occupations are comprised of substantial proportions of minority group members, the use of nonwhites has been the practice for some time.

The characteristics of the workers, particularly in the case of the LPN's, combined with the limited employment alternatives for someone trained in the occupation, are important factors in explaining the rather modest response of

[e] The recent much more militant attitude, largely under professional auspices, may force alteration in these policies. At the time of the study no such movements were observed but in recent months several strikes of nurses have taken place.

wage levels to the shortage situation. Salaries of medical technologists seem somewhat more in line with the demands of the occupation and the market situation. In part, this reflects labor market factors that differentiate the occupation from LPN's. There are more males in the field, a smaller proportion of the workers are secondary workers, a much smaller proportion are nonwhites, and the hospitals must compete with other employers (industrial firms, for example) for workers with similar qualifications.

A number of other items with respect to the relationship between salary levels and the shortage are of interest. One is that there appears to be a rather tenuous relationship between salary levels in any given hospital and how it is affected by the shortage. Table 3-6 shows average starting salaries for hospitals classified by whether or not they were experiencing labor shortages at the time of the survey. Considering the two cities together, the relationship is as one would expect for LPN's, but average salaries are the same in the two groupings of hospitals for medical technologists. The data are more meaningful for the cities considered independently, but the small number of cases in most of the "no shortage" categories makes interpretation difficult. In the case of the Chicago LPN's, which is the most suitable for analysis, there appears to be little difference in salaries paid by "shortage" and "no shortage" hospitals. In any event, the data do not provide a clear basis for concluding that shortages in particular hospitals are strongly related to salary levels.

Hospital adminstrators and employees in the occupations were asked their views on the importance of pay as a factor related to the supply of labor. The administrators were asked to note what they believed the positive and negative attraction of their hospitals to be when attempting to hire personnel in the two occupations. For both occupations, only a small minority of hospital administrators, about 15 percent, listed lower pay than in other hospitals as a hindrance or liability in hiring labor. None had any understanding of the long-run competitive implication of their salaries compared to other alternative occupations as a factor. In other words, they interpreted this question only in the context of other hospitals. Somewhat higher numbers, however, listed higher pay than in other hospitals as an asset in obtaining personnel. The higher pay factor was cited by 30 percent of the hospitals with respect to hiring LPN's and about 20 percent in hiring medical technologists. Altogether, about half of the hospitals mentioned salary as either an asset or a liability in their efforts to attract LPN's and nearly 40 percent did so with respect to their ability to hire medical technologists. Hospitals in the "no shortage" category were much more likely to mention higher pay as an asset than were hospitals in the "shortage" category. For LPN's, for example, over half of the "no shortage" hospitals compared with one-tenth of the "shortage" hospitals listed their higher pay scales as an advantage in recruiting help. This relationship was not so striking in the case of medical

Table 3-5

Racial Distribution of Licensed Practical Nurses and Medical Technologists, Chicago and St. Louis Sample Hospitals

	Cities Combined			
Occupation		*White*	*Black*	*Other Nonwhite*
	N	*Percent*	*Percent*	*Percent*
Licensed Practical Nurse				
Recent Entrants	99	30	70	- -
Veterans in Occupation	59	23	75	2
Medical Technologist				
Recent Entrants	85	62	27	11
Veterans in Occupation	94	66	33	1

Chicago			St. Louis		
White	*Black*	*Other Nonwhite*	*White*	*Black*	*Other Nonwhite*
Percent	*Percent*	*Percent*	*Percent*	*Percent*	*Percent*
35	65	--	25	75	--
38	59	3	7	93	--
58	27	15	67	26	7
70	30	--	61	36	3

Source: Worker interviews.

Table 3-6

Mean Starting Salaries for Licensed Practical Nurses and Medical Technologists, Chicago and St. Louis Sample Hospitals at the Time of the Survey (1964)

		Combined Cities		Chicago		St. Louis	
Occupation		*Shortage*	*No Shortage*	*Shortage*	*No Shortage*	*Shortage*	*No Shortage*
Licensed Practical Nurse	N =	22	15	9	13	13	2
		$265	$306	$299	$306	$242	$304
Medical Technologist	N =	28	7	18	4	10	3
		$357	$357	$362	$381	$348	$339

Source: Hospital interviews.

technologists, where the size and facilities of the hospital and the existence of training programs were viewed as more decisive factors in attracting personnel.

The context of these responses is the view of the individual hospital with respect to the labor market and is not germane to the question of the relationship of general salary levels to the supply of labor. The hospital administrators were not viewing the results of the relationship of their wage levels to wages in general and evaluating how they stood relative to other types of employers. Nevertheless, although the results suggest a considerable sensitivity of the hospitals to the importance of wages in attracting labor, vis-a-vis other hospitals, less sensitivity was evidenced in regard to wage scales in hospital occupations compared to alternatives requiring similar attributes in the general economy.

Occupants of the occupations, on the other hand, seemed to attach secondary importance to pay. This is not to say that they thought pay was irrelevant, but when asked what they thought was the most important thing that could be done to persuade more people to enter the occupation only a small minority suggested increasing prevailing salary levels. About 11 percent of the LPN's (but twice as many in St. Louis as in Chicago) and 13 percent of the medical technologists cited prevailing salaries as the most important deterrent to larger numbers entering the occupation.[f] While the judgments of neither the hospital administrators nor the incumbents in the occupations can be regarded as impressive

[f]Much larger proportions, however—about 4 of 10 LPN's and 6 of 10 technologists—spontaneously included higher wages in their list of things they thought would be helpful in attracting more people to the occupation.

evidence for rejecting wage levels as a crucial factor in the shortage situation, they do suggest that nonwage factors are also important determinants of career choice. Undoubtedly, if one had access to the judgments of persons who because of low pay considered but rejected these occupations as careers, however, the relative importance of wages and salaries would have appeared somewhat greater.

Three general conclusions emerge from the evidence on pay levels: (1) The shortage situation is reflected only partially in recent salary trends in the two occupations, although it is probably true that there has been at least a moderate improvement in pay relative to other occupations. (2) Although relatively low salary levels are a contributing factor to the continued shortage of qualified personnel, they are not the only explanation and may not be the most important. (3) The personal characteristics of those who are dominant in the occupations explain to an important degree why it has been possible to continue to attract substantial numbers, although fewer than demanded, of qualified personnel in spite of relatively low pay scales.

Other Evidence of Shortages

The interviews with head nurses and laboratory directors indicated that, in some hospitals at least, the shortages were having definite effects on operations. In some nursing offices, for example, it appeared that much of the work involved moving personnel from one floor or ward to another or scheduling personnel from the day shift to evening shift so that at least the minimum number of staff would be available at all times and in all departments. In some cases head nurses indicated that it was necessary to centralize the staffing function on a shift basis because of the shortage of personnel, rather than allow individual departments to do their own staffing. The reason was to assure similar nurse-patient ratios throughout the hospital. In a few hospitals the shortages of nurses meant that the nurses could pick and choose, and generally chose the day shift. Then, the relatively lesser number of LPN'S on the day shift complained that they were used as nurse aides, while LPN's in the same hospitals on the night shifts because of the dearth of nurses, complained they had to perform functions usually reserved for nurses and jobs for which they were not specifically trained. The shortage contributed to a misuse of resources and to a deterioration of quality of services provided.

In the laboratories, as well as in nursing offices, one level of staff was often substituted for another in order to meet work loads. As one laboratory director put it, "What a hospital needs is hands, and if we can't get them from one classification of workers, we'll hire them in another." Thus, in the absence of other alternatives, the laboratory would hire someone off the street, usually a high school graduate, and provide that person with on-the-job training to do specific tasks that needed to be performed. Another laboratory indicated that it was set up to train six people in the program leading to ASCP creditation but had only one in the program at the time. In the meantime, it was getting along without the highly trained people it would like by using less qualified people on tasks for which they had been trained on the job. Complaints about the large proportion of testing errors indicate that this substitution may affect quality.

In circumstances such as these the hospitals had the number of personnel necessary to get work ostensibly done, but neither at maximum efficiency nor at the desired quality level. Patients were not turned away, but neither were they getting the service that the hospital could provide if the requisite personnel could be hired. These qualitative dimensions represent circumstances difficult to document in terms of a shortage, but the bulk of the evidence in regard to quality of service would seem to indicate that a shortage indeed existed.[g]

In sum, the data presented in this chapter make it clear that there was a shortage of licensed practical nurses and medical technologists at the time of the survey in the two metropolitan areas. These shortages existed in spite of the relatively loose character of the labor market at that time. Evidence for this conclusion was found in the numbers of hospitals with vacancies and in the vacancy rates in the two occupations, the difficulties expressed by hospital administrators in recruiting personnel, the experiences of the workers in the job market, and the administrative problems faced by the hospitals in accomplishing their work. The data on pay scales and trends were not entirely conclusive, but the concerns expressed by the hospitals about the relationship between pay levels and recruitment, and the evidence of advancing relative pay scales, are consistent with the conclusion that workers in the two occupations were in short supply.

It was also clear from the data presented that the shortage of LPN's was much more serious in St. Louis than in Chicago. The wage data would suggest that the much lower level of wages, and a somewhat greater degree of wage nonresponsiveness to the shortage resulting from a greater degree of wage restraint, explains the difference in part.[h] Other contributing factors will be explored in subsequent chapters. The shortage of medical technologists was more pervasive, affecting both cities and more hospitals.

It is difficult to give a quantitative measure of the severity of the shortages. A reasonable judgment would seem to be, except for the case of LPN's in Chicago, that the shortages were serious but not critical. Necessary hospital functions were being carried out but not with the efficiency and effectiveness that would

[g]A recent study (Harkness) would seem to indicate that, judged by testing errors, not so well trained personnel are as apt to perform as well as those better trained.

[h]The lower wages in St. Louis for LPN's means that in St. Louis, more so than in Chicago, the occupation stands at a disadvantage compared with alternative occupational possibilities. Since the labor markets for LPN's are local, no direct comparisons between the two labor markets are meaningful. Only relationships between the given occupations and other comparable alternatives in the same labor market areas are meaningful in relationship to the shortage.

be possible and desirable. That the situation was not critical was probably largely a function of the nature of the supply of labor. The propensity of the hospitals to rely on female workers who were in large proportions secondary workers and members of minority groups provided at least a minimum supply of labor in spite of the relatively unattractive salaries provided. The ability of the hospitals to substitute lower level categories of workers in both the nursing services and in the laboratories also kept the situation from being a desperate one.

4 Factors Affecting Supply: Information, Counseling, Guidance, and Recruitment

The general premise underlying the analysis in this chapter is that the supply of labor available to an occupation is related to knowledge about and access to the occupation. The extent to which adjustment to a shortage situation is effectuated by increased efforts to attract additional personnel into the occupation and the extent to which shortcomings exist in informational and recruitment channels will be examined.

Is the potential supply of labor being adequately exposed to information about and opportunities in the occupation? What actions are successful in attracting recruits to the field? These questions are explored primarily by investigating the channels through which current workers came into the occupation and the efforts of employers, training schools, and others to encourage or direct people into the occupations. The questions are particularly crucial in the cases of licensed practical nurses and medical technologists because the occupations are not only expanding rapidly but their major growth period is of comparatively recent vintage. It cannot be assumed, therefore, that the general population will know of the occupations or the requirements for entry into them, as one might, for example, in more established occupations such as carpenter or lawyer.

In an effort to evaluate the relationship between shortages in the two occupations and knowledge and access to them, the routes through which entry to the occupations is made are traced, the characteristics of workers who have been attracted into them are summarized, and specific attempts to tap potential workers for the field are analyzed.

Sources of Occupational Information and Knowledge

In the interviews with the employed practical nurses and medical technologists, a number of questions were asked which were designed to determine the route by which they entered training for these occupations. The responses to some of these questions are summarized in Table 4-1. The first line in the table shows the responses to the question: "How did you get into the training program for your present occupation? Were you counseled on the training available?" The answer to the second part of the question is "generally not." About 70 percent in both occupations said they received no counseling at all concerning opportunities for training in the occupations. Much of the counseling they did receive was through informal channels – usually from a personal friend working in the occupation. Over half of the LPN's who said they received counseling cited this as the source. Only about 15 percent of the LPN's indicated the source of counseling was an agency established for the purpose. These sources consisted of high school counselors (7 percent), the public employment service (3 percent), an employer (4 percent), or a college counseling service (1 percent). The minority of medical technologists who received counseling, on the other hand, more frequently obtained it from a formal counseling service. Over one-fifth of them were counseled about training opportunities from a college (11 percent) or high school (6 percent) counselor, an employer (3 percent), an employee organization (1 percent), or a private employment agency (1 percent). Only 8 percent were counseled by a friend in the occupation and none received counseling from the public employment service.

Despite the relatively small number working in the occupations who were able to recall being formally counseled, most felt they had adequate information about the occupations before they entered training. They were asked: "Do you think you knew enough about the occupation before training so that you could make an intelligent decision?" Approximately two out of three in both occupations responded in the affirmative (Table 4-1).[a] Apparently many, therefore, were able to obtain access to the relevant information without benefit of formal advice. Examination of the replies to the question of how they got into training reveals the general process involved in becoming informed about the occupations. The replies, which were free responses, were susceptible to classification from two points of view. In some cases the respondent interpreted the question to mean why he chose the occupation. Others interpreted the meaning to be how they became acquainted with the occupation. Table 4-1 shows the results of classifying the responses both ways. In some cases, the reply could be classified with respect to both meanings. The percentages shown in Table 4-1 are based on the number of cases which could be categorized under the particular heading. Of the 162 LPN's in the study, the replies of 126 were placed in the "why chose" category and the replies of 125 were placed in the "how became acquainted" category. Of the 182 medical technologists, the comparable figures were 122 and 119. For both occupations, therefore, a considerable number of responses were coded both ways.

From whichever point of view the replies are viewed, three factors stand out. First and most important is the tremendous influence of acquaintances. Half of the respondents indicated that a friend, relative, or someone in the occupation was the primary source of information, and roughly a third claimed such persons were the primary influence in affecting their choice of occupations. Second, a large group, 37 percent of the LPN's and 20 percent of the medical

[a] Only a bit over one-half of the St. Louis LPN's, compared with four-fifths of those in Chicago, were satisfied with the information they had prior to entry into training. What appears to be an inferior information system in St. Louis may partially explain the more serious shortage situation there.

Table 4-1

Factors Related to Entry into Training, Licensed Practical Nurses and Medical Technologists (Percent Distributions)

		Licensed Practical Nurses Combined Cities		
		Total	*Recent*	*Veteran*
Counseling Received on Training Available	N =	162	102	60
No Counseling Received		69	64	78
Received from High School or College Counselors		8	8	7
Received from Personal Friend in Occupation		16	21	7
Other (S.E.S. or Employer)		7	7	8
Parent in Same or Related Occupation		6	9	2
Felt had Sufficient Information Prior to Training		68	63	76
Why Chose Area of Training	N =	126	78	48
Wanted Hospital Work, Help Sick, or Higher Level Occupation in the Field		37	39	35
Suggestion of Friend or Relative		29	32	25

Licensed Practical Nurses					
Chicago			St. Louis		
Total	Recent	Veteran	Total	Recent	Veteran
85	52	33	77	50	27
61	51	76	78	76	81
9	10	9	5	6	4
20	31	3	12	12	11
10	8	12	6	6	4
9	13	3	3	4	0
79	74	88	56	52	58
70	42	28	56	36	20
39	41	36	36	36	35
27	31	21	32	33	30

(continued)

Table 4-1 (*continued*)

Why Chose Area of Training (*cont.*)		Licensed Practical Nurses Combined Cities		
		Total	*Recent*	*Veteran*
Previous Hospital or Military Experience		21	18	25
Other		13	11	14
How Became Acquainted with Occupation	N =	125	79	46
Friend, Relative, or Someone Else in Occupation		46	47	44
From Working in Hospital		26	25	26
Training School Literature		12	10	15
Counselor Advised		6	8	2
Newspaper		9	6	13
Employment Agency		2	4	0
		Medical Technologists Combined Cities		
Counseling Received on Training Available	N =	182	86	96
No Counseling Received		70	64	76
Received from High School or College Counselors		17	22	12

Licensed Practical Nurses					
Chicago			St. Louis		
Total	*Recent*	*Veteran*	*Total*	*Recent*	*Veteran*
21	14	33	20	22	15
12	13	10	13	9	20
76	47	29	49	32	17
47	49	45	43	44	41
22	19	28	31	34	24
17	17	17	4	0	12
4	6	0	8	9	6
7	4	10	12	9	18
3	4	0	2	3	0

Medical Technologists					
Chicago			St. Louis		
88	40	48	94	46	48
65	55	73	75	71	79
19	27	13	14	17	10

(continued)

Table 4-1 (*continued*)

Counseling Received on Training Available (*cont.*)		Medical Technologists Combined Cities		
		Total	*Recent*	*Veteran*
Received from Personal Friend in Occupation		8	10	8
Other (S.E.S. or Employer)		5	4	4
Parent in Same or Related Occupation		9	7	11
Felt Had Sufficient Information Prior to Training		63	60	66
Why Chose Area of Training	N =	122	61	61
Wanted Hospital Work, Help Sick, or Higher Level of Occupation in the Field		29	25	35
Suggestion of Friend or Relative		34	34	34
Previous Hospital or Military Experience		21	23	20
Other		15	18	11
How Became Acquainted with Occupation	N =	119	57	62
Friend, Relative, or Someone Else in Occupation		52	53	52

Medical Technologists					
Chicago			St. Louis		
Total	*Recent*	*Vet-eran*	*Total*	*Recent*	*Vet-eran*
10	11	9	8	9	6
6	8	4	3	2	4
6	0	11	13	20	10
65	58	70	62	61	63
65	31	34	57	30	27
32	19	45	27	30	22
32	42	24	37	27	48
19	19	18	24	27	22
17	19	15	12	16	7
57	30	27	62	27	35
45	41	48	60	64	57

(continued)

Table 4-1 (*continued*)

How Became Acquainted with Occupation (*cont.*)	Medical Technologists Combined Cities		
	Total	*Recent*	*Veteran*
From Working in Hospital	20	21	19
Training School Literature	13	9	15
Counselor Advised	10	12	8
Newspaper	3	1	6
Employment Agency	2	4	0

Medical Technologists					
Chicago			St. Louis		
Total	*Recent*	*Veteran*	*Total*	*Recent*	*Veteran*
27	31	23	10	7	13
15	10	19	10	11	10
3	7	0	17	18	17
7	3	10	2	0	3
3	7	0	0	0	0

Source: Worker interviews.

technologists, indicated simply that hospital work and/or helping the sick was something they had always wanted to do. In part, this type of response can be interpreted to mean the respondent was motivated to engage in an activity that provided opportunity to serve those in need. And in part the response indicates interest in the intrinsic nature of the work involved in the occupation. In some instances the respondent's initial interest was in a related occupation, such as registered nurse or pathologist, which was for some reason beyond reach. In any event, for relatively large numbers in the two occupations, the work itself has an attractiveness that pulls people into it. It is apparently not a matter of indifference to these people whether they are doing this kind of work rather than something else. It is also apparent that those who responded in this fashion must have had some contact or acquaintance or information about the occupations in order to have developed a strong interest in them. Third, another substantial group in both occupations, somewhat more than one-fifth of the total, became exposed to the nature of the work and were influenced in their choice of the occupation by their experience in previous hospital or military work.

In addition to these three major factors related to obtaining information about and choosing these occupations, it is noteworthy that a substantial minority of the practitioners attributed their initial exposure to information about the occupation to more formal aspects of the informational network. Well over a quarter of the respondents said they got into training as a result of exposure to training school literature, the advice of a counselor, a newspaper advertisement, or contact with an employment agency. Obviously, therefore, the formal communication apparatus had an important impact on decisions to prepare for these occupations.

A number of writers have emphasized that the phenomenon of occupational choice is a process rather than a decision reached at a particular period of time.[1] It is, therefore, somewhat of an oversimplification to list *the* factors which influence a person to enter into training for a particular occupation. The final decision to do so is influenced by a history of experiences and steps which lead up to the final decision. Nevertheless, a definite decision is finally made, and the respondents to this survey were in general able to identify, in some cases more specifically than in others, those factors which were influential in their decision.

The importance of information, guidance, and counseling in attracting individuals to the occupations is suggested by the responses to a variety of other questions asked in the interviewing program in this study. In general, the responses indicate that a serious gap exists in the process of getting the relevant occupational information to potential entrants.

On the question of the availability of occupational information, the administrators of training schools for LPN's differed from those administering schools for medical technologists. Officials of four of the six LPN schools interviewed felt adequate information was available to potential entrants. Most (62 percent) of the officials of the 16 medical technology schools contacted, on the other hand, felt there was a lack of information concerning the occupation of medical technologist. In both cases, training school officials felt that high school counselors did an inadequate job of counseling students on career opportunities in the occupations. This was the judgment of two-thirds of the officials of LPN schools and four-fifths of the officials of schools of medical technology. These responses can be interpreted as suggesting that reasonably adequate information is available for the occupation of LPN but not for medical technologist and that for both occupations there is a serious barrier to getting the relevant information to those potential entrants who are confronted with occupational selection decisions while at school. Results of the interviews conducted with high school counselors in Chicago indicate that part of the problem is a reluctance on the part of counselors, particularly those in suburban, middle-class schools, to urge any of the students to consider occupations that do not involve college education.

Practitioners in the two occupations were also asked for their views on the adequacy of counseling concerning the availability of training opportunities. Only about one in ten in both occupations rated counseling as excellent or good (and the same proportion described it as adequate), about one in three rated it fair or poor, and the majority said they didn't know enough about it to reach a judgment. Of the third who claimed counseling was inadequate, over half in each occupation (56 percent) attributed the shortcomings to the lack of information available to counselors and potential entrants and a quarter or more to the shortage or poor quality of high school and college counselors.[b]

Of greater interest are the views of the practitioners on what the barriers are to attracting more people into the two occupations. Those who thought that there was a shortage of personnel in the two occupations were asked: "What do you think can be done to persuade more people to enter the occupation?" The proportions who cited the three most frequently mentioned factors are shown in the following tabulation.[c]

[b]The mail questionnaire responses of the Chicago recent trainees gives a somewhat different picture of counseling. These respondents were asked to evaluate the advice or counseling they received before entering training. Of those who completed training, about 2 out of 3 LPN's and 4 out of 10 medical technologists gave an evaluation of excellent or good. The fact that these responses deviate so strikingly from all the other evidence available in the study suggests that the subject was probably inadequately presented in the mail questionniare.

[c]The percentages are of the total number in the sample, including those who weren't asked the question because they believed there was no shortage. The figures would be higher if based on only those answering the question.

	Percent who mentioned the factor without prompting or suggestion that it might be a factor			Percent who named it the most important factor		
	Information to potential entrants	*Quality of guidance and counseling*	*Pay*	*Information to potential entrants*	*Quality of guidance and counseling*	*Pay*
LPN	56%	31%	21%	36%	13%	11%
MT	65%	52%	34%	39%	20%	13%

Source: Worker interviews.

The extent to which the dissemination of information and the quality of guidance and counseling predominate in the minds of practitioners as the most important factors related to the attraction of people to their occupations is striking. The characteristics of the occupations, prevailing pay rates, working conditions, and the nature and extent of fringe benefits all received lesser note compared to these two factors as methods for attracting people to the field. Three times as many respondents mentioned the need for better information, as the most important incentive in attracting candidates to the field, as mentioned increasing pay rates, in spite of the relatively low pay scales in both occupations.

When possible remedial areas were suggested to the respondents and they were asked to judge whether improvement was likely to help in attracting candidates, some of the other areas, particularly pay, were given more support. But even then, as the following tabulation shows, the factor getting by far the strongest support is more effective provision of information to potential entrants.

Percent of Practitioners Mentioning Factors Helpful in Attracting More People to the Occupation (Spontaneous Plus Prompted Responses)

Occupation	*Information to potential entrants*	*Quality of guidance and counseling*	*Pay*	*Characteristics of occupation*	*Working conditions*	*Fringe Benefits*
LPN's	72%	51%	48%	28%	13%	11%
MT's	75%	64%	54%	16%	7%	4%

Source: Worker interviews.

It should be noted that the opinions of those working in the occupation are not necessarily expert in the sense that these persons are in the best position or the best qualified to make judgments concerning the questions asked. They were, it should be emphasized, attracted to the professions and fields despite these informational and counseling deficiencies. Even if more information or even guidance were available it is not certain that these would attract others who did not have similar motives for entry into a medical field. However, their direct involvement in the process of choosing the occupations, training for them, and working in them gives them insights that no one else has. And the evidence they presented appears to be generally consistent with that obtained from other sources. What conclusions are suggested concerning the role of information, guidance, and counseling in supplying an adequate number of candidates for these occupations?

The occupations under consideration are relatively new and expanding. There is, therefore, relatively little acquaintance or knowledge of them by the population in general. They are also parts of occupational hierarchies, the separate parts of which are not always known or distinguishable to the candidate. Potential candidates must therefore be drawn to the field in some way other than through natural familiarity. Few of those in the occupation, for example, could use their parents as a direct source of information; at least few of them had parents who were engaged in the same or similar work.

Yet most of those working in the field did not come to a knowledge of or interest in the occupations through formal informational, guidance, or counseling channels. The most important stimulus to interest in the occupations came from contacts with friends or relatives or persons working in the occupations. Many indicated that the work they were doing was just something they had wanted to do, and something in their general experience had led them in the direction of their present work. Also, previous hospital work was an important factor in their decision to enter training for their particular occupation. All of these can be considered general environmental factors; that is, influences arising from where they happened to be, who their associates were, and where they happened to find jobs prior to entering specialized training.

In spite of the primary use of informal sources of information, most of the practitioners felt they had adequate information upon which to make their choice to enter training for the occupation. On the other hand, most of them also felt that the most important need for attracting more people into the occupations was more adequate dissemination of information. What this suggests is that the informal sources of information provide generally adequate information for those who get it but that the information reaches inadequate numbers of potential entrants. The opinions of training school administrators, in general, lead to the same conclusion.

From a policy point of view, the implication would seem to be that an important payoff would occur in the form of increased supplies of entrants to shortage occupations by efforts to widen and enrich the environment in which the exchange of occupational information takes place. This would seem to be particularly important in culturally disadvantaged areas. While this study has directly investigated only the career choices of those who actually entered the occupations under study, the importance attached by these people to information, and their dependence for information on friends and relatives, suggests that people with rather narrow and limited contacts are likely to be excluded from considering many occupational possibilities. Use of the classroom for occupational instruction and the development and expansion of work experience opportunities would appear to be prime possibilities for the suggested widening and enrichment of the informational environment. Also, more attention to existing formal channels for distributing occupational information (e.g., expansion of the number and improvement in the training of counselors) would help overcome a serious gap in access to information.

Access to Information and Entry: Characteristics of Trainees and Workers

The supply of labor to an occupation may be affected by how adequately information about the occupation is brought to the attention of sectors of the population that are most likely to be interested and whether or not employment opportunities are made available to these groups. The only direct evidence in the study on this question is the information provided by employers about their minimum hiring qualifications. However, the characteristics of trainees and workers in the occupations provide indirect evidence on who has had access to information and employment opportunities. This section beiefly presents evidence of these two types.

The hospital administrators were asked to state the minimum education and training requirements for new hires into the occupations and to comment on whether or not they were satisfied with the hiring standards. For practical nurse positions none of the hospitals required both licensing and experience. However, three-fourths of the hospitals required that the practical nurse be licensed. The other fourth hire persons without the license provided it is obtained within a specified period of time. The one-fourth willing to hire on this condition were almost all large hospitals; perhaps they had a greater number of qualified persons to supervise the work of the practical nurse. About 80 percent of the hospitals also cited certain minimum personal or physical requirements, which varied widely from hospital to hospital, as conditions of employment of practical nurses. The most frequent requirement (mentioned by 35 percent of the hospitals) was that the candidate be clean, neat, and tidy. Others had requirements or at least preferences, with respect to such factors as weight, personality, age, and ability to write legibly. No one of these personal factors or characteristics was mentioned often and it is doubtful that they have any general significance. They seem to be preferences distributed randomly among personnel people.

The requirements for hiring into laboratories indicated a good deal of flexibility. About 30 percent of the hospitals required that the candidate be either ASCP registered as a medical technologist or have a B.A. or B.S. college degree. Another 30 percent were willing to substitute experience for the formal training requirements. An additional 30 percent required only a high school education and no experience; they were willing to do their own training. The remaining 10 percent usually required either registration or the college degree, but would sometimes hire people with neither advanced training nor experience. Again, the larger hospitals tended to have the more flexible hiring standards. Half of them were willing to hire high school graduates without previous training or experience. Few of the hospitals cited any minimum hiring requirements for laboratory personnel other than those related to education, training, or experience.

Nearly all of the personnel officers, chief pathologists, and directors of nursing thought that the hiring standards in their particular hospital were about right. Three-fourths or more of those interviewed in the three administrative or supervisory positions were satisfied with the qualifications required for hiring LPN's and medical technologists. The greatest degree of dissatisfaction occurred among the chief pathologists, 22 percent of whom felt that hiring standards were too low. Presumably these pathologists were at hospitals where advanced training and education were not required and the shortages precluded the raising of standards.

The process by which the workers in our sample qualified themselves for the two occupations is shown in Table 4-2. Almost all of the LPN's had become licensed practitioners by enrolling in approved training schools and passing the examination required by state law. Substantial proportions of the veterans, however, had become licensed by waiver by virtue of their experience on the job. Among the technologists, however, qualification had come through a variety of routes. Over one-third had been registered by the American Society of Clinical Pathologists by meeting the formal requirements for recognition as medical technologists. The ratio of those with a college degree to those without was about two to one. A higher proportion of technologists in Chicago than in St. Louis had both registration and degrees. About the same proportion in both cities had either ASCP registration or a college degree or both. On the other hand, flexibility in the utilization of laboratory personnel is indicated by the fact that well over one-third of the technologists had neither formal registration nor a college degree; and 13 percent of the sample group had no college education whatsoever. However, the trend is clearly in the direction of increasing formal qualifications. Substantially higher proportions of the recent entrants than of the veterans had obtained ASCP registration and fewer were without either the registration or a college degree. In spite of the shortage situation the qualifications of the technologists being used were on the upgrade.

Table 4-3 shows various characteristics of the Chicago and St. Louis samples of practical nurses and medical technologists.

Table 4-2

Training Qualifications of Sample Licensed Practical Nurses and Medical Technologists, Chicago and St. Louis
(Percent Distributions)

		Combined Cities		
Occupation		*Total*	*Re-cent*	*Vet-eran*
Licensed Practical Nurse	N =	162	102	60
Licensed by Examination		92	97	83
Licensed by Waiver		8	3	17
Total		100	100	100
Medical Technologist	N =	182	86	96
ASCP Registered		37	48	28
With College Degree		25	36	16
No College Degree		12	12	12
Bachelor's Degree (Non–Reg.)		25	21	28
With 1–Year Lab. Training		18	16	20
Without Formal Lab. Training		7	5	8
Other (Non–Degree, Non–Reg.)		38	31	44
Some College Work		25	19	30
No College Work		13	13	14
Total		100	100	100

Chicago			St. Louis		
Total	*Re-cent*	*Vet-eran*	*Total*	*Re-cent*	*Vet-eran*
85	52	33	77	50	27
95	98	91	88	96	74
5	2	9	12	4	26
100	100	100	100	100	100
88	40	48	94	46	48
42	63	25	33	35	31
33	48	21	18	26	10
9	15	4	15	9	21
19	12	25	30	28	31
8	2	12	28	28	27
11	10	12	2	--	4
39	25	50	37	37	37
23	15	29	26	22	31
16	10	21	11	15	6
100	100	100	100	100	100

Source: Worker interviews.

Table 4-3

Characteristics of Workers Employed as Licensed Practical Nurses and Medical Technologists, Chicago and St. Louis Samples (Percent Distributions)

	Two Cities Combined							
	LPN				Medical Technologist			
	N	*Total*	*Recent*	*Veteran*	*N*	*Total*	*Recent*	*Veteran*
Sex								
Male	4	3	1	5	37	20	17	23
Female	158	97	99	95	145	80	83	77
Race								
White	44	28	30	24	115	64	62	66
Nonwhite	114	72	70	76	64	36	38	34
Wage Earner Status								
Primary	81	51	47	58	130	71	77	66
Secondary	79	49	53	42	52	29	23	33
Marital Status								
Single	40	25	29	17	84	46	55	38
Married	79	49	52	43	85	47	38	55
Other	43	26	19	40	13	7	7	7
Educational Level								
8th Grade or Less	4	3	2	3	0	0	0	0
Grades 9-11	31	19	11	33	3	2	2	1
High School Grad.	97	60	70	43	30	7	14	19
Beyond H. S.	30	18	18	20	148	81	83	80
College Graduate					(82)	(45)	(52)	(39)

Table 4-3 (*continued*)

Two Cities Combined

	LPN				Medical Technologist			
	N	*To-tal*	*Re-cent*	*Vet-eran*	*N*	*To-tal*	*Re-cent*	*Vet-eran*
Hours								
Full Time	159	98	98	98	177	97	98	97
Part Time	3	2	2	2	5	3	2	3
Years in Metro. Area								
Native Entire Life	74	46	53	33	68	38	40	36
Moved into Area	88	54	47	67	111	62	60	64
Reasons Moved to Area								
To Seek Employment	17	20	28	11	38	34	33	34
For School or Training	6	7	6	8	28	25	28	23
Accompanied Spouse	25	30	32	27	18	16	14	18
Other and Unknown	36	43	34	54	28	24	25	24

Chicago

	LPN				Medical Technologist			
	N	*To-tal*	*Re-cent*	*Vet-eran*	*N*	*To-tal*	*Re-cent*	*Vet-eran*
Sex								
Male	2	2	2	3	21	24	19	28
Female	83	98	98	97	67	76	81	72
Race								
White	30	36	35	38	56	64	58	70
Nonwhite	53	64	65	62	31	36	43	30

(*continued*)

Table 4-3 (*continued*)

	Chicago							
	LPN				Medical Technologist			
	N	*Total*	*Recent*	*Veteran*	*N*	*Total*	*Recent*	*Veteran*
Wage Earner Status								
Primary	48	56	52	64	62	70	76	66
Secondary	37	44	48	36	26	30	24	34
Marital Status								
Single	23	27	31	21	36	41	51	32
Married	35	41	46	33	45	51	41	60
Other	27	32	23	45	7	8	7	8
Educational Level								
8th Grade or Less	3	4	2	6	0	0	0	0
Grades 9–11	22	26	19	36	3	3	5	2
High School Grad.	46	54	62	42	17	20	12	26
Beyond H. S.	14	16	17	15	67	76	82	72
College Graduate					(41)	(47)	(55)	(40)
Hours								
Full Time	82	97	96	97	84	95	95	96
Part Time	3	3	4	3	4	5	5	4
Years in Metro. Area								
Native Entire Life	31	37	46	21	26	30	25	35
Moved into Area	54	63	54	79	60	70	75	65
Reasons Moved to Area								
To Seek Employment	10	20	29	9	27	45	41	48

Table 4-3 (*continued*)

	Chicago							
	LPN				Medical Technologist			
	N	*Total*	*Recent*	*Veteran*	*N*	*Total*	*Recent*	*Veteran*
For School or Training	3	6	4	9	7	12	14	9
Accompanied Spouse	20	39	39	39	8	13	10	16
Other and Unknown	18	35	28	43	18	30	34	26
	St. Louis							
	LPN				Medical Technologist			
	N	*Total*	*Recent*	*Veteran*	*N*	*Total*	*Recent*	*Veteran*
Sex								
Male	2	3	0	7	16	17	15	19
Female	75	97	100	93	78	83	85	81
Race								
White	14	19	25	7	59	64	67	61
Nonwhite	61	81	75	93	33	36	33	39
Wage Earner Status								
Primary	33	44	41	50	68	72	78	67
Secondary	42	56	59	50	26	28	22	33
Marital Status								
Single	17	22	28	11	48	51	59	44
Married	44	57	58	56	40	43	35	50
Other	16	21	14	33	6	6	6	6

(continued)

Table 4-3 (*continued*)

	St. Louis							
	LPN				Medical Technologist			
	N	*Total*	*Recent*	*Veteran*	*N*	*Total*	*Recent*	*Veteran*
Educational Level								
8th Grade or Less	1	1	2	0	0	0	0	0
Grades 9–11	9	12	2	30	0	0	0	0
High School Grad.	51	66	78	44	13	14	15	12
Beyond H. S.	16	21	18	26	81	86	85	88
College Graduate					(41)	(43)	(50)	(38)
Hours								
Full Time	77	100	100	100	93	99	100	98
Part Time	0	0	0	0	1	1	0	2
Years in Metro. Area								
Native Entire Life	43	56	60	48	42	45	53	38
Moved into Area	34	44	40	52	52	55	47	62
Reasons Moved to Area								
To Seek Employment	7	21	26	14	11	21	23	20
For School or Training	3	9	11	7	21	40	45	37
Accompanied Spouse	5	15	21	7	10	19	18	20
Other and Unknown	18	55	42	71	10	19	14	23

Source: Worker interviews.

As was indicated in the previous chapter, both occupations attract a mainly female labor supply. Ninety-seven percent of the sample LPN's and 80 percent of the medical technologists were female. The breakdown by recent-veteran entrants indicates no change in respect to the sex ratio. The mail survey of recent trainees in Chicago, in which 99 percent of the LPN's and 97 percent of the medical technologists were women, likewise shows that the occupations continue to attract virtually no men to the fields. Undoubtedly, unattractive wage levels and other working conditions, as well as the tradition of employing mainly females, operate as a deterrent to entry to the occupations by male, primary earners. The resulting concentrations of females in the two occupations is an portant limiting factor to expanding supply, since so much of the newly trained supply is required for replacement of those leaving the labor force.

The data on race, on the other hand, give no indication that supply is limited because of failure to utilize minority groups. Nonwhites nearly all of whom were black comprised 72 percent of the LPN worker sample and over a third of the medical technology sample. In general, the evidence *does not* indicate that different criteria were being used in the hiring of white and nonwhite candidates for employment. As Table 4-4 indicates, the educational qualifications of white and nonwhite employees were quite similar in both occupations. The exception is the Chicago LPN's, among whom the nonwhites had attained substantially higher education levels. This does not necessarily mean, of course, that Chicago hospitals and training institutions are more selective among nonwhite applicants than among white. It may be that nonwhite applicants have higher qualifications than white applicants. In any event, the evidence is fairly strong that qualified nonwhites have access to job opportunities in these two occupations and that, in general, they compete on about the same footing as whites. The data on race also show that the use of minority groups in the two occupations is not a new phenomenon; the proportion of nonwhites is high among both recent and veteran entrants to the occupations.[d]

The data in Table 4-3 also show that employers make heavy use of secondary workers, particularly for LPN positions (see data on wage earner status and marital status). Nearly half of the LPN's are married women who are second earners in their families. The smaller proportion of secondary workers among the medical technologists is due to the greater number of men and of single and

[d]The St. Louis interviewers reported, however, that some of the St. Louis training schools for LPN's appeared to operate on a racial quota system which limited the number of blacks who would be accepted into training programs and resulted in whites being accepted for immediate training. In fact, the smaller proportion of nonwhites in the recent entrants category for St. Louis LPN's may indicate some use of race as a selective factor, since a waiting list for admission to training aggregating 1400 persons, primarily nonwhite, existed at the time of the study.

Table 4-4

Educational Attainment, by Race, Worker Samples (Percent Distributions)

	LPN			
	Chicago		St. Louis	
Educational Level	*White*	*Nonwhite*	*White*	*Nonwhite*
Less Than High School	40%	25%	7%	15%
High School Graduate	50	56	71	64
Some College	10	19	21	21
Total	100	100	100	100
	Medical Technologist			
High School Graduate or Less	25%	20%	14%	17%
1–3 Years College	25	32	36	45
College Graduate	50	48	50	37
Total	100	100	100	100

Source: Worker interviews.

younger women in the occupation. In both occupations, however, there is great dependence on the willingness of married women to participate in the labor force. Many of them appear to be in the labor force because of the necessity to support dependents; nearly half of the LPN's (46 percent) had two or more dependents to support, and one-third had three or more.

It is also noteworthy that apparently the LPN occupation offers frequent opportunity for older women to start a new work career. As the following age distribution of the recent trainees in Chicago shows, a third of the LPN's who had just completed their training program were over the age of 35. And the average age of the LPN trainees was much higher than that of the medical technologists.

Ages of Recent LPN and Medical Technologist Trainees, Chicago
(Percent Distribution)

Occupation	*Total*	Age: *Under 20*	*20–24*	*25–29*	*30–34*	*35–44*	*45 & over*
LPN	100	8	35	12	9	18	18
Medical Technologist	100	15	59	17	4	3	1

Source: Mail questionaire

Presumably the relatively short training period (one year) makes it feasible for married women (57 percent of the recent trainees were married) whose home duties have been lessened, to invest at relatively late ages the time and resources necessary to start a new career. This suggests that the age group above 35 or 40 might be an important source of reserve manpower that could be further tapped to staff the expanding requirements for nursing services at the practical nurse level. This age group might also be a potential source of additional manpower for the training of laboratory personnel. Older high school graduates could qualify for laboratory assistant (CLA) positions with one year of laboratory training. And older college graduates, particularly those who have worked in the sciences, could also qualify for medical technology positions with only a year of further specialized training.

The data in Table 4-4 showing the educational attainment of the practitioners are a reflection of the minimum educational requirements for entry into training for the two occupations. The main point of interest is comparison of the distributions for recent and veteran entrants to the occupations. In the cases of both occupations it is clear that educational requirements are rising. For LPN's, for example, 35 percent of the veterans but only 13 percent of the recent entrants had less than a high school education. For medical technologists, 52 percent of the recent entrants compared with only 39 percent of the veterans had completed college degrees. Thus, during the same period of time that shortages have been developing, entry has been limited to those with higher levels of education.

The remaining characteristics summarized in Table 4-4 are less directly related to the question of the sources of labor supply, but they are of general interest regarding the characteristics of incumbents in the two occupations. Virtually all of the practitioners interviewed were full-time employees, suggesting that strong efforts were not being made to attract persons to work who could work only part time.[e] Well over half of the practitioners in both occupations were migrants to the two metropolitan areas. A large proportion of these among the medical technologists had moved to the two areas for training or employment. Most of the LPN's, on the other hand, had moved for other reasons.

The labor market implications of this section may be summarized as follows:

1. The hiring standards applied by the hospital employers appear to conform reasonably well to the job requirements of the two occupations. The variance in practices is considerable among the hospitals in the hiring of laboratory personnel. For the most part, personnel administrators, nursing supervisors, and pathologists are satisfied with the hiring practices being followed. To the extent that there is dissatisfaction, it is primarily directed toward the need to hire some laboratory personnel who have less adequate training than the pathologists would like.

2. Access to the two occupations does not appear to be unduly limited by the personal characteristics of potential entrants. The major limitation is the predominate reliance upon a female labor supply. This is due to the traditional image of the two occupations as female occupations and is perpetuated by the existence of salary levels that are not very attractive to male primary breadwinners. An important source of new entrants to practical nurse positions is the married woman past age 35 or 40 who is prepared to train for a new occupation after homemaking responsibilities have been lessened. It was suggested that this source might be tapped even further and that it might also be an important source of personnel for laboratory positions, for which a training period of a year or so is sufficient.

Recruitment – Efforts to Tap Potential Supply

The efforts of hospitals and training schools to recruit entrants into jobs and training and the experiences of workers in the two occupations in locating jobs are examined in this section. The objective is to determine whether there is a relationship between recruiting practices and the shortages of personnel in the two occupations. The assumption is that investment in recruitment is one of the avenues open to employers and training schools for attracting more people into the field or into employment.

[e]This may be related to some extent to the process of selecting interviewees. Since interviews were done on the job, the chances of selecting part-time workers may have been less than their proportional representation in the labor force.

Hospital Recruitment

Heavy emphasis was placed by the sample hospitals on obtaining additional personnel from among new graduates of training schools. For both occupations, a majority of the hospitals listed training schools as their primary source of new workers, and most of them said training schools were either their primary or secondary source (see Table 4-5). Walk-in applicants and referrals by present employees were the most important sources for those hospitals that did not rely primarily on recruits from the training schools. Public or private employment services and advertising are of some importance in recruiting, but few hospitals emphasize them. To the extent that they were used, it was mainly after the training schools, walk-ins, and referrals by employees failed to produce enough candidates.

The primary method of recruitment differed very sharply with the size of the hospital. In the search for LPN's, all of the large hospitals indicated that their primary source was training schools. Less than half of the medium-sized hospitals (47 percent) and only 21 percent of the small hospitals, however, said they relied primarily on this source. The smaller hospitals tended to rely much more commonly on walk-ins and referrals from present employees. Fifty-eight percent of the small hospitals and a third of the medium-sized establishments depended primarily on these sources. The differences in recruiting practices by size of hospital is partly explained by the fact that the larger hospitals were more likely to have their own training schools or be connected with a training program. Seventy percent of the larger hospitals named their own training schools as their primary source of new recruits; the same was true of only 34 percent of the medium-sized and 7 percent of the small hospitals. Clearly, whether or not the hospital was connected with a training program was a most important factor determining its recruitment practices.

Size of hospital was also important in the recruitment of medical technologists, although not so dramatically as in the case of LPN's. About three-fourths of the large hospitals recruited primarily from the training schools; less than half of the smaller hospitals relied primarily on this source. Unlike the case for LPN's, there was no close relationship between the size of the hospital and whether or not it relied primarily on recruits from its own training school. Apparently it was more a matter of the larger hospitals having better access to the new trainees, probably because they were able to offer more attractive laboratory facilities. Similar to the recruiting of LPN's, none of the large hospitals relied primarily on walk-ins and employee referrals, whereas substantial minorities of the smaller hospitals did (17 percent of the small and 42 percent of the medium).

The data on primary sources of recruits show that the training schools are the most effective source of new hires for both occupations. The hospital authorities were also asked to specify what the least effective sources of manpower were. For both occupations, the commercial schools were mentioned most often in this regard.[f] For LPN's, advertising was also mentioned fairly frequently as ineffective, and for medical technologists the public employment service was often noted as a poor source of recruits.

[f] That is proprietary training schools. They are generally not approved by the registration bodies.

Table 4-5

Sources of Additional Employees for Chicago and St. Louis Hospitals
(Percent Distributions)

	Licensed Practical Nurse		Medical Technologist	
	Primary Source	*Secondary Source*	*Primary Source*	*Secondary Source*
Training Schools	56%	41%	55%	41%
Walk-ins and Employee Referrals	31	26	20	30
State or Public Employ. Serv.	9	12	5	16
Advertising	2	7	9	9
Other	2	14	11	4
Total	100	100	100	100

Aside from the particular recruitment practices followed, the hospitals were able to identify various factors which they considered to be either advantages or hindrances in recruiting personnel. In order of frequency of mention, hospitals felt they were at an advantage in comparison with others in the recruitment of LPN's because of higher pay rates (30 percent), participation in a training program (20 percent), better working conditions (18 percent), and location (13 percent). Sixteen percent felt they had no advantages over other hospitals. The most important disadvantages mentioned were location (30 percent), lower pay rates (14 percent), and undesirable clientele (11 percent). Over one-fourth felt they were encumbered by no particular liability. The ranking of factors important to the recruitment of medical technologists was somewhat different. The most important assets cited by hospitals were participation in a training program (44 percent), size and quality of the hospital staff and facilities (26 percent, including 57 percent of the large hospitals), and higher pay than other hospitals (21 percent). Those listing their disadvantages in recruitment of medical technologists most frequently cited location (25 percent) or low pay rates (16 percent). The largest group (44 percent) indicated they suffered no particular disadvantage.

Although substantial proportions of the hospitals saw their training programs as their chief asset for the recruitment of both LPN's and medical technologists, very few hospitals saw the absence of a training program as their major liability in recruitment. Possible explanations for this are that other factors were deemed more important as liabilities, or the hospital officials were insensitive to the advantages of participation in a training program.

The liabilities cited by those hospitals who were experiencing labor shortages at the time of the survey are of particular interest because these hospitals are the ones most likely to be sensitive to recruitment problems. For the recruitment of LPN's, the location of the hospital (31 percent) and lower pay rates (15 percent) were the dominant liabilities cited. Only one of the 22 hospitals in this category cited the lack of a training program as a prime disadvantage. In the recruitment of medical technologists, location was also the most frequently cited liability; size and quality of facilities, which were often mentioned as an advantage in recruitment, were not mentioned by any of the hospitals in the shortage category as a liability in recruitment.

The factors cited by the hospital authorities as relevant to the degree of their success in recruiting personnel are probably not of much importance in explaining the general problem of shortages in these occupations. They are of more importance in affecting how the limited supply of labor is distributed among the various employers.

However, the terms in which the hospital administrators see the recruitment problem is important. The fact that most of the hospitals recruit most of their employees through training schools and from walk-ins and employee referrals is understandable. These are prime and natural sources of new employees. But the lack of evidence of any extensive effort to go beyond these obvious methods of recruitment in the face of labor shortages reflects a rather passive reaction to the problem. For example, no systematic efforts to attract inactive practitioners into the work force were apparent, either for LPN's or medical technologists. When asked what actions were taken when the hospital was unable to obtain sufficient help, about 70 percent of the hospitals indicated they did one of two things: substituted persons with similar but lower level occupational qualifications or got along with the staff they had. Since few of the hospitals said they curtailed services under these circumstances, the implication is that the quality of services was reduced. In addition, a small minority of hospitals filled in for shortages of LPN's with student nurses, and laboratories hired unqualified candidates and gave them the training necessary to do certain tasks. None of the hospitals made such investments in recruitment as nurseries for children, transportation assistance, or out-of-area recruitment to attract additional workers.

In spite of the relatively passive approach to recruiting in the face of the shortages, only a minority of the personnel administrators indicated dissatisfaction with their hospitals' recruiting policies. When asked to evaluate the adequacy of these policies, only 15 percent said they were dissatisfied with their recruitment efforts for LPN's, and about 40 percent were not satisfied with their recruitment of medical technologists.[g] Those who expressed dissatisfaction were asked for suggestions as to how recruiting might be improved. Among the recommendations were increased pay, more career education in high school and college, establishment of a hospital training program, and in one case, reorganization of the hospital personnel department.

The evidence from the hospital interviews is that the hospitals responded to the shortages to only a minor extent by adjusting their recruitment efforts. There is little, if any, evidence that hospital management gave very serious consideration to the possibility of bringing forth an increased supply of labor through additional investment (or expenditure) in recruitment activities.

Training School Recruitment

We turn next to the policies and practices of the training schools in the recruitment of students. We start with the fact that most of the schools were operating at less than full capacity. The number of trainees could have been expanded within existing facilities. To some extent, therefore, the shortages could be attributed to a failure to recruit all of the students that could be accommodated at the training schools.

The following tabulation shows the number of training schools and the extent to which they were at full capacity.

[g]Perhaps it's not realistic to expect that administrators will generally express dissatisfaction with company policy.

Whether Training Schools Were Operating at Full Capacity

	Combined Cities			Chicago		St. Louis	
	Total	*Yes*	*No*	*Yes*	*No*	*Yes*	*No*
LPN	6	3	3	1	3	2	0
Medical technologist	16	5	11	4	10	1	1

Source: Hospital interviews.

As the tabulation shows, the LPN schools had a somewhat better record of utilization than did the medical technology schools. Both of the St. Louis LPN schools were at full capacity, as was one of the laboratory schools. The schools not operating at full capacity had room for substantial expansion in enrollment. At the LPN schools, expansion potential varied from 30 to 100 percent. At least one of the LPN schools indicated, however, that while physical facilities would allow a large increase in the number of students, difficulty in finding qualified instructors greatly limited the possibility of rapid expansion. At the medical technology schools, expansion possibilities were much greater. Seven of the 11 schools with vacancies indicated enrollment could be increased by 100 percent or more. At 4 schools, the school administrators indicated they were in a position to take four times as many students as they had. Clearly in both occupations the situation at the schools was in general one of a shortage of trainees.

Recruitment of students for both types of schools was generally limited to the metropolitan area in which the school was located. Five of the 6 practical nursing schools and 10 of the 16 medical technology schools concentrated all or most of their recruiting efforts in the Chicago and St. Louis metropolitan areas.[h] Most of the others confined their recruiting to a 200-mile or so radius of the two cities. One medical technology school claimed to recruit all over the country and even beyond, and two obtained students regularly from the Philippines through an exchange program.

The schools were assisted in their recruiting through a variety of contacts with other institutions. For the practical nursing schools these included high school counselors, governmental agencies such as the employment service and the administrative apparatus of the Manpower Development and Training Act program, the Chicago Health Careers Council, and churches. For the medical technology schools the main help came from certain colleges, but the relevant professional associations such as the American Society of Clinical Pathologists and the American Medical Association, high school counselors, and the Chicago Health Careers Council were also of some assistance.

A variety of recruiting techniques was used. All of the practical nursing schools and most of the laboratory schools distributed brochures describing their training programs. Among the practical nursing schools, newspaper advertising

[h]It may be noted again, however, that about one–third of the technologists had moved to the two areas to seek a job or to go to school or take training.

and participation in high school career days were common. Most of the schools had also established contacts with high school counselors or with hospital personnel that were helpful in turning up candidates, and a couple used either their personal representatives or direct mail to make contact with potential candidates. Among the medical technology schools, contacts with colleges was the most common technique used in recruiting, many participated in college career days, and a number used newspaper or magazine advertising and other techniques. For both types of schools, however, the method cited by the largest number of schools as the one producing most of the students was word-of-mouth referrals; that is, someone in the occupation referring a candidate to the school. This fits, of course, the data described earlier in this chapter which showed large numbers of practitioners becoming acquainted with the occupation through a friend or someone working in the occupation. Career days were listed by the second largest number of schools as the source of most of their students. Other sources of significant numbers of students for a number of training schools were counselors, notices of training opportunities by professional organizations, and contacts by personal representatives of the schools.

Most of the training schools had made no changes or innovations in their recruitment methods in the past 10 years or, in cases where the school was not that old, since the school had begun operations. This was the case for 5 of the 6 schools of practical nursing and 13 of the 16 technology schools. One practical nursing school had started newspaper advertising, apparently with poor results. Two of the medical technology schools had begun direct recruitment at high schools, presumably for candidates for lower level training. One had initiated the use of a film at career days. Further, none of the practical nursing schools planned any changes in their recruitment policies. Half of the medical technology schools did anticipate changes, but for the most part the changes involved intensification of present efforts. Exceptions were that one school planned to make home visits to potential candidates and one planned to provide some stipends to assist candidates in the financing of their training. Some of the reasons cited for not planning recruitment changes were lack of funds, the shortage of qualified candidates, and a judgment that expansion of recruitment efforts would not be worth the time and expense. Most of the schools, however, did not give reasons for their lack of interest in increasing recruitment activities.

The training school directors were asked to give their opinion on whether or not the recruitment of qualified candidates for their schools was becoming easier or more difficult. The respondents were rather evenly split as to whether the task was easier, more difficult, or about the same as always. The differences in opinion seemed to depend upon the emphasis put by the director on various trends. Among practical nursing school directors, for example, some thought recruitment was easier because the educational level of the population was rising and the quality of high school training was improving. Others felt it was more difficult to recruit because more people were going on to college or other types of more advanced training, leaving a smaller group of high school graduates to draw on. Among the medical technology schools, some felt recruitment was easier because more people were now interested in the field, colleges had developed more relevant curricula, or high schools were better and providing more science and mathematics. Others felt recruitment was becoming harder because educational requirements for entry had risen, and a number said their particular schools were affected by competition from a growing number of schools offering training in medical technology.

The picture of recruitment efforts by training schools presented above has mixed elements. On the one hand, one finds a variety of techniques in use which can be described as positive efforts to attract potential candidates into training. On the other hand, unusual efforts to intensify recruitment in the face of relatively serious shortages of trainee candidates are generally lacking. It also appears that most of the recruiting is carried out by individual training schools, each going its own way. Intensified joint efforts by training schools might offer possibilities for increased effectiveness and might overcome some of the resistance to expanded efforts evidenced by the concern of some schools for the costs and time involved.

Worker Experience

Additional evidence on the role of recruitment is found in the experiences and reactions of the practitioners in getting into training and finding jobs.

The importance of hospital participation in a training program in obtaining personnel is indicated again by the practitioner responses to how they obtained their first jobs after completing training. Nearly a quarter (23 percent) of the practicing LPN's and half (47 percent) of the medical technologists said that they stayed on at the hospital where they had received their training. Most of the others had found their jobs by making direct application to the hospital where they obtained employment; in general the applications appeared to be made on the initiative of the practitioner. The practitioners were also asked to indicate the primary reason for taking the particular job they did. Again, the fact that they had been trained at a particular hospital had a strong influence on their decision. Twenty percent of the LPN's and 30 percent of the medical technologists gave this as the primary reason for accepting their first employment. In both occupations, this was the reason most often cited.

Other reasons cited by the practitioners for accepting their first jobs, however, indicate quite a variety of influences affecting their decisions. Among the LPN's the location of the hospital in close proximity to their homes (18 percent), the hospital working conditions, including shift arrangements (19 percent), the salary offered (13 percent), and knowing others in the employ of the hospital (10 percent), were cited by approximately equal proportions of the practitioners as reasons for taking the job they did. Similar factors were cited by the medical technologists, except that the hospital location (3 percent) and salary offered (6 percent) were cited less often than among the LPN's. Working conditions (21 percent) and knowing other workers at the hospital (10 percent) received about the same emphasis as in the case of the LPN's.

These responses suggest what factors are important to practitioners in these occupations in their choice of employers. The factors may not be conclusive in determining whether or not a person will choose to work or not; undoubtedly that decision is based primarily on a different set of conditions. On the other hand, such factors as the working conditions or terms of employment may have importance at the margin, thus affecting to some degree the supply of labor available. In addition, the analysis gives an indication of what factors in the work situation might be susceptible to exploitation by a hospital in its attempts to recruit an adequate labor supply.

The practitioners were asked in the interviews to give their personal evaluation of recruitment efforts to attract persons into training programs for the two occupations. A majority, 54 percent of the LPN's and 61 percent of the technologists, said they didn't know enough about the situation to venture an opinion. Those offering an opinion, however, judged these efforts unsatisfactory by about a four to one margin. Thirty-seven percent of the LPN's and 31 percent of the technologists rated recruiting efforts only fair or poor; only 9 and 8 percent in the two occupations, respectively, judged them excellent or good. Large majorities of those who had a low estimate of the efforts to recruit trainees felt that the quantity of recruitment was inadequate. A substantial group indicated that they had never witnessed any recruiting efforts. The fact that so many were unwilling to express any judgment on the matter also indicates that recruitment activities are not very evident. A few expressed opinions about what kinds of recruitment efforts were needed, and these suggestions included the need for more advertising, the sending of recruiters to high schools, and the encouragement of individuals in lower level occupations (such as nurse aides and laboratory technicians) to enter training programs.

The practitioners themselves are not necessarily a good source for evaluating recruiting. On the other hand, it is noteworthy that so few of them had had enough exposure to recruitment activities to have an opinion about them and that so few of those who were willing to judge had a good word about the subject. This suggests that there is at least room for some experimentation with new and/or expanded recruitment programs.

In summary, occupational information, counseling and guidance, and recruitment activities are all potentially useful mechanisms for meeting an occupational shortage situation. As in the case of attempts to reduce a shortage by increasing rates of pay, costs are involved in trying to increase the supply of labor by use of these mechanisms. It is not satisfactory, therefore, merely to say that increased efforts in these areas will bring forth a larger labor supply. It is also necessary to examine the costs of various proposed activities and weigh them against the likely benefits. While this study has not been addressed to the question of costs of programs in these areas, it does offer evidence of areas in which efforts to expand the labor supply of practical nurses and medical technologists are likely to be effective. The following are the major relevant points:

1. Most of the training schools for the two occupations were operating well

below their full capacity. It is highly probable, therefore, that additional expenditures to attract students so that the schools could operate at full capacity would be an economical investment.

2. The major exception to the above generalization was the case of practical nursing schools in St. Louis. Here there was no underutilized capacity; in fact, the schools had long waiting lists of candidates for entry into training. Obviously, the shortage here could be met only with additional investment in training facilities.

3. Few of the training schools had experimented with or had plans for new programs for the recruitment of additional students. Little effort had been made to meet the shortage through innovations in recruitment. The possibilities for increasing the number of students through joint recruiting efforts of training schools and other institutions seemed largely unexplored.

4. Most of the practitioners in both occupations obtained information that led to their choosing of the occupation through informal means – mainly friends or the happenstance of their previous work experience. Improved dissemination of occupational information is needed. A number of suggestions were made for enriching the environment in which the exchange of occupational information takes place, including more emphasis on occupational education in the school curriculum and more systematic exposure of youngsters to the world of work.

5. Hiring requirements by employers seemed to be realistic in view of the work requirements in both occupations. Particularly in the case of laboratory personnel, employers adjusted to the shortage by hiring at whatever levels persons were qualified. In general, employers were satisfied with the hiring standards that were being used. The major exception was pathologists, a number of whom felt that too many laboratory people with inadequate qualifications had to be hired. The possibilities for adjusting to the shortages in the hospital by the further substitution of lower level for higher qualified personnel did not seem great.

6. In recruiting new employees, very heavy reliance was placed on new graduates of training schools, but very little emphasis seemed to be placed on trying to recruit from among inactive practitioners or from other geographic areas. On the other hand, large numbers of secondary earners, mainly married women, were already being used. Examples of special efforts or programs that would make it possible or attractive for additional married women to enter the labor force, however, were not apparent. Since both occupations rely almost exclusively on female employees, the inactive married woman would appear to be the major source, other than greater numbers of trainees, of additional labor. The older woman also appears to be a potential source of new trainees for the two occupations. The LPN training schools were already tapping this source to a considerable extent; new trainees could probably also be drawn from the same age group for laboratory positions. As a general proposition, however, recruitment policies and practices of the hospitals and training schools followed a rather routinized path and were not used as positive elements to try to adjust to the occupational shortages.

7. The experiences and evaluations of the sampled LPN's and medical technologists support the generalizations described above. If their judgments are accurate indicators of worker behavior, then improved dissemination of information, better counseling and guidance, and more active and directed recruitment efforts would have a marked effect on entry into training and employment in both occupations.

The subject areas discussed in this chapter have implications both for public policy and private practices. On the public front, for example, recognition by the schools of the importance and relevance of occupational education is needed. At the private level, appreciation by hospital administrators for the possibilities of using information, guidance, and recruitment policies as positive labor market instruments was lacking.

5 Factors Affecting Supply: Training and Placement

The relationship between training and the supply of licensed practical nurses and medical technologists has received some attention in previous chapters. It was shown, for example, that hospitals with their own training facilities have a hiring advantage over other hospitals because of their easier access to new trainees. Many trainees cited as the main reason for accepting their first job the fact that they did their training at the hospital where they first accepted employment. It was also shown that, in general, the inadequate supply of new trainees, with the exception of the LPN labor market in St. Louis, was a matter of inability to attract sufficient numbers of people into training programs. Most of the training schools were operating at less than their full capacity.

Characteristics of training and training schools that may be related to the attraction of people into training for the two occupations are explored more fully in this chapter. The chapter begins with some background information on the characteristics of the sample training schools and follows with a discussion of factors possibly related to the output of trained persons in the two occupations. Finally, the chapter considers the labor-market experiences of workers and trainees in an attempt to evaluate the efficiency of the labor market in utilizing the available supply. The main concern here is whether serious impediments to the process of matching workers and jobs are apparent.

The Nature of Training Schools

The interview sample of practical nursing and medical technology training schools examined in the study was as follows.

Type of School	*Chicago*	*St. Louis*	*Total*
Practical nursing	4	2	6
Medical technology	14	2	16
Medical laboratory assistants	1	3	4

The practical nursing school sample included all of the training schools in the two metropolitan areas. The medical technology school sample was taken from the 18 schools in Chicago and the 9 in St. Louis that were approved for the training of medical technologists at the time of the study by the Council on Medical Education of the American Medical Association.[1] A few of these schools also conducted one-year training programs for high school graduates as laboratory assistants (certified laboratory assistants). In addition, 4 schools in the sample provided training for laboratory assistants or technicians in programs which did not have the approval of the American Medical Association.[a]

The recent rapid growth in employment in the two occupations is reflected in the age of the training school. As the following tabulation indicates, many of the schools were relatively new.

Years School Had Been Established

	2 and under	*3–5*	*6–10*	*Over 10*	*Total*
Practical nursing	0	1	3	2	6
Medical technology	2	2	4	8	16
Medical laboratory assistant	2	2	0	0	4

Three of the practical nursing schools were operated by boards of education of the public school system (city boards in Chicago and St. Louis and a township board in the Chicago area). In St. Louis a hospital operated a practical nurse school and in the Chicago area one school was operated by an order of Catholic nuns and one by the Cook County Board of Commissioners. All of the approved schools of medical technology were operated by hospitals, some of which were affiliated with universities for the purpose of gaining approval of the year of training as credit toward the bachelor's degree. Of the laboratory assistant or technician schools, three were private organizations established for the purpose of training and one was operated by a hospital.

As indicated above, some of the medical technology schools are affiliated with colleges or universities. Affiliation means that the college or university has agreed to accept the year of specialized technology training as the equivalent of the fourth year of college and therefore this training is credited toward the bachelor's degree. Apparently, it has been difficult for the training schools to establish such relationships; those which had them were generally affiliated with only one or two colleges. Failure of the training schools to be tied in more broadly with colleges and universities is probably one of the major problems connected with their difficulties in recruiting students.

Enrollment in the practical nursing schools at the time of the study varied

[a]The programs of some of these schools, however, were approved by the Registry of American Medical Technologists.

from about forty to over four hundred students. Enrollment in the approved schools of medical technology was generally quite small, varying from one to sixteen students. Three to 6 students was typical. The number of students in the schools for laboratory assistants or technicians was larger, and was typically forty to sixty students.

The sources of finance for the schools varied considerably, depending, among other things, on the nature of the sponsorship. Various combinations of tuition and fees, taxes, patient charges, and voluntary contributions supported the training programs. Costs to students are considered in the following section.

Training and the Supply of Labor

Training Capacity

The majority of training schools were operating below the maximum number of students that could have been accommodated with existing facilities. Three of the six practical nursing schools, eleven of the sixteen schools of medical technology, and three of the four laboratory schools had fewer students than they could have accommodated and would have liked. In general, therefore, the situation was not one in which expansion in supply was being held up by a lack of training spots. The major exception to this generalization was that there was no room for expanding the number of practical nurse trainees in St. Louis. In fact, one of the St. Louis practical nursing schools had a waiting list of some 1,400 applicants.

In spite of excess capacity, a number of the school administrators saw a need for expanding facilities. Obviously, new training facilities or expansion of existing facilities is essential to meeting the shortage of LPN's in St. Louis. Even in Chicago, however, one of the nursing school administrators felt that additional facilities were required. Her main argument was for the need for school facilities in additional locations. Most of the students in practical nursing are nonresident or commuting students. For this reason, access to training facilities is a factor in determining whether or not a person is able or willing to enter training. One of the Chicago schools is located in a largely black residential area and about 90 percent of its students are blacks. Concern was expressed that the occupation will eventually become identified in Chicago as a black occupation and whites will refuse to enter it. If this should happen, it was felt that the shortage would tend to become more critical because a large segment of the potential supply of students will refuse to consider it. Whether or not this is likely to occur, it is probable that additional training facilities will not be forthcoming, at least through public programs, until the utilization of present facilities has been exhausted. However, in large metropolitan areas, the location and accessibility of training facilities, as well as the total training capability, is probably a factor in determining the number of candidates who will enter training. This study provides no direct evidence on the importance of this factor. A related factor, about which this study also offers no evidence, is the adequacy of public transportation. In a large metropolitan area, where most of the students live at home, the availability of public transportation between home and the training facility is undoubtedly a factor of some importance in determining the number of persons who will avail themselves of the training opportunity.

In the case of the medical technology schools, the school administrators had conflicting views about the need for additional training facilities. It was clear, of course, that the number of trainees could have been expanded substantially within existing facilities. The main problem was that of finding more candidates who were interested. Nevertheless, some of the training directors spoke of the great need for more hospitals to establish training programs. In part at least, this view reflected the interest of the laboratory director in securing the use for his own laboratory of those trained in his hospitals. Hospitals without training programs must rely on technologists trained in other hospitals; this poses the threat to training hospitals that they will lose their investment in trainees. The more hospitals with their own training programs, the less risk there is that a hospital will lose personnel it has trained to other employers. And, if a hospital does lose personnel to other employers, the more widespread and general the training programs are, the greater the probability the hospital can hire replacements trained elsewhere. On the other hand, some laboratory directors attributed the difficulty they were having recruiting trainees to increased competition for recruits from the growing number of hospitals with training schools. There is, therefore, some ambivalence on the need for more training hospitals. The more there are, the more competition there is for an apparently limited number of students. However, as the number of training schools increases, the less danger there is of losing the training investment through the loss of trained personnel to other employers.

The ambivalence results because the training hospitals are not confident that if the number of training programs are expanded the industry will be able to expand proportionately the number of trainees. Any given training institution would naturally regard the over-all supply of potential trainees, especially for ASCP technologists, as beyond its control. The result might be more training schools competing for the same number of students. The resulting ambivalence is a clear indication of the link between recruitment policies and training policies. Expansion of the number of training facilities can be successful in increasing the supply of technologists only if a more successful recruitment program can be established.

Although the shortage of personnel in the two occupations cannot be attributed primarily to a lack of training facilities, except in the case of St. Louis practical nurses, a number of the training schools had plans for further expansion of their training facilities. Two of the six practical nursing schools (one in each city) said they planned to increase their facilities, as did four of the sixteen schools of medical technology (all in Chicago) and two of the four schools for laboratory assistants (one in each city). Others had plans (hopes?) to increase the number of students and faculty within existing facilities. Two of the practical nursing schools indicated the reason for their expansion plans was the establishment of MDTA training programs for practical nurses at their schools. Apparently the subsidized training programs were having an effect on training capacity and on the number of trainees.

The four schools of medical technology with plans to expand training facilities gave as a reason for doing so the fact that their hospitals were expanding and they would have need for additional technologists. They were planning expansion, in other words, solely to meet their own needs for additional personnel. This is characteristic of the approach generally taken by the hospital training schools; that is, their training programs were nearly always viewed as designed to meet their own personnel needs and not the general needs of the market for technologists. The small size of the schools is to a considerable extent a function of the objective of the hospitals to limit training to fulfilling the expansion and replacement needs of the individual hospital. Given the small size of the typical training establishment it is quite conceivable that costs are much higher than they would be if training were centralized. These higher costs probably limit the number of training posts and may result in training that is inferior to what would be possible were training more concentrated in larger schools. The limiting of training to the hospital's own staffing needs is due to the high training costs discussed below.

In the case of the schools for laboratory technicians, the schools are attempting to train for the general needs of the market for technicians. Most of them could handle a substantial expansion in enrollment with their existing facilities. However, the products of many of the commercial schools are suspect; many hospitals will not hire their graduates. Their contribution to solving the problem of shortages of laboratory personnel, even with expanded enrollments, is therefore decidedly limited.

What can be said, in summary, concerning the adequacy of training facilities? For practical nurse training, the total training capacity in Chicago was adequate. Training facilities had expanded sufficiently as demand increased over the years to take care of the demand for training. Room existed, in fact, for further expansion of enrollment. The location and accessibility of training facilities, however, raises questions about the possibilities for meeting the long-term training needs of the occupation. As the existing training facilities are filled, the question will have to be raised concerning the desirability of expanding existing facilities compared with the advantages and disadvantages of establishing new training facilities at new locations. At the time of the study, two Chicago schools were planning expansion at their present locations.

In St. Louis, the limiting factor in expanding the training of practical nurses was that the training schools were filled to capacity. Long waiting lists of candidates for training existed. There is no solid explanation as to why St. Louis had been unable to respond to the need for additional training capacity. In the face of the fact, however, that there was a heavy demand for entry into training and that St. Louis hospitals were willing to hire all LPN's, whether white or black, one would expect that the community would respond by providing additional training facilities. It can be contended that a subtle form of racial discrimination is at least partially responsible for the failure to increase the size of the public training establishment. In an attempt to "prevent the floor from becoming all black," as one personnel director put it, the large St. Louis training institution apparently accepts all qualified whites immediately (i.e., for the next class) and fills out the remainder with blacks. The result is a long waiting list of candidates, virtually all black. Although there is no strong evidence to support the view that the desire to maintain racial balance has resulted in a formal discriminatory policy, the proportion of nonwhites in the recent sample (75 percent) was substantially below the proportion of nonwhites in the veteran sample (93 percent).[b] It appears probable, therefore, that the desire to preserve some modicum of racial balance explains why the length of queue did not result in an expansion of training facilities given that the system was able to train nearly all the whites who could be recruited into the occupation.

In the case of medical technology, the total training capacity was adequate to meet the demands for training. Most of the schools had room for additional students. In the short run the question of how to attract more students was of more importance than the question of expanding facilities. The long-run problem, however, is different. Most of the training facilities are small; typically the hospitals have a training capacity of less than a dozen students. The primary motivation of the hospitals operating the schools is to meet their own needs for trained personnel. A number of the hospitals, in fact, were planning expansion of their training facilities in anticipation of increased needs for technologists at the hospital. Few, however, were training any personnel for the general needs of the market. Since only a minority of the sample hospitals (about one-third) conducted training programs for medical technologists (although greater numbers were engaged in the training of lower level laboratory personnel), the long-term needs of the market for technologists were not being met with existing facilities. Insufficient personnel will be trained even if the training schools manage to fill all of their training slots. The question remains, therefore, of how training facilities can be expanded to meet long-run needs.

The Costs and Financing of Training

The specialized preparation of practical nurses and medical technologists costs money. How these costs are met and by whom, and the likely payoff that results, are factors in determining to what extent the training will be offered and whether or not offers of training will be accepted. These relationships are examined in a general way in this section. The calculus of the payoff to those involved is not computed.

For the most part, the training of practical nurses has not been the responsibility of hospitals, although hospitals participate in the practical or

[b]See Chapter 4, Table 4-3.

on-the-job aspects of the training. Only one training program of the six examined in this study was conducted by a hospital. A more common form is sponsorship by a public school system. In the case of hospital sponsorship, financing of the training comes from the resources of the hospital; namely, patient fees, contributions, and, if it is a public hospital, taxes. In the case of school board sponsorship the financing comes from taxes. In both cases, these costs to the sponsoring agent are offset to the extent that the student is charged tuition and other fees. In cases where the school participates in an MDTA training program, the financing is again done by taxes, but from a different source.[c]

The six practical nursing schools examined here all charged the student some form of tuition or fee for the one-year training program. The lowest charge was a fee of $100 for uniforms, books, and other necessary supplies.[d] The highest charge was $140 plus books and required uniforms.[e] In return, the student received the necessary instruction and on-the-job experience and usually a free lunch. In only one of the schools did the student receive a stipend for any part of the training program. Those students taking training under an MDTA program, of course, received a weekly training allowance. Except in those cases where the school provided one free meal per day, the student was responsible for the costs of board and room. Since most of the students lived at home, these costs were probably minimal in many cases. The costs of the training, therefore, were in all cases shared by the sponsoring training institution and the student. Clearly the fees paid by the student do not cover the training costs at any of the schools. The instructional costs of the cooperating hospitals, however, are probably largely offset by the services rendered by the students in their on-the-job training.

The largest cost to the student is in wages foregone during the training program. Most of the schools offered loan programs and/or installment arrangements for needy students. Three of the schools had a very limited number of tuition and/or fee scholarships. While the training costs are subsidized by the training institutions and the direct fees charged the student are modest, the student must make a substantial investment in his training, primarily by foregoing earning possibilities. Because training is generally a full-time responsibility of the student, opportunities for employment while in training are

[c]Commercial schools also offer training in practical nursing. They are often correspondence schools and are not approved by the states. In these cases the costs, and then some, are met out of student fees.

[d]This was the charge for residents of the school district. Non-residents paid, in addition, a tuition charge of $320.

[e]$190 for nonresidents of the school district.

limited.[f] Some of the schools discouraged the student from engaging in any part-time work.

Unlike the practical nurse training programs, almost all of the schools of medical technology are operated by hospitals in hospital facilities. The general pattern is that the student does either three or four years of college or university work followed by the one year of specialized laboratory training in the hospital school. The college or university training is the entire responsibility of the student. That part of the training, of course, is applicable to many occupations other than medical technologist. Unlike the case of practical nurse training, the costs and benefits to the student for the specialized laboratory training varies greatly among the training schools. A fairly typical case, however, is one in which the student pays no tuition, received a modest monthly stipend (e.g., $25 to $50 per month) during the period of training, is given free board and room, and provides his own uniforms, books, and necessary supplies. These items, however, are handled and combined in a variety of ways, and the result is not always as attractive to the student as the case cited above. One school, for example, charges tuition of $150 and provides no stipend and no room or board. Other schools pay relatively high stipends, and room and board is the responsibility of the student. One school in this category offered free tuition and a monthly stipend of $200. At some schools room and board was granted on a scholarship basis. At one of these the scholarship was conditioned on the agreement by the student that he would work at least one year following his training in the hospital's laboratory. Frequently, the hospitals also offer part-time employment opportunities to students outside school hours.

In general, then, the specialized training of the medical technologist is subsidized by the training school to a much larger degree than is the training of the practical nurse, although some of the costs are offset by the services rendered by trainees. Some idea of the extent of the subsidization is revealed in a comparison of the charges and benefits of the hospital schools with those of the commercial schools. Three of the laboratory technician schools included in the study provided information on the tuition and fees charged their students. The tuition charges in the three schools were $780, $1,000, and $1,100. In addition there were substantial charges for required books and other fees ($140 in one case) and the schools offered no such perquisites as room, board, and stipends.[g]

[f]Some schools, however, offered part-time night school programs spread over a longer time period, such as 72 weeks.

[g]These schools were not approved for training in medical technology as the term is used by the ASCP, although in their pamphlets they put themselves forward as trainers of medical technologists and tell their readers they are authorized to use the initials "MT" after their names after the completion of their training program.

The financial implications of providing and expanding training facilities for practical nurses are quite different from those for medical technologists. To a considerable extent the decision to provide opportunities for practical nurse training is a public one. A school board must weigh the costs and needs for practical nurse training against the costs and needs of other types of education and training. The decision-making process is essentially political. Other forms of sponsorship are, of course, alternative possibilities, and to some extent private organizations have accepted responsibility for providing training opportunities. And the availability of MDTA programs for practical nurse training has helped stimulate an expansion of vocational education courses for practical nursing.

The decision to offer training opportunities in medical technology, on the other hand, rests primarily with the individual hospital. In public hospitals the decision involves the political process in a way similar to that in the case of practical nurse training. At least the public interest becomes a factor in the decision. In hospitals, generally, the decision involves weighing the benefits of conducting a training program in the context of the hospital's budgetary constraints. The costs of the training program are relatively high, as the discussion above indicates. The costs must be met primarily out of the income from patient fees. The result is that if the hospital engages in training at all, it is likely to limit its efforts to training for its own needs. It is difficult to justify imposing the cost burden on its patients for training personnel that will be serving other hospitals. In any event, it is dubious that the need for medical technologists can be met with the existing structure for financing training. There is insufficient motivation for hospitals to provide training to the extent required by the market.

From the students' point of view, the decision to accept training opportunities depends upon an assessment of the relationship between training costs to himself and anticipated payoff in future earnings, as well as on the relative attractiveness of the occupation as a type of work to be in. On the monetary benefits side of the equation, compared to other alternatives involving similar competences and levels of education, neither occupation offers a very attractive payoff in earnings. Yet, both occupations apparently possess a considerable attraction to those who enter them. On the cost side both occupations demand a substantial investment in training expenses by the student for the year of specialized training.[h] This year of specialized training is generally subsidized to a

[h] For medical technology the required college education demands a much larger investment. Since the college education has a much wider applicability than to medical technology alone, the relevance of cost to the decision of whether or not to go on for the specialized training must be made by comparing the relative payoff of medical technology with other uses to which the education investment can be put. It is probably the case that the year of specialized training adds little, if any, future income to the student over and above what his college education provides, particularly if the specialized training is taken in addition to the bachelor's degree. In 1965, for example, beginning level chemists, engaged in mainly routine analyses, tests, and operations, had average monthly earnings of about $550. At the same time average monthly earnings of all (not just beginning) medical technologists in Illinois were about $485. And the chemist could look forward to much higher salary increments than the technologist. For chemist salaries see Bureau of Labor Statistics, *National Survey of Professional, Administrative, Technical, and Clinical Pay, February–March 1965,* Bulletin No. 1469 U. S. Department of Labor (Washington, D. C.: U. S. Government Printing Office, October 1965) p. 16.

much greater extent for medical technology than for practical nursing. In general, the payoff in both occupations is insufficient to attract enough candidates into training to meet either the demands of the market or to fill available training slots. This could be overcome either by increasing the payoffs (earnings) in the occupations or increasing the training subsidies to the students. At present, subsidies to some practical nursing students are being made through MDTA programs. For medical technology students, for whom there is a much more serious shortage, no subsidization is being given outside the training schools themselves with the exception of a relatively small number of scholarships.

Table 5-1 gives an indication of the sources of financial support that recent trainees in the two occupations turned to. The 17 percent figure for medical technology trainees is surprisingly low in view of the reports from the training schools on the extent of the benefits they offer students in the form of stipends, room, and board. It may be that some respondents classified these forms of aid under part-time work, viewing the stipend as a form of wage for services rendered during the on-the-job training period. Of particular note is the large proportion of students who relied on financial assistance from parents, particularly among the technologists – probably due to the long and expensive education in college. If support provided by a working spouse is included, a large proportion of the practical nurses also depended upon family support. Also, a relatively small proportion of the trainees indicated that they had received a stipend or any other form of scholarship during their training. Data are based on the mail questionnaire responses of recent trainees in Chicago training schools. The heavy reliance on family financial support suggests that financial barriers might be of some significance as a factor limiting the enrollment of trainees in both occupations; that is, students who do not have access to family help might be precluded, or at least discouraged, from seeking training.

On the other hand, those in the worker sample who had completed training and were working in the two occupations did not generally indicate that the costs of training had caused undue hardship. Had either drop-outs or those who did not enter the fields been cited, generalizations about hardship might have been different. Each respondent was asked: "Did you have to overcome any problems in order to take or complete this training?" Nearly 60 percent of the LPN's and 75 percent of the medical technologists answered no to the question. Only 12 percent of the LPN's and 14 percent of the medical technologists said they faced financial problems during their training period.[i] Among those who indicated having some problem, however, financial problems were by far the most frequently mentioned.

The discussion of the costs and financing of training for practical nursing and medical technology suggests the following conclusions:

1. The provision and financing of facilities for practical nurses training is largely a political decision since most of the training is done in public facilities. In states like Illinois, which are placing a heavy emphasis on the development of junior or community colleges, facilities will probably be adequate to meet

[i] The question was not asked, however, in a context of training costs. It followed a question for which they were asked to evaluate their classroom and on the job training. If the context had been training costs or had they been asked directly whether financing training was a problem, it is possible that more would have identified training costs as a problem.

Table 5-1

Percent of Recent Chicago Trainees Who Received Financial Support from Various Sources, Practical Nurses and Medical Technologists

Source of Support		*Practical Nurse Trainees*	*Medical Technology Trainees*
	N =	307	69
Part-Time Work		19	45
Parents' Assistance		24	64
Working Wife or Husband		22	3
Loans		3	4
Stipend or Scholarship		9	17
MDTA		14	--

Source: Mail questionnaire

training needs. This assumes that the stated goals of emphasizing technical and practical training in these schools is actually followed. In states where such schools are not adequately supported by the public, facilities for practical nurse training, as well as for other technical areas, will probably be inadequate.

2. The present structure for providing and financing facilities for training in medical technology is inadequate to meet the need for trained personnel. Most of the training is done in hospitals, and the incentives for hospitals to accept the responsibility for the costs of training personnel in numbers sufficient to meet the needs of the market are weak. If facilities and training programs are to be expanded sufficiently, it will probably be necessary to provide public subsidy to the hospitals for this purpose.

3. Direct costs to the trainee for the year of specialized training in each of the occupations are substantial but not overwhelming. Costs to the trainee are a barrier to entry in both occupations in two ways: (a) The costs probably keep some potential entrants from considering training because they lack the resources, and (b) some potential trainees, while they might have the resources, view the likely benefits as not justifying the expenditure. The problem can be met by either increasing the benefits (earnings) that accrue to practitioners or by further subsidizing the students. Thus far, the market has not sufficiently adjusted earnings to solve the problem. In part, at least, this is a phenomenon of a dynamic shortage. Demand continues to expand and the adjustments in earnings never catch up to the expanding demand. Further subsidization of students will probably be required. For practical nurse students, the MDTA approach appears to be effective so long as facilities are underutilized. For medical technology students, something approaching full subsidization of the costs of the last year of college and the year of specialized laboratory training through special scholarships might be an effective approach.

Evaluation of Training

Training school and hospital administrators, the practitioners, and the recent graduates of training schools were asked a number of questions that provide evaluative information about the nature of training. Some of this information bears to some extent on the supply (either quantity or quality) of labor in the two occupations. The responses to these questions are summarized in this section.

A factor of direct relevance to the supply of labor to the occupations is the proportion of entrants into training who actually complete the training course. The completion rate is of particular importance to the practical nurse and medical technologist occupations because, by and large, entry to the occupations is exclusively through the prescribed training programs. Therefore partial completion of the training programs does not ordinarily qualify a person for entry at any level. There is some exception to this in the laboratories, since some hospitals accept unqualified persons for on-the-job training for the more routine laboratory tasks.

Drop-out from medical technology training programs is apparently a very minor problem. All of the training schools in the sample reported completion rates of 85 percent or higher, and most indicated that well over 90 percent of their students complete the program. The six schools for practical nurse training, on the other hand, reported drop-out rates from their programs ranging from about 25 percent to 33 percent. One school reported substantially higher drop-out rates (over 40 percent) among students in MDTA programs. The reasons for the relatively high drop-out rates included a combination of personal, ability-related, and financial causes. The sample of recent trainees surveyed by mail questionnaire included 69 students of practical nursing schools who had not completed their training, and most of them reported their reasons for dropping out.[j] Nearly half of these (49 percent) reported that they failed to complete the training because they were dropped from the program by the school for failure to do acceptable work or they left voluntarily because the material was too difficult for them. Other important reasons for leaving training before completion were financial problems (12 percent), home responsibilities or other factors that created a time problem (14 percent), and illness or accident (13 percent).

While some of the drop-out problem is unavoidable, the high proportion of drop-outs apparently due to failure or inability to measure up to performance standards suggests the possibilities that either the performance standards are too rigorous or that the criteria for selecting students are not quite rigorous enough. The selection criteria generally include a minimum educational requirement, a satisfactory grade in an entrance examination, and a personal interview. The educational requirement varied somewhat among the six schools. Two schools required a minimum of a tenth-grade education (but in one school this could be waived) and four schools required high school graduation (and in two of these schools this requirement could be waived). Five of the six schools had raised educational requirements during the past 10 years because general educational levels were rising and the schools felt they could be more selective. Four of the six schools had no plans for further changes in entrance requirements and two were considering raising requirements, one of them by elimination of the practice of waiving minimum requirements.

The general entrance standards of the practical nursing schools can probably not be faulted too seriously, in spite of high drop-out rates and frequent performance failures by students. The demand for trained practical nurses was strong and most of the schools had excess capacity. These factors, plus the fact that screening criteria are never faultless, probably argue for a reasonably liberal entrance requirement and a rigorous holding to performance standards. The high completion rate among medical technology students gives no cause to question the entrance requirements. All of the approved schools in the sample required the minimum three years of college and the minimum course work in mathematics and science required of the ASCP for program approval.

[j]The mail questionnaire sample included only three drop-out respondents from schools of Medical technology. These schools, as indicated above, had few drop-outs from their programs. No analysis, therefore, of reasons for dropping out is possible.

The alternative explanation for high drop-out rates in practical nursing, namely that the training programs were unnecessarily difficult, can be tested to some extent by the evaluations of training programs given by the students and practitioners who went through them and by the hospitals which employed the product, as well as from the evaluation of the training schools of their own students.

For the most part, the training schools themselves were satisfied with the students they were getting. Four of the six practical nursing schools and eleven of the sixteen medical technology schools said they were generally satisfied with the students entering their programs. The two nursing schools which were dissatisfied expressed concern about the high drop-out rate, but had no specific plans for dealing with the problem. The dissatisfied medical technology schools indicated concern about such matters as inadequate mathematical and verbal skills, lack of ambition, and lack of interest in the field among some of their students. In general, however, both types of schools were reasonably satisfied with the quality of students attracted to the field.

The hospitals which hire the products of the training schools give the training schools high ratings. Of the hospital supervisory personnel interviewed, 88 percent gave "very good" or "good" ratings to the approved practical nursing schools and 77 percent gave the same ratings to approved schools of medical technology. Only 10 to 12 percent of the hospital supervisory personnel rated either type of school "fair" or "poor." Two percent did not rate the practical nursing schools and 11 percent did not rate the medical technology schools because they did not use the graduates of these schools. Most of the hospital supervisors who gave high ratings to the schools indicated that they based their judgment on the fact that they were satisfied with the performance of the graduates of the schools; some, however, referred to the excellence of teachers and instructors and to the high standards of admittance and retention of the schools.

The commercial (unapproved) schools of practical nursing and medical technology, however, were rated very poorly by the hospital supervisors. Most of them rated these schools as "poor" or said they were unable to judge them because they didn't hire their students. For both types of schools, only five percent of the hospital supervisors gave "good" ratings. Again, those hospitals which gave unfavorable ratings to the commercial schools generally based their judgment on the performance of the schools' graduates; most said they were unable to perform satisfactorily. Others mentioned the absence or poor quality of laboratory or training facilities, low admission standards, lack of interest in training (interested only in the student's money), and poor quality teachers. Very few hospitals had any praise for the training programs of the commercial schools.

The approved training school programs also received high marks from the practitioners who had successfully gone through them. Among the practical nurses interviewed, 87 percent gave "excellent" or "good" ratings to the classroom instruction they received, and 83 percent gave the same ratings to the internship or on-the-job aspects of the training. Among the practicing medical technologists, 72 percent gave the same favorable ratings to their classroom instruction and 86 percent to the on-the-job training.

The minority of LPN's who rated their classroom instruction unfavorably indicated several shortcomings in this aspect of their training. Over a quarter (27 percent) said too little time was devoted to the classroom or insufficient attention was given to theoretical materials. About a third of the dissatisfied put the blame on poor teachers. And substantial proportions claimed that classes were too large (18 percent) or that the classroom instruction was insufficiently applied to the work situation (also 18 percent). The major complaints of those dissatisfied with the on-the-job training were that they received poor treatment by supervisory or other employees at the work place (37 percent) and that they were not given enough variety or responsibility in their work experience. All of these complaints, it should be emphasized, were expressed by relatively small proportions of the practitioners.

Among the medical technologists, most of the dissatisfaction about the training program was related to the classroom instruction. The most frequent complaint, voiced by 39 percent of those who gave unfavorable ratings to the classroom instruction, was that not enough time was devoted to classroom instruction and/or theoretical materials. Poor teachers (22 percent) and unsatisfactory application of classroom instruction to the work situation (17 percent) were also relatively frequent complaints. For the relatively small number of technologists dissatisfied with the internship portion of the training, the dominant complaint was poor teachers. Poorly organized training programs, poor equipment, and insufficient contact with patients comprised most of the other sources of dissatisfaction (16 percent each). The concentration of the complaints among technologists with the classroom part of the training program is probably closely related to the severe shortage of technologists' services. The training is done in the hospitals, and it is likely that the pressure to get work out of the laboratory results in a shortcutting of classroom instruction in the interest of getting the student into the laboratory where he can contribute to output.

Following evaluation of their training experience and their reasons for it, the practitioners were asked to suggest ways in which the training could be improved. Relatively few had suggestions to make, responses were given by only 38 of the LPN's and 26 of the medical technologists, and their suggestions covered a rather wide range. The most common suggestion given by the LPN's, made by about 30 percent of those responding, was that training should include more practical and less theoretical orientation (which appears to be at variance with most of the criticism of training). The dominant theme among the suggestions of the medical technologists was the reverse; close to 30 percent of the respondents suggested that the training should be more theoretical and less practical. On the other hand, close to another 20 percent suggested training should be less theoretical and more practical. The conflicting views among both groups of practitioners may well be due to differences in the emphasis given theory and practice in the various training programs. Undoubtedly there is considerable variation in approach among training programs.

In general, the views of the practitioners toward their training indicates that the training given is appropriate for the two occupations. Only a small minority in each occupation indicated serious dissatisfaction with the training they received, and the diversity of complaints appears to reflect rather minor deviations in training practices and in personal preferences. Further, most of those who gave unfavorable judgment on their training experience made their response in the "fair" category; few practitioners felt so strongly that they gave a rating of "poor," and those who were critical in no cases based their criticism on the fact that the training was too difficult. There is no evidence from the practitioners themselves, therefore, that the performance standards of the schools are too rigorous. On the contrary, most of the criticisms referred to possible deficiencies in the programs offered. As a general proposition, on the basis of those who completed training then, no serious fault can be found with either the admission standards of the approved schools or with the general quality of the training programs offered.[k]

The practitioners were questioned along a number of other lines regarding their training experiences that are less directly related to the adequacy of the supply of labor. One of these, however, is worthy of some attention. The practitioners were asked to indicate any supplementary training they had taken since coming on the job and any plans they have for further training. About 80 percent in each occupation had undertaken no further training, other than orientation to their specific job required by the employer. Of those who had, most of the LPN's had undertaken the training to satisfy their own curiosity or to improve their competence as a practical nurse. A very few had taken or were engaged in training which they hoped would lead to advancement in the occupation. The same pattern applied to the medical technologists, except that a somewhat larger proportion had taken the training in hopes of advancement in the profession and a few had completed the work for the bachelor's degree while on the job.

The small amount of additional training engaged in for the purpose of professional advancement, particularly among the practical nurses, emphasizes a matter that might be a problem in recruitment of people to the occupations. In the case of the practical nurse, the training qualifies the candidate for the position of practical nurse but has no applicability to nursing occupations higher in the occupational hierarchy. Thus, a practical nurse interested in becoming a registered nurse would have to start at the beginning of the RN training program; she would receive no credit for the practical nurse training or experience. The practical nurse position, in other words, is a dead-end occupation. The extent to which this characteristic of the occupation acts as a deterrent to entry to the occupation cannot be determined from this study, but on the face of it one would presume that it has a negative effect. Earning possibilities in the occupation are quite limited in the first place, and it is difficult to move on to

[k]The mail questionnaire survey of recent Chicago trainees also asked the respondents to rate their training experience. Again the responses were very favorable; 88 percent of the LPN's and 80 percent of the medical technologists rated their training as excellent or good.

higher occupations where the returns are more attractive.[l] In addition, inability to apply practical nurse training toward RN and associate nurse training programs probably also reduces the potential supply of labor to these shortage occupations. What is suggested is that a better coordination of training programs for the various nursing occupations might increase the supply of labor to all of them.[m] As training programs are now designed, very few practical nurses take training beyond the requirements for the practical nurse positions.

The problem of advancement is not quite so extreme in the case of medical technologists. Their training qualifies them for relatively high level work to begin with. Also, there are some opportunities in the laboratories for advancement to supervisory positions as well as opportunities for some to engage in independent research.

The difference between the two occupations with respect to opportunities for advancement is illustrated by the replies of the practitioners to the question: "What do you think your chances are of advancing to a better job as a (LPN or medical technologist)? Explain." While 45 percent of the medical technologists rated their chances excellent or good, only half as many LPN's, 22 percent, did so. Over two-thirds of the practical nurses who did not rate their chances good gave as a reason the fact that practical nursing is a dead-end job – there is no place for a practical nurse to go. Most of the rest, about 20 percent, said advancement would require additional training in nursing. Among the medical technologists who saw little chance of advancement, less than half (48 percent) attributed the difficulty to the fact that medical technology is a dead-end occupation. Most of the rest, 37 percent, indicated that advancement would require additional training. Over half of the latter group were technologists who had neither ASCP registration nor the bachelor's degree, and their unfavorable rating of advancement opportunities was a recognition of their own training deficiencies rather than a commentary on the nature of the occupation. While the perceptions of the practical nurses verify the limited opportunities for advancement in the occupation, the importance of this limitation in attracting people to the occupation, as indicated above, is not certain.

The practitioners were also asked whether they had plans to take any further training. Nearly half in both occupations claimed that they had such plans. In view of the small proportion who had taken supplementary training in the past,

[l]Candidates may, of course, enter the RN and associate nurse training programs in the first place. However, the longer initial training periods in these occupations may also be a deterrent to entry. If a practical nurse, after a period of time on the job, were able to continue training toward a higher level occupation, however, the length of the training period might be less of a deterrent.

[m]This discussion ignores difficulties that might be involved in accomplishing this. They may be considerable.

this statistic should perhaps be accepted with some skepticism; perhaps the stated plans should more realistically be viewed as distant hopes. In any event, it is of interest to note what specific goals the respondents had in mind. Among the LPN's claiming plans for further training, 42 percent indicated their goal was to become registered nurses, 21 percent planned to train for occupations entirely outside the nursing field, and 37 percent were interested only in improving their skills as practical nurses. Among the medical technologists who claimed they had plans for further training almost all (72 percent) had in mind training to improve their skills and competencies as medical technologists; a number planned for training that would lead to ASCP registration (12 percent) and a few indicated plans to become medical doctors or to train for occupations outside the medical field.

The main conclusion that can be drawn from these stated training plans of the practitioners is that most of the medical technologists saw training as a way to improve or maintain their status in the profession, while most practical nurses viewed further training as a way to advance in the nursing services hierarchy. Among the practical nurses considerable interest and motivation to advance to higher occupational levels appears to exist. The barriers to attaining this goal are formidable, however, and it is doubtful that many of them with the interest will succeed in reaching the goal. If the training program for practical nurses could be better integrated with the training programs for other nursing occupations, practical nursing would likely become a more attractive entry occupation and more practical nurses would move up the occupational hierarchy.

Placement

The relationship of placement to the supply of labor is primarily a matter of the effectiveness of labor market institutions in allocating available qualified persons to available jobs. A number of questions used in this study bear on the matter.

Some evidence of the effectiveness of the labor market in matching workers with jobs is the speed with which an available worker located a job. The interviews with the practitioners and the mail questionnaire responses of recent trainees indicate the length of time it took persons in both occupations to find jobs after the completion of their training. The results are in Table 5-2.

The data show that qualified persons generally obtained positions in a relatively short period of time. Both surveys indicate that most persons found a job within a month of completing their training. The work histories gathered for both surveys were not complete enough to determine whether the 10 to 15 percent who took longer than a month to find a job were in the labor force and looking for work the entire time between completing their training and finding a job. It may well be that the picture would be even more favorable if allowances were made for time spent on vacation or for other purposes following training and before entry into the labor force. The relative speed with which jobs are found is probably more a function of the shortage of personnel in the

Table 5-2

Length of Time to First Job Following Training, Practitioners and Recent Trainees (Percent Distribution)

Months to First Job	*Licensed Practical Nurses*	*Medical Technologists*	Recent Trainees (Chicago Mail Questionnaire) *Licensed Practical Nurses*	*Medical Technologists*
Total	100%	100%	100%	100%
Less Than One Month	90	85	85	82
One to Two Months	6	9	6	6
Over Two Months	4	6	9	11

Source: Worker interviews and recent trainee mail questionnaire.

occupations than it is of effective labor market organization. A qualified worker can find a job by applying almost anywhere. In fact, as was indicated in an earlier chapter, many of the practitioners found their first job by direct application to hospitals. Seventy-one percent of the practical nurses found their first job this way. Most of the rest (23 percent) took jobs at the hospital where they received the internship part of their training. Among the medical technologists, on the other hand, twice as many (47 percent) stayed on at the hospital where they were trained and 30 percent found jobs by direct application. And a substantially larger proportion than among the practical nurses (18 percent) found positions through public or private employment offices, recommendations from their training schools or others, and by answering newspaper or journal advertisements. These findings indicate that in a situation of shortages of skilled personnel a formal labor market mechanism is not essential in order for available workers to find employment. Whether the informal channels resulted in an optimum allocation of the available labor is another question.

The informality of the placement function, indicated by the responses of the practitioners to the question of how they found their first job, may be somewhat overstated. It will be recalled from the discussion of hospital recruitment practices that, particularly for LPN's, hospitals relied to a considerable extent on their contacts with the training schools for identifying potential new employees. Although few of the training schools for either occupation operated formal placement services for their graduates (an exception is the commercial schools for laboratory technicians), most of them indicated that they had close contact with the labor market through their relationships with hospital administrators. Undoubtedly these contacts are used to a considerable extent in putting their students in contact with potential employers. In some cases, what the practitioner labeled a direct application may have been initiated by the training school by referring or putting the student in touch with a hospital in need of personnel.

A number of characteristics of the post-training employment experience of the recent Chicago trainees surveyed by mail questionnaire are also of interest as indicators of the effectiveness of the labor market in the placement of qualified personnel in jobs. In the first place, nearly all of the recent trainees had had some work experience since the completion of their training. About 93 percent in both occupations had worked for some period of time.[n] At the time of the survey the current labor force status of the respondents was as follows:

	LPN's	*Medical Technologists*
Employed	82%	81%
Unemployed	4%	3%
Out of the labor force	14%	16%
Total	100%	100%
	(N=307)	(N–69)

As indicated, most of the recent trainees were employed, a few were unemployed, and about 15 percent in each occupation were out of the labor force at the time of the survey. Of those not active in the labor force, nearly two-thirds of the practical nurses and over one-third of the medical technologists were engaged in household activities, and most of the others were in school continuing their education or training. Nearly all of the employed – 96 percent of the practical nurse trainees and 98 percent of the medical technologist trainees – were working in the occupations for which they were trained. And nearly all were employed by medical institutions. Eighty-one percent of the practical nurses were working for hospitals and 15 percent for other medical institutions. The comparable figures for the technologists were 63 percent and 32 percent. Excluding those who had not worked at all since completing their training (7 percent in each occupation), the work experience of nearly all of the recent trainees had been entirely in the occupations for which they were trained. Ninety-three percent of the practical nurses and 91 percent of the medical technologists had worked in no other line of work. Finally, 94 percent of the

[n]Although some variation existed among training schools in the time periods covered in the lists of graduates they provided, most of the recent trainees had completed their course of training in late 1963, 1964, or 1965. The questionnaires were sent out and returned between September 1965 and February 1966.

employed practical nurse and 89 percent of the employed medical technologist respondents were working in the Chicago area. Only 3 and 4 percent in the two occupations, respectively, were working outside the state of Illinois.

As a contrast to the labor market experiences of the recent trainees who had completed their training, it is of interest to look at what happened to those trainees who dropped out of training before completing the training program.[o] Twice as many dropouts from practical nurse training (15 percent) had no working experience after leaving training as was the case for those who completed training. And at the time of the survey, only 64 percent of the drop-outs were employed (83 percent), three times as many, 12 percent, were unemployed (4 percent), and nearly twice as many, 24 percent, were out of the labor force (14 percent), over half of whom were occupied as housewives.[p] Those who were employed took much longer to find a job than did the practical nurses who had completed training. Only 31 percent found a job within a month of dropping out of the training program (compared with 85 percent of those completing the training). As would be expected, most of them (51 percent) were employed in occupations unrelated to practical nursing. However, 42 percent were working in related occupations such as nurse aides, and 7 percent claimed to be employed as practical nurses. Nearly half of them, 46 percent, were employed by hospitals or other medical institutions. Clearly, as compared with the experience of the drop-outs, completion of the practical nurse training program paid off in higher employment rates, lower unemployment rates, greater participation in the labor force, speedier job finding, and jobs making use of their training.

We now return briefly to a line of questioning conducted in the interviews with the practitioners that relates to the stability of their attachment to jobs as LPN's and medical technologists. They were asked whether they intended to remain in these two occupations. About 80 percent in each occupation said they did; the remainder said they expected to leave it or were uncertain about it. Among the minority of practical nurses who thought they might leave, most (88 percent) felt they might prefer to be in a different line of work and the rest planned to leave to raise a family. The comparable figures for the medical technologists planning or thinking about leaving were 61 percent and 25 percent; in addition some technologists cited pay (7 percent), the difficulty of the work (4 percent), or plans to move (4 percent) as reasons for leaving the occupation.

[o] Because the mail survey included only three medical technology dropouts from training, it is not possible to compare this group's experience. The analysis above is based on the experience of 69 respondents to the mail survey who dropped out of a practical nurse training program before completion.

[p] Figures in parentheses are the comparable figures for those who completed training.

With respect to plans to remain with their present employer, the practitioners exhibited a somewhat higher propensity to move. Sixty-eight percent of the practical nurses and 62 percent of the technologists indicated they had no intentions of leaving their present employers; the remainder said either that they planned to change employers or were uncertain. The main reasons given by the practical nurses for thinking about changing jobs were to enter other occupations (48 percent) and dissatisfaction with working conditions at the hospitals (28 percent). The most common reasons cited by the medical technologists with intentions to change employers were plans to move their residence (28 percent), to change occupations (24 percent), and dissatisfaction with pay (13 percent) or working conditions (11 percent).

Most of the practitioners in the two occupations, therefore, are committed to remain in their present line of work. Mobility is mainly in and out of the labor force and between employers.[q] Relatively small proportions indicated intentions of leaving the occupation; probably smaller proportions actually carry out their intentions.

The main conclusions to be drawn from the information on the post-training labor market experiences of persons in the two occupations are as follows:

1. No evidence was found of serious labor market malfunctioning in the matching of workers and jobs. Although informal channels of placement predominate, jobs are found quickly following completion of training, employment rates are high in jobs directly related to the training received, and unemployment is low.

2. Trainees who complete training for practical nursing have clear advantage in the labor market over those who drop out before completing training. This was evidenced in higher employment rates, lower unemployment rates, greater labor force participation, and much speedier placement in jobs.[r]

3. The practical nurses and medical technologists have strong attachments to these two lines of work. Most of the mobility that occurs among them relates to changes in labor force status and in employers, not to changes in occupation.

[q]Information was gathered in the work histories of the practitioners on the number of different employers they had worked for and on periods out of the labor force. The first of these are difficult to work with because of the differences among the workers in how long they have been in the labor force. The second is difficult to interpret because the sample does not contain persons who were not employed at the time of the survey.

[r]Although lower labor force participation of the dropouts may in part be for the same reasons that the trainees had to drop out of training (e.g., family responsibilities, illness, etc.).

6 Factors Affecting Supply: Internal Adjustments and Employee Benefits

The extent to which hospitals have availed themselves of the possibilities for adjusting to the shortages through changes in utilization patterns of nursing and laboratory personnel as well as through systems of worker benefits and employee relations will be considered in this chapter.

Utilization Patterns

When it is not possible for an organization to go to the market to hire the quality and quantity of labor it desires in sufficient numbers to meet the demand for its services, it may turn to other methods to generate the needed or desired volume of services. These methods include the lowering of minimum hiring qualifications, establishing on-the-job or other training programs, job redesign (e.g., job dilution, the process of breaking down jobs into simpler tasks) and the substitution of lesser trained for highly skilled labor, substitution of capital for labor, and the lowering of the quality of services offered customers. The sample hospitals in this study used various combinations of these devices in their attempts to adjust to the shortage. However, in general it must be indicated that the available evidence showed that the extent of the possibilities for adjusting through these methods was not fully and perhaps not even significantly realized.

Hiring Policies

Hospital hiring policies were summarized earlier in the discussion of recruitment practices and in the discussion of entry into training programs. The tendency over the years in both occupations has been to increase educational requirements for entry into the prescribed training programs. The requirements for entry into training carry over to hiring policies, since for the most part only persons completing the training programs are considered for employment. Thus, there has been no effort to meet the shortage situation by diluting the requirements for qualifying for employment; rather, the reverse is true. If anything, the shortage has become more acute by making access more difficult. In practical nursing, entry requirements for training have generally moved from one to two years of high school to a high school diploma. In medical technology, the requirement had moved up from two years of college to the requirement of three years of college level work at the time of the survey of the medical occupations.

Hospital administrative and supervisory personnel were generally satisfied with requirements for entry as they stood. Large proportions of these persons interviewed in this study thought that standards for entry were about right. In the minority of cases where dissatisfaction was expressed, personnel administrators tended to think that requirements for medical technologists were too high and chief pathologists in charge of laboratories tended to think they were too low.

It is difficult to assess the appropriateness of qualification standards. The use of educational attainment level as a screening device is itself somewhat arbitrary, regardless of what cut-off point is used. It is undoubtedly the case that some persons with only a year or two of high school would make perfectly acceptable practical nurses, and that some persons with two years of college completed would make excellent medical technologists. On the other hand, in the interest of efficiency in selection, it is usually necessary to establish some qualification floor beneath which persons are not ordinarily given consideration. In the cases of practical nursing and medical technology, however, it might be feasible to develop objective tests that could be substituted as entry criteria for persons who do not meet the minimum educational requirements, particularly in periods when insufficient students with normal qualifications are available. For practical nursing such tests are already given as a supplemental screening device and, if they are reasonably valid predictors of success, could be extended to persons without the formal educational requirements. Presumably such tests ought to measure general intelligence level and writing, verbal and comprehension abilities.

For medical technologists the relevant requirements for entry into specialized training are mainly a level of proficiency in certain scientific subjects and some minimum level of intelligence. The common requirement in scientific subjects was 16 semester hours each in chemistry and biology and a one-semester course in college mathematics. A beginning course in physics and in bacteriology were often recommended. The level of required scientific proficiency can only be obtained at the college level, but it does not necessarily follow that three or four years of college education are required. It is quite possible that the desired level of proficiency could be gained by other shorter routes that would tend to increase the supply of technologists. If, for example, special programs could be set up offering the necessary scientific instruction in community or junior colleges, they might provide an alternative two-year route to entry into specialized training in medical technology. A test of relevant scientific knowledge might be administered at the completion of the college level training to screen these students for admission into the year of specialized training in medical technology.[a] Two advantages of such an alternative route to preparation for the occupation would be the shorter training period and the reduction in training costs that would accrue. An additional advantage would be the more than marginal increase in number of potential applicants if this type of institution with its lower opportunity costs for students could be employed as a base for recruitment. Both advantages should have a favorable effect on increasing the supply of persons available for the occupation. An additional advantage might be that such a training program could add visibility to the occupation and be a factor in bringing opportunities to the attention of potential students. The present program for preparing for a career in medical technology could be retained, and students taking this route would be presumed to be better prepared for the more complex and advanced work in medical technology (particularly for research responsibilities).

The suggestions for changes in the formal qualifying requirements for the two occupations accept as valid the criteria implicit in the existing formal entrance requirements for training. They merely indicate possibilities for increasing the supply of entrants to the occupations with the required abilities and qualifications by making the formal entrance requirements less rigid. Whatever the merits of the specific suggestions, it is important that consideration be given to the feasibility of altering the minimum formal entrance requirements so that access to the occupations by potentially qualified individuals is maximized. A key problem in both occupations, and particularly in medical technology, is a shortage of candidates for training positions. For this reason attention to ways in which individuals are screened out of consideration by formal entrance requirements is called for.

Training

The relationship between training programs and the supply of labor was discussed at length in the previous chapter. None of that discussion will be repeated here. The purpose of including training in this chapter is to highlight it as a potential force in adjustment by the firm to a shortage situation. The focus will be mainly possibilities for using training as a short-run adjustment device.

In the case of practical nursing there is little opportunity and should be little need for the individual hospital to meet a shortage situation by establishing a training program. The established training program for practical nursing is relatively short, and when a shortage situation is recognized it should not take an extraordinary length of time for training facilities to expand and begin to turn

[a]Students completing such a program would have several career options available to them. They might continue their college work to the bachelor's degree, they might go on immediately to the specialized training in medical technology, or if they failed the qualifying exam, they might go to work in laboratories in lower level positions, perhaps with some on-the-job training.

out students to meet the need.[b] In fact, the MDTA approach of subsidizing certain students and instructional costs would appear to be the appropriate type of response to a shortage situation in an occupation like licensed practical nurse. Failure of facilities to expand, of course, does leave open the option for a hospital to establish a formal training program.

There is little possibility, however, for a hospital to meet shortages by substituting on-the-job training for the formal practical nurse training programs. Only a very small proportion of the sample hospitals in this study made use of unlicensed practical nurses who had been trained on the job or in any fashion outside the approved programs. The four hospitals which did so were all located in St. Louis where the shortage was severe, indicating that it is a last resort practice. When the practice is resorted to, it is likely that the duties of the individual used are closer to those of a nurse aide than they are to those of a licensed practical nurse. Hospital affiliation with training programs for the purpose of providing the internship part of the training, however, is a possible device for trying to meet a shortage situation. Affiliation puts students on the floor who can make some contribution to providing nursing services and, in addition, may be a help in the hospital's recruiting efforts. The device, however, does not lead to an increase in the total supply of labor; it affects only the distribution of the supply among hospitals.

Similarly, on-the-job training cannot be substituted for a formal training program in an attempt to increase the supply of medical technologists. As indicated elsewhere, however, under the present structure of training for the occupation, the supply is affected by the number of hospitals which establish formal training programs, and in response to the shortage of technologists, increasing numbers of hospitals have done so. Also, many hospitals have tried to increase the number of hands available in the laboratory by hiring unqualified persons and giving them on-the-job training in routine laboratory tasks. While this does not increase the number of qualified technologists, it may release qualified technologists from routine tasks and increase the effective supply. This possibility is further discussed below when job redesign is considered.

The newest approach to training in the laboratories is the program for certified laboratory assistants (CLA). Although the program was very new at the time this survey was conducted, and little opportunity was available to evaluate it, most hospital supervisory personnel were strongly in favor of it. Its main attraction, however, is not as a solution to the shortage of medical technologists but as a program for supplying more highly qualified and skilled personnel for the simpler laboratory tasks. Again, the program may have some effect in increasing the effective supply of technologists by releasing them for more complex duties, and it will probably reduce the need for hospitals to hire unqualified personnel. MDTA programs can probably be effective in bringing about an increased supply of certified laboratory assistants.

Since both occupations by their very natures require relatively extensive, formal preparation, adjustment to the shortages through the establishment of hospital training programs has only limited possibilities. Efforts of hospitals in

[b]Although the failure of facilities in St. Louis to expand to meet the need indicates that it is not always as easy to do as it should be.

this direction are likely to result more in a redistribution of the available supply of labor than in an increase in the total supply. Exceptions to this generalization were discussed in the previous chapter.

Job Redesign

To what extent is it possible to ease the shortage of practical nurses and medical technologists by reorganizing jobs in nursing services and in the medical laboratory? Job redesign becomes a possible device for adjusting to a shortage of skilled or technical personnel if, with reference to our cases, nursing and laboratory tasks performed by practical nurses and medical technologists can be broken down or subdivided into simpler tasks for which, to some extent, unskilled or lesser skilled labor can be utilized. If this can be done, the time of the practical nurse and the medical technologist can be released for the most complex and highly skilled tasks and a closer equilibrium between demand and supply attained through a reduction in effective demand. The reduction in demand for practical nurses and medical technologists would be accomplished by shifting the demand to lower level personnel for whom the supply would presumably be more readily available.

The rapid expansion in the demand for practical nurses in recent years is itself largely the result of extensive redesign of nursing services. The occupation has been largely cut out of the duties previously performed by registered nurses and to some extent those performed by nurse aides. As the national employment trends summarized in Chapter 2 show, the job redesigning has resulted in rapid growth in the relative number of practical nurses employed in hospitals and other medical institutions and has been an important factor in adjusting to the shortage of nursing personnel.

In the interviews conducted at the sample hospitals in this study, administrators were asked to indicate relative employment trends in their hospitals in nursing occupations over the past five years. Seventy-one percent of the hospitals, 55 percent in Chicago and 86 percent in St. Louis, were using relatively more practical nurses at the time of the survey than they were five years earlier, indicating that the process of substituting practical nurses for other nursing personnel was a continuing one in most hospitals.

Changes in the employment ratios of the three nursing services occupations indicate the extent to which redesign of nursing tasks has occurred (see Table 6-1). The changes in ratios are difficult to interpret because they are based on surveys covering differing groupings of institutions, but they indicate that the increased demand for nursing services has been met by proportionately larger increases in the employment of practical nurses than of registered nurses and nurse aides. They also show, however, that there are large differences in the extent to which practical nurses are used in different areas of the country. And, although this is not shown in Table 6-1, great variations between individual hospitals occur in the composition of nursing services employees. In Chicago hospitals, for example, the ratio of practical nurses to registered nurses ranged from 1 to 1.2 to 1 to 20 in 1965. In St. Louis, practical nurses comprise a much larger proportion of nursing employment than they do in the country as a whole or in Chicago. And the rate of substitution of practical nurses for registered nurses and nurse aides has moved much more rapidly. In Chicago this trend appears to have started late, but the available data indicate that the substitution of practical nurses for registered nurses proceeded rapidly after 1960. The more intensive utilization of practical nurses in St. Louis probably explains, in part, why the shortage of licensed practical nurses showed up as much more serious in St. Louis than in Chicago.[c] Apparently the employment mix of nursing service employees is not a fixed ratio and, as a result, considerable flexibility exists for reorganizing and redesigning nursing services tasks. The actual mix used is a function of relative wage rates, the availability of personnel, and the degree of recognition by hospital administrators, supervisors, and doctors of the possibilities for making substitutions.[d] As indicated above, a majority of hospitals in both cities are moving in the direction of increasing the relative proportion of practical nurses in the nursing services team. There would appear to be considerable opportunity to continue this trend, particularly in Chicago, as a means of meeting the present and expected future shortage of nursing personnel. Accomplishing this will depend, of course, on training a sufficient supply of practical nurses.

The main reasons given by our sample hospitals for the shift toward greater utilization of the LPN were the shortage of RN's (49 percent),[e] desire to increase the quality of patient care by substituting LPN's for nurse aides (24 percent), and attempts to lower costs by substituting LPN's for higher paid nurses (19 percent).[f] These are all factors that are likely to be important in the future; job redesign and the substitution of practical nurses for other nursing personnel will most likely continue, therefore, to be very important adjustment factors for meeting the nursing shortage. The process of shifting the shortage from RN's to practical nurses, however, cannot be applied very extensively further down the nursing hierarchy; that is, the possibilities for meeting the practical-nurse shortage by further job redesign and substitution of nurse aides for practical nurses is limited. The tendency is in the opposite direction; that is, hospitals attempt to replace nurse aides with practical nurses to the extent that

[c] On the other hand, it is probable, although the point wasn't under direct investigation in this study, that the shortage of registered nurses was viewed by hospital administrators as more serious in Chicago. Nearly all of the Chicago sample hospitals indicated a shortage of registered nurses.

[d] On the latter point, the hospital interviews provided considerable evidence that many supervisors, particularly doctors, were not fully aware of the capabilities and potential of the practical nurse as a member of the nursing team. In fact, many hospitals had a strong preference for meeting nursing needs with registered nurses, and hired LPN's only when they couldn't hire RN's. Also, substantial numbers of the LPN's interviewed for the study (37 percent) claimed that their present jobs were not making full use of their capabilities and training. The most frequent complaint of these LPN's was that doctors and nurses prevented them from doing tasks they were trained to do. To the extent that this is the case, there is room for not only using more LPN's, but for making further use of those who are employed.

[e] The interviews with hospital personnel also indicated that substitution of lower for higher level personnel is a common form of adjustment to short-term personnel shortages. Fifty-six percent of the hospitals, when asked what action they take when they are unable to obtain licensed practical nurses, indicated that they substituted with lower

Table 6-1

Employment Ratios for Nursing Occupations, Selected Years

Employment Ratios	*1950*[1]	*1959*	*1960*[1]	*1963*	*1964*	*1965*[4]	*1966*[6]
LPN to RN							
United States	1–2.9	1–2.4[2]	1–2.8	1–1.8[5]	1–2.3[2]		1–1.7
Illinois	1–3.8		1–3.8				
Chicago	1–4.9		1–4.9	1–2.6[4]		1–2.6	1–4.2
Missouri	1–2.2		1–2.1				
St. Louis	1–3.4	1–2.5[3]	1–2.4		1–1.6[3]		1–1.4

[1]Census data computed from employment figures in U. S. Census of Population Reports, "Detailed Characteristics of the Population" (Washington, D.C.: U.S. Government Printing Office, 1950 and 1960).

[2]U. S. Department of Health, Education and Welfare, Public Health Service, *Health Resource Statistics*, Interagency Conference on Nursing Statistics, 1964 (Washington, D. C.: U. S. Government Printing Office, 1965), p. 111.

[3]Employer interviews. From employment figures reported in interviews with administrators of the St. Louis sample hospitals.

[4]From employment figures reported by the Chicago sample hospitals in the 1963 and 1965 Salary Surveys of the Illinois Hospital Association. Copies of the completed questionnaire forms were supplied through the courtesy of the Illinois Hospital Association. The Association supplied returns for 17 of the 22 Chicago sample hospitals for 1963 and for 18 of the hospitals for 1965. The others were nonrespondents to the association salary survey and, with two exceptions, were small hospitals.

[5]Based on data from Bureau of Labor Statistics hospital surveys in Standard Metropolitan Statistical Areas reported in "Earnings in Hospitals in Mid–1963," *Monthly Labor Review*, (May 1964), p. 552.

Table 6-1 (*continued*)

Employment Ratios	*1950*[1]	*1959*	*1960*[1]	*1963*	*1964*	*1965*[4]	*1966*[6]
LPN to Nurse Aide							
United States				1-2.2[5]		1-2	1-2.5
Chicago				1-3.5[4]		1-3.2	1-3.4
St. Louis		1-5[3]			1-2.7[3]		1-3.1
RN to Nurse Aide							
United States				1-1.2[5]			1-1.5
Chicago				1-1.4[4]		1-1.2	1-1.3
St. Louis		1-2[3]			1-1.7[3]		1-2.2

[6]Based on data from Bureau of Labor Statistics survey of hospitals throughout the country and reported in "Earnings of Hospital Nurses, July, 1966," *Monthly Labor Review* (June 1967), pp. 56–57.

practical nurses are available. Using nurse aides when practical nurses are unavailable is viewed as a temporary or emergency measure. To the extent that job redesign of nursing services is feasible as a long-term solution to the nursing shortage, its limits are at the level of the practical nurse.

As with the case for practical nurses, a majority of the sample hospitals (63 percent) indicated that the utilization of medical technologists had increased in the past five years compared with other hospital personnel. The reasons for the increase, however, were different. By far the most common reason cited was that the number and complexity of laboratory tests required by doctors in the care of their patients had increased rapidly. In addition, many hospitals said that technologists were in greater demand because more research was being conducted in the laboratories.

Trends in the utilization of qualified medical technologists compared with other laboratory personnel are difficult to quantify. Published employment data tend to lump all laboratory personnel together. Also, variation in the use and meaning of job titles complicates measurement of ratios of qualified medical technologists to other laboratory personnel.

Whatever the precise trends in laboratory employment are, however, it is clear that a strong tendency exists to intensify the utilization of technologists in the laboratory. It is also clear that the shortage of laboratory personnel is heavily concentrated at the medical technologist level. Eighty-seven percent of the respondent hospitals indicated that their need was for bachelor-degree holders and/or ASCP-registered personnel. Only 14 percent indicated there was a shortage at their hospital for experienced but unregistered people; none faced a shortage of inexperienced, lower level technicians.

The question is, to what extent could the unmet need for technologists be met by job redesign and the substitution of lower level personnel for some of the work being done by technologists? In the view of most laboratory supervisors, this as a partial solution to the shortage problem is, at best, limited and imperfect. The fact that most of the work requires people with scientific backgrounds, is in some cases becoming more complex, and involves more research than previously, makes it dubious that much can be accomplished by attempts to substitute people with less training for the technologist.[g]

On the other hand, the pressure of the shortage had clearly resulted in the

---

level personnel (40 percent) or filled in with student nurses (16 percent).

[f]Most of those hospitals which were not increasing the proportion of LPN's (58 percent) cited as the reason the shortage of LPN's; that is, they were unable to hire more. Thirty-six percent said they were satisfied with the present ratio and 6 percent said it was hospital policy not to increase the ratio of LPN's to other nursing personnel.

[g]While pathologists frequently reported trends toward more complex laboratory tests, the technologists themselves did not appear to be particularly sensitive to this. When asked whether any major changes had occurred in their jobs since they began them, only a minority (about one-third) reported such changes. Most of the changes reported were said to be the result of advances in laboratory methods and equipment (28 percent) and the assignment of more responsibility to them (54 percent). None of the technologists reported that their work required more skill than previously.

utilization of lower qualified people in the laboratory when qualified people could not be found. About half of the hospitals indicated that in such a situation they either substituted with lower level technicians (38 percent) or hired unqualified people and trained them to do some of the tasks in the laboratory (13 percent). The remainder either got along with the available staff (e.g., by working overtime hours), (33 percent), curtailed service (5 percent), or had never encountered the problem (11 percent). The utilization of technicians when technologists are unavailable, however, tends to be a short-run imperative; it does not result in a reduced need for technologists. If technologists become available, they would be used in place of the technicians.

The evidence from the hospital interviews, therefore, indicates that job redesign is used primarily as a temporary expedient in meeting the demand for medical technologists and, furthermore, that it offers only limited possibilities as a device for adjusting to the shortage. The interviews with the technologists themselves provided little to change the picture. The most relevant question directed to them was whether or not they felt they were making full use of their training. If they felt they were not, one might have some basis for concluding that they were being underutilized and that perhaps some of their tasks could be done by people with less skill and training. Two-thirds of them, however, felt that their training was being fully utilized. Most of those who felt otherwise indicated that their work was too specialized, and some expressed the wish that they could be engaged more extensively in research work. While these replies suggest possibilities for some upgrading among technologists, they do not reflect a situation of widespread underutilization. In addition, most of the technologists (82 percent) found their jobs in conformity with what they anticipated when they entered training. Only 12 percent, in comparing their work with what they had expected of the occupation, expressed negative sentiments about their work experience; 8 percent said they found their jobs routine or lacking in variety compared with their expectations.

It cannot be concluded from the evidence in this study that job redesign offers any substantial hope for meeting present and anticipated shortages of medical technologists.[h]

Capital Substitution

Technological changes often have profound effects on labor demand. In a labor shortage situation, one would expect great pressure to introduce machines to do work formerly performed by labor. At the least, technological innovation can be viewed as a possible adjustment device to meet a labor shortage situation.

This study made no intensive investigation of the impact of technological changes on the demand for practical nurses and medical technologists. Most of what is said is based on casual observation and conversation with hospital personnel.

It is of some significance, however, that when asked what actions the hospital

[h] This conclusion is not based on engineering or scientific investigation of the laboratory work place. It is unlikely, in fact, given the state of hospital personnel practices, that any of the hospitals in the study had conducted such a study. It is probable, therefore, that the evidence in the study tends to understate the possibilities for job redesign.

took when it was unable to hire needed practical nurses and medical technologists, none of the hospital administrators or supervisory personnel indicated that they pressed for the introduction of available capital equipment. All of their responses dealt with their attempts to recruit or utilize the available work force. Nevertheless, substantial and significant technological innovation has occurred in hospitals and laboratories in recent years. Some of these innovations have labor-saving implications and results. In hospital wards, for example, improvements in the preparation and packaging of medicines have simplified and increased the efficiency with which medications can be given. Various monitoring devices have done the same for observing and checking the current condition of patients. While these and other innovations have increased the efficiency of labor, their introduction is apparently not very closely related to the supply availability of labor available.

The situation is apparently similar in the laboratory. Great strides have been made in the introduction of machines for making laboratory tests. Many of these are many times more efficient in labor requirements than older methods and apparently more accurate and dependable as well. But their introduction into the laboratory is more a function of their availability and the economies they provide than it is a function of the availability of labor. In addition, their labor-saving qualities apply more to the utilization of technicians than to that of technologists. In the view of laboratory directors, this is likely to be the case in the future as well, mainly because of increased need for research work. The major possibility for capital substitution might be from pooling the work of smaller hospitals so that major technological innovations will be economically feasible.

The conclusion seems to be that technological innovations with labor-saving implications are made largely independent of labor market conditions. In addition, many innovations, particularly in the nursing area, have results more related to the quality of patient care than to savings in labor. In the laboratory, although major innovations have and will probably continue to occur, the volume of laboratory work expands along with the innovations. Further, the demand for technologists is not heavily affected by the introduction of machines, in large part because increased research needs require the skill of the technologist.

Quality of Service

When we turn to the question of the relationship between labor shortages and the quality of hospital and laboratory services, we encounter a very difficult problem of measurement. The subject is a very sensitive one with hospital authorities. Unlike the case in much of the economy, the quality of service rendered is not just a matter of customer satisfaction or convenience; in some cases it might be a matter of life and death. High quality service is an expected norm in hospital ward and laboratory.

As a result most hospital authorities are not anxious to discuss the problem in any detail; when they do they are likely to say that the labor shortage has not resulted in a deterioration in the quality of services. Scattered evidence from interviews with various hospital personnel suggests, however, that some of the adjustment to the shortages was made through reductions in the quality of service rendered. Occasionally, for example, a practical nurse would speak of her concern that her ward was understaffed and the frustrations of being unable to care for all of the needs of the patients for whom she had some responsibility. And some of the technologists, in discussing characteristics of their jobs that they did not like, complained of the time pressure in getting out work.

The most direct approach to the question of quality was taken with the directors of training schools. They were asked: "Do you feel that the services provided for patient care have in any way been affected as a direct result of the shortage? How?" Five of the six directors of the practical nursing schools responded to the question and all five of them felt that quality of service had been lowered. The laboratory school directors were split on the question; half of them felt that services had been lowered and half either felt that services had been unaffected (38 percent) or expressed no opinion. Understaffing and the employment of unqualified personnel were cited as explanations for the declines in quality. There has also been considerable public attention to the problem of quality of medical laboratory work. Testimony before a committee of the U. S. Senate indicates that "as high as 25 percent of the tests conducted by clinical laboratories are erroneous."[1]

The matter of quality of service goes to the heart of the central questions associated with the supply of manpower to the two occupations. The maintenance or improvement of quality services must be in the background in considering many of the policy questions affecting the supply of labor, including entry qualifications for training, the length and content of training programs, the expansion of teaching and training facilities, minimum hiring qualifications, and job redesign and the substitution of lower level for highly qualified personnel at the work place. And there are vicious circle elements in the relationship of the shortages to the quality of service. To the extent that the shortages result in understaffing and the work of the practitioner becomes more difficult, frustrating, and unrewarding, the more difficult it becomes to retain them on the job and attract new ones to the occupation. And to the extent that the shortage results in delays and errors in laboratory work, hospital stays are likely to lengthen, thus aggravating the nursing shortage.

The relationships between the shortages and the quality of services cannot be finely documented from the evidence in this study. One probable result of the shortage, however, is a quality of medical services lower than that which the existing levels of technology, including knowledge, could provide if hospitals were adequately staffed. And the need and value in maintaining a high level of quality in services offered is an inhibiting factor in finding easy solutions to the shortage problem.

Employee Benefits and Employee Relations

Employee benefits of various kinds stand in a crucial position with respect to the adequacy of the supply of labor to an occupation. The most important of these benefits is the rate of pay.

Our earlier discussion of salaries and salary trends in the two occupations noted that salaries of practical nurses and medical technologists have advanced somewhat more rapidly than salaries generally, but that average salaries in both occupations are below those for occupations that require similar training and skill levels. It was also noted that some evidence exists of artificial depression of salaries through informal agreements among hospital authorities not to compete too strenuously for the limited amount of personnel available.

One further fact about salaries in the two occupations requires emphasis; namely, that the wage structure is relatively narrow. The average starting salary for Illinois LPN's in 1963 was $244 per month and the average going salary was only $265. For medical technologists, the comparable figures were $411 and $456 (see Table 3-4, Chapter 3). These narrow ranges suggest that length of service is relatively unimportant in salary administration, which means relatively little force or pull is present to keep people on the job. Since length of service gets relatively little reward, an employee loses little by changing employers or leaving the labor force for either short or extended periods of time.

With respect to salary levels in the two occupations, adjustments were taking place in response to the labor shortages. In Chicago, in fact, salaries for LPN's were close to the equilibrium level for equating supply and demand. Salaries for LPN's in St. Louis fell short of this mark, and the same was true for medical technologists in both cities. Considerable sensitivity to the salary problem existed, however, and over 40 percent of the hospitals indicated that they tried to adjust to the shortage of technologists by raising salary levels (55 percent in Chicago but only 23 percent in St. Louis). Attempts to adjust salaries of technologists to close the demand-supply gap is complicated by the fact that the training period is lengthy and by the fact that the market for technologists to some degree extends beyond the bounds of the local market. For these reasons actions beyond the capabilities of individual hospitals are required for effective action against the shortage.

Nonwage benefits for workers in the two occupations were identical or very similar and can be treated together.[i] The normal work week in well over 90 percent of the hospitals was between 35 and 40 hours. About nine out of ten hospitals made group hospital and medical insurance (usually Blue Cross-Blue Shield) plans available to its employees. In most hospitals, however, the employee paid the entire cost of the insurance. In about one of ten hospitals with plans, the hospital paid the entire premium, and in about one in four the cost was shared between the hospital and the employee. The typical vacation provision (in about 70 percent of the hospitals) was 10 days of vacation after one year of service and a maximum vacation for long-service employees of 21 days. Most hospitals allowed about 12 days of sick leave per year and six paid holidays. Only about 60 percent of the sample hospitals provided pension plans

[i] Small difference in coverage of fringe benefits existed for the two occupations due to the fact that not all hospitals employed both practical nurses and medical technologists.

for the practical nurses and medical technologists. Size of hospital was an important factor. Nearly 90 percent of the large hospitals had pension programs, compared with about two-thirds of the medium sized and less than a third of the small hospitals. Contributions to the pension plans were made jointly by the hospital and the employee in about 80 percent of the plans; the remaining 20 percent were noncontributory plans. About half of the hospitals provided their employees with uniforms and about one in five provided one free meal per shift. None of the sample hospitals provided day-care facilities for the children of working mothers nor assisted in the transportation of employees to and from work. Nor were housing facilities provided for employees by any of the hospitals.

Nearly all of the sample practitioners were full-time employees. Somewhat less than a third of the hospitals indicated, however, that they were attempting to make greater use of part-time workers as a way of attracting additional people into the work force. Also, over half indicated that they were attempting to adjust to the shortage by allowing adjustment in hours or work schedules to meet the requirements of individual workers.

Only one of the 37 sample hospitals engaged in collective bargaining with a labor union representing practical nurses or laboratory personnel. This hospital, located in St. Louis, engaged in collective negotiations with representatives of both occupations.

The workers in the two occupations were questioned about their likes and dislikes concerning the jobs they held. Prominent among their likes were the content of their jobs (mentioned by about 90 percent in each occupation) and, to a lesser extent, working conditions (mentioned by 31 percent of the practical nurses and 44 percent of the technologists). Interestingly, working conditions were also the most frequently mentioned dislike among practical nurses (45 percent) and stood second on the list among technologists (32 percent). Co-worker conflicts, working hours, and the difficulty and pressure of the work were the main complaints listed by both groups concerning working conditions. Pay was the most common element of the job disliked by the technologists (45 percent) and took second place among the practical nurses (26 percent). It is of interest to compare these dislikes with the reasons given by the practitioners for leaving previous jobs. Among those who had worked on other than their current job, the explanations given for changing jobs by the practical nurses were spread evenly among a dozen different reasons. Among the technologists, however, low pay was the predominant reason given for leaving previous jobs; over a third of the quits were primarily for this reason.

Salaries aside, employee benefits, while affording room for improvement at several points, are reasonably attractive and compare well with what would be available in comparable employment. On the other hand, various characteristics of the two occupations, particularly working hours and pressure to get work done well under conditions of understaffing and a shortage of personnel, tend to discourage participation in the work force. Over-all, the hospital authorities have not given systematic attention to personnel and employee relations problems.

For the most part, hospitals have not had union or other organizational pressure to force them to think through their policies. Many of the sample hospitals had only recently added professional personnel administrators to their administrative staffs and were only beginning to give thought to regularizing and systematizing personnel practices.

Relatively few examples of designing personnel practices to meet the specific problems of the hospital and the market were provided. In addition to unduly low wage levels, wage structures seemed generally unresponsive to the problem of labor turnover and shortage. In general, hospitals had done little experimentation with various part-time work arrangements in an effort to accommodate to the primarily female labor reserve available. Nor were there any hospitals in the sample operating or trying to establish day-care centers for working mothers who might be available for employment if their young children could be cared for. Hospitals in locations that presented transportation problems for employees in getting to and from work provided no solution to the problem. Hospitals that might be right up to date with the latest equipment in the ward and laboratory exhibited little capacity for developing programs to find people to run the equipment.

These and other practices that bar better internal adjustment to labor shortages are likely to be modified and, as a consequence, become more flexible and responsive as professionalization of personnel functions in hospitals increase, as employee organizations become more active in policy making, and as personnel shortages and rising medical care costs intensify. In the meantime, rising salaries are likely to be the major form of adjustment to the shortage. While this is required, and to a considerable extent desirable, the cost will be very high and even prohibitive unless other adjustment mechanisms are brought more fully into use.

III: The Industrial Occupations

7 Extent of the Shortage

The four industrial occupations selected for study, tool and die maker, tool and die designer, engineering technician-electronics, and engineering technician-metalworking, were chosen because there was apparent evidence based on aggregative trend data that severe shortages of workers in these occupations had existed over a long period of time. For shorthand purposes, hereafter the four occupations will be referred to as tool maker, tool designer, electronic technician, and metal technician. This evidence was buttressed by almost universal beliefs, especially verbalized by employers, that serious shortages prevailed. Statements about these alleged shortages were frequently being cited in the popular mass communication media.

Much of the evidence concerning shortages for the entire economy was cited in Chapter 2. The very rapid expansion of technician employment during the decades of the 1940's and 1950's and the projections for continued rapid growth in the 1960's and 1970's were cited. One projection, for example, estimated that employment of technicians in manufacturing would increase about 78 percent between 1960 and 1970 (National Science Foundation) and most analysts predicted that adequate supplies of qualified workers would not be available to fill the demand. Allegations concerning chronic and persistent shortage of workers throughout the country in the tool and die trades were also cited. Employment expansion in these occupations has been more modest than for technicians, but reports from industry and governmental sources have indicated great shortages of qualified workers. These reports often have been buttressed by statements that the shortages were resulting in serious losses in production and income. In the case of tool makers, projections for the future were conflicting. Some suggested substantial increases in the demand for qualified workers, both for replacement needs and new positions. However, at least one major projection showed a very sizable drop in employment between 1960 and 1980. The differences were due primarily to different assumptions about the effects of the introduction of new technology in tool making.

The purpose of this chapter is to look in more detail at the two labor markets of Chicago and St. Louis in order to assess the degree of shortage that existed at the time of the study. In short, what is proposed is to examine the specific operation of the labor market and the behavior of those on the demand and supply side to ascertain whether the labor market manifestations of behavior were consistent with the generalized belief about the prevalence of shortages. These specific labor market behavioral patterns are much more indicative than apparent conclusions resulting from aggregated trend projections.

It should be recalled again that most of the field work for the investigation was done between mid-1964 and mid-1965 when the labor market in both cities was moving toward balance. One of the objectives of the analysis is to determine the extent to which shortages of skilled and technical workers can exist at times of general labor surplus. The analysis includes examination of employment and earnings trends, employer experiences and perceptions of staffing problems, the extent of job vacancies, worker labor market experiences and perceptions of job mobility, characteristics of workers and trainees in the occupations, and other matters indicative of the extent of the shortages.

Employment Trends

The data regarding employment of workers in the four occupations in the sample firms shown in Table 7-1 strikingly indicate a very modest change in employment between 1959 and 1964 in all four occupations. In the tool and die trades employment actually declined during the five-year period and the decline in tool maker employment in Chicago was substantial.[a] With the possible exception of the metal technician case in St. Louis, one must conclude that the rapid expansion of technician employment that was characteristic of the 1940's and 1950's did not extend into the early 1960's for the sampled firms in the electronics and metalworking industries in the two labor markets studied. In the same industries, employment in the skilled tool and die trades generally declined.

Employment trends in individual firms, however, varied widely from the norm. While some firms doubled or tripled their employment of persons in one or more of the occupations, others had drastic reductions. In general, substantial expansion tended to be concentrated in smaller firms while some large firms had substantial cutbacks in employment. In one large Chicago firm, for example, employment of tool makers and electronic technicians declined from 300 to 150 and from 300 to 200, respectively, and offset fairly substantial percentage gains in employment in a number of smaller firms. Nevertheless, on the whole, only a minority of sample firms experienced employment gains in the five-year period. Only for electronic technicians in Chicago and metal technicians in St. Louis did as many as a majority of the sample firms expand their employment between 1959 and the time of the survey in 1964.

For the minority of firms in which employment had expanded between 1959 and 1964, the major reason given for the expansion was increased business for the firms (see Table 7-2). For tool designers and the technician occupations, changes in technology requiring more skilled and technical workers were also of some importance in bringing about increased employment.

The early 1960's employment trends in the four occupations in Chicago and St. Louis in electronics and metalworking industries, then, were at considerable variance with the national trends in these occupations in earlier years. The market was not receiving heavy pressures from rapidly increasing demands. Any major pressure on supplies would have to come from previously existing

[a]This picture is at variance with some published data. Bureau of Labor Statistics data, for example, indicate that between 1958–1959 and 1964 tool and die maker employment in the machinery industry in Chicago increased 36 percent. The difference may be due to the sample used in this study, which consisted mainly of the larger firms and was not representative of the smaller job shops.

vacancies and replacements needs resulting from either death, retirement, health, or transfer out of the occupation or area. A subsequent section assesses the effects of these factors on the demand-supply situation.

Employer Views of the Market

Employers (mainly personnel directors and supervisors) in the sample firms were questioned along a number of lines in an attempt to get a qualitative evaluation of how serious a shortage of workers existed in the four occupations. Replies to these questions are summarized in Table 7-3.

Representatives of approximately one-half to three-quarters of the companies said that there was a shortage of workers in the various occupations. Substantially larger proportions of the firms indicated a shortage of workers in the tool and die trades than in the technician occupations. The pattern of responses was similar in the two cities, and the views of larger employers differed little in most cases from those of smaller firms. The proportion of firms with vacancies at the time of the study, another indicator of the extent of the shortage, was substantially less for each occupation than the proportion indicating there was a shortage. This is not necessarily indicative of contradictory evidence from personnel administrators. For instance, positions may have been filled with workers deemed less than satisfactory in amount of education and training. In short, employer representatives were answering on the basis of what they believed was taking place in establishments other than their own, thus setting up a type of self-fulfilling prophecy syndrome. In this case, more firms indicated vacancies in technician positions than in tool and die positions.

A large majority of firms that indicated there was a shortage said that the shortage was serious for their company. The evidence for the seriousness of the shortages, however, is, to say the least, not very persuasive. Only a minority of firms, as already indicated, had unfilled openings in the four occupations at the time of the study. And the vacancy rates, computed on the basis of the total number of open positions compared to total employment in the sample firms, do not indicate a particularly severe shortage situation (see Table 7-4). In general, the vacancy rate pattern for the four occupations conforms closely with the pattern of responses to the question of how serious the shortage was considered to be by the companies which claimed a shortage existed; that is, the shortage was most serious for tool designers in Chicago and metal technicians in both labor market areas. For none of the occupations, however, does the vacancy rate suggest either a desperate or even serious shortage. They seemingly are of a magnitude that most companies could adjust to with only minor changes in practices, without serious consequences.

This conclusion is supported by employer replies to questions that were designed to determine the extent to which companies were pressed into what might be termed drastic action as a result of labor shortages. In general, such

Table 7-1

Employment in Sample Firms, Four Occupations, Chicago and St. Louis Labor Markets, 1959 and 1964

	Tool and Die Maker		Tool and Die Designer	
	1964	*1959*	*1964*	*1959*
Chicago				
Employment	1790	2046	226	235
Percent Change, 1959–1964	−12.5%		−3.8%	
Average Employment Per Firm	48	55	10	11
Sample Firms with Expanding Employment	26%		17%	
St. Louis				
Employment	753	735	169	170
Percent Change, 1959–1964	+2.4%		−.6%	
Average Employment Per Firm	44	43	24	24
Sample Firms with Expanding Employment	39%		43%	
Two Cities				
Employment	2543	2781	395	405
Percent Change, 1959–1964	−8.6%		−2.5%	

Electronic Technician 1964	Electronic Technician 1959	Metalworking Technician 1964	Metalworking Technician 1959
835	785	286	278
+6.4%		+2.9%	
46	44	18	17
55%		38%	
59	74	127	100
−20.3%		+27.0%	
15	18	16	12
None		62%	
894	859	413	378
+4.1%		+9.2%	

Source: Employer interviews.

Table 7-2

Reasons Employment in the Selected Occupations has Increased (Percent Distributions)

	Tool and Die Maker			Tool and Die Designer		
	Total	*Chicago*	*St. Louis*	*Total*	*Chicago*	*St. Louis*
N =	19	12	7	8	5	3
Business Expansion	79	83	71	50	40	67
Business Recovery	5	8	--	12	20	--
Technological Change	5	--	14	38	40	33
Doing Work Formerly Contracted Out	5	8	--	--	--	--
New Department or Reassignment of Work	5	--	14	--	--	--
Total	100	100	100	100	100	100

	Electronic Technician			Metalworking Technician		
	Total	*Chicago*	*St. Louis*	*Total*	*Chicago*	*St. Louis*
N =	11	11	0	11	6	5
Business Expansion	64	64	--	55	67	40
Business Recovery	--	--	--	--	--	--
Technological Change	36	36	--	27	33	20
Doing Work Formerly Contracted Out	--	--	--	--	--	--
New Department or Reassignment of Work	--	--	--	18	--	40
Total	100	100	100	100	100	100

adjustments were not required. Few companies, for instance, had been faced with the unhappy necessity of turning down any business, and equally small numbers felt the shortages had affected their ability to compete. On the other hand, a substantial minority had put workers in the occupations on layoff during the past few years for reasons of poor business, not an action firms would likely take if the market were very tight for workers in the occupations and they were deeply concerned about their ability to find replacements when business expanded. These layoffs of primary male breadwinners could be contrasted with the nonlabor force reasons why the largely female members of the medical field study were not working at any given time. Although it is expensive to keep workers on in times of poor business, particularly highly paid tool and die tradesmen, it is nevertheless of some significance that some companies opted for short-term cost savings and took their chances on being able to find the necessary labor when business expanded. If serious long-run shortages were in reality a significant aspect of their long-run expectations and planning horizons, it would have been rational to have behaved differently. Thus, an assessment of behavior in the context of rational adjustment to shortages cited as serious over a long-run period would conclude that these employers did not act as though a serious long-run shortage situation had prevailed.

Basically, only a relatively small minority of firms indicated inability to find eventually the number of qualified people they wanted. The shortage was reflected mainly in the length of time it took to fill vacancies. With the exception of the electronics technician case, a majority of firms indicated it took a month or more to fill a vacancy, and for 15 to 20 percent of the firms, more than three months were required to fill vacant positions.

In addition to the matter of time involved in filling vacancies, seriousness was defined in some cases in terms of other effects of the shortages on plant operations. While at least a majority of firms, ranging from 56 percent for tool makers to 73 percent for electronic technicians, said the shortages had no significant effect on plant operations, some firms indicated that the shortages required more overtime work, substitution of either higher or lower level persons to fill vacancies in the four occupations, a slowing of operations and/or decreased efficiency, and, for tool and die work, the contracting of work to other firms. Yet these other firms had enough tool and die workers to fulfill contracts, a situation which is certainly not indicative of a generalized shortage. In fact, such vertical disintegration of specialized functions to job shops might have added to over-all efficiency in utilization of these personnel.

Employer replies to questions concerning the existence of unfilled openings also indicate that most firms felt there had been little change in the seriousness of the shortage over the past five years. Except for tool designers, only a minority of firms – in the case of technicians, only small minorities– said that the time required to fill vacancies had increased in the five-year period. Otherwise, most of the firms, 51 percent for tool makers and 65 percent for technicians, indicated that the time required was about the same as five years earlier.

Table 7-3

Factors Reflecting the Extent of the Shortage, Four Occupations, Chicago and St. Louis (In Percents)

	Tool and Die Maker			Tool and Die Designer		
	Total	*Chicago*	*St. Louis*	*Total*	*Chicago*	*St. Louis*
N =	57	39	18	31	24	7
Is There a Shortage—Yes	75	77	72	74	67	100
Under 2000 Employees	89	89	73	74	71	100
2000 Employees and Over	73	75	67	75	60	100
Current Unfilled Openings—Yes	33	33	33	29	29	29
How Long to Fill Vacancy						
One Month or More	51	58	42	66	63	80
Three Months or More	16	16	18	20	16	40
Longer Than 5 Years Ago	44	42	47	52	50	60
How Serious is Shortage?						
Companies Who Said Shortage Existed- - Serious for Company	66	57	75	83	77	100
Serious in General, Not for Company	27	33	--	13	18	--
Not Serious	6	9	25	4	6	--
Has Company Turned Down Business Because of Shortage? Yes	11	13	6	3	4	--
Have Orders Been Delayed by Shortage? Yes	33	26	50	16	17	14
Has Shortage Affected Ability to Compete? Yes	11	8	17	3	4	--

Electronic Technician			Metalworking Technician		
Total	*Chicago*	*St. Louis*	*Total*	*Chicago*	*St. Louis*
26	20	6	24	16	8
62	65	50	54	62	38
62	70	50	59	73	29
60	60	--	50	40	100
50	50	50	42	50	25
36	26	67	50	71	12
12	--	50	14	14	12
23	17	40	29	36	17
71	64	100	92	100	67
6	7	--	--	--	--
24	28	--	8	--	33
4	5	--	8	12	--
27	20	50	17	25	--
8	5	17	8	12	--

(continued)

Table 7-3 (*continued*)

	Tool and Die Maker			Tool and Die Designer		
	Total	*Chicago*	*St. Louis*	*Total*	*Chicago*	*St. Louis*
Any Layoffs of Persons in the Occupation in Last Few Years?						
Yes	32	41	11	23	29	--
Reason—Poor Business	67	62	100	86	86	--
Reason—Changing Technology Reduces Need	11	12	--	--	--	--
Anticipated Demand, Next 5 yrs.						
Increase	65	61	75	61	56	83
Decrease	8	11	--	4	--	17
Remain the Same	27	28	25	35	46	--
How Operations Affected by Shortage						
More Overtime Work	9	10	6	10	4	28
Substitute with Lower Level People	2	--	6	--	--	--
Substitute with Higher Level People	--	--	--	--	--	--
Slows Operations and/or Decreased Efficiency	18	18	17	10	8	14
Farm Out Work	16	15	17	13	13	14
No Significant Effect	56	56	56	68	75	43
Whether Able to Find Sufficient Number of Persons with Minimum Qualifications. No	29	24	43	31	19	80

Electronic Technician			Metalworking Technician		
Total	*Chicago*	*St. Louis*	*Total*	*Chicago*	*St. Louis*
35	35	17	22	33	--
75	71	100	60	60	N.A.
--	--	--	--	--	N.A.
74	76	67	70	80	50
--	--	--	--	--	--
26	24	33	30	20	50
4	5	--	12	12	12
4	5	--	--	--	--
4	5	--	4	6	--
15	5	50	17	19	12
--	--	--	--	--	--
73	80	50	67	63	75
22	21	25	10	14	0

Source: Employer interviews.

Table 7-4

Vacancy Rates, Four Occupations, Chicago and St. Louis

	Tool and Die Maker	*Tool and Die Designer*	*Electronic Technician*	*Metalworking Technician*
Two Cities				
Employment in Occupations	2543	395	894	413
No. of Vacancies	64	24	31	32
Vacancy Rate	2.5%	6.1%	3.5%	7.7%
Chicago				
Employment in Occupations	1790	226	835	286
No. of Vacancies	35	10	22	25
Vacancy Rate	2.0%	8.8%	2.6%	8.7%
St. Louis				
Employment in Occupations	753	169	59	127
No. of Vacancies	29	4	9	7
Vacancy Rate	3.9%	2.4%	15.3%	5.5%

Source: Employer interviews.

How can the views of employers on the extent of the shortages be summarized? Most felt that there was a shortage of labor for all four occupations. Only a minority, however, had unfilled openings at the time of the survey. Large majorities of those who felt there was a shortage described the shortage as serious. Seriousness seems to mean primarily that vacant positions could not be filled immediately. Except for electronic technicians, a majority of firms indicated that a month or more was required to fill vacancies in the occupations. Because of inability to fill vacancies quickly, relatively minor adjustments in plant operations were sometimes required, such as working more overtime, contracting out some work, and delaying the completion of some orders. Only a minority of firms, however, found these adjustments to be necessary.

The existing market situation seemed to be one in which there was little, if any, labor reserve in the four occupations. The tightness of the labor market was somewhat more severe for tool and die tradesmen than for technicians. Because of the absence of a labor reserve, excessive time, from the point of view of employers, was required for the market to produce a worker for an unfilled opening. This situation had been in existence for at least the five past years, probably longer. Because a majority of employers were faced with approximately the same situation, few felt that their ability to compete had been adversely affected by the market situation. Based on the views and experiences of employers, the shortage in all four occupations could at the most pessimistic stage be described as chronic, but certainly not serious, and definitely not critical.

Other Views and Market Experiences

Additional clues to the extent of the shortage are available from the interviews with trade school administrators and practitioners in the occupations and from the experiences of the practitioners and recent trainees in locating jobs.

In this connection, the most direct question asked of training school administrators was whether they thought enough students were being trained in the four occupations. Almost all of them replied in the negative. Negative replies were received from all 12 of the schools for skilled tradesmen, 10 of the 11 technician schools, and both of the correspondence schools for electronic technicians. Presumably, the basis for these replies was their experience in placing graduates and the requests they received from employers for referrals. Most of the school administrators, two-thirds from the skilled trade schools and 55 percent from the technical schools, believed that the deficiency in training would get worse in the years ahead. The majority based their prognosis on a belief that business expansion and increased demand for workers in these occupations would outrun the supply of students turned out by the training schools. These views were expressed by over 80 percent of the training school administrators. The possible influence of their bias in the direction of favoring more students in their schools, however, should not be overlooked. Nine of the 12 trade schools, 10 of the 11 technician schools, and both of the correspondence schools were operating at less than their full capacity of students at the time of the survey. About a third of the skilled trades schools and a quarter of the technical schools felt that insufficient training facilities would be available to meet future demand.

Another indicator of the tightness of the labor market is the time required for workers to find a job following completion of their training. The length of time required for both the practitioners and the Chicago recent trainees to locate their first jobs is shown in Table 7-5. Most of the practitioners found jobs within two weeks of completing training. The major exception was Chicago electronic technicians, one-fifth of whom required over a month to locate a job. The experience of the recent trainees in locating employment is quite similar. In part, however, the favorable experience of the recent trainees is due to the fact that large proportions of them, except for tool makers, were already employed when they entered training. They were, therefore, automatically in a job at the completion of their training program.

The tool and die designers and the electronic technicians had the least favorable experience in locating jobs quickly. For the electronic technicians, this result fits well the data presented in the previous section on employer views of the market; that is, it probably reflects a looser market for electronic technicians than for the other occupations. For tool designers, the explanation for a more lengthy job search is that the demand for experienced workers is stronger. The shortage, in other words, is for people with both the required training and experience in tool and die making and other shop tasks. A majority of the recent trainees were people holding jobs who also were attending school to get the training necessary to move into tool design positions. It is likely that the trainees and practitioners who took some time to locate a job lacked the requisite experience.

The practitioners' perceptions of their chances of obtaining a similar or better job in their occupation at another company is another indicator of the tightness of the market. Assuming some knowledge on the part of the workers of alternative job opportunities, the more favorable their rating of their chances for a similar job the tighter the job market is likely to be. The workers' perceptions in this regard are summarized in Table 7-6. Abour four-fifths of the tool and die tradesmen and two-thirds of the technicians rated their chances as excellent or good, indicating again that the shortage was more serious for tool and die tradesmen. This proportion, while high, is significantly lower than that for the hospital occupations studied. Also, most of the tool and die tradesmen who rated their mobility chances high cited the high demand for workers in their trades as the reason. Among technicians rating their chances high, there was more inclination to refer to their own experience and training as giving them a favorable market position, particularly among electronic technicians.

Among the tool and die tradesmen, the proportion giving high ratings to their job chances in other companies actually appears to understate the tightness of the market. Among the tool makers who rated their chances of finding a similar or better job only fair or poor, over 80 percent gave as their reason for the lower rating their advanced age or their belief that their present job was the best available in the market. For tool designers, over 60 percent gave the same two reasons or the fact that they had insufficient experience to command an equal or better job in the market. Only 4 percent of the tool makers and 14 percent of the designers felt a lack of demand inhibited their chances in the labor market.

Among the technicians, age and a judgment that their present job was the best available in the market also played an important part for those giving low ratings to their alternative job opportunities. A feeling that their training and experience was too specialized to be of use to other companies, however, was also in the picture. Again, few cited a lack of demand as a restricting factor; only 8 percent of the electronic and 12 percent of the metal technicians cited this as an explanation.

The practitioners were also asked for their judgments on whether or not enough people were being trained in their occupations. About the same pattern of responses emerged as in other lines of questioning of workers and employers. The tool and die tradesmen more than the technicians felt that inadequate numbers of workers were being trained. A majority in all occupations, however, felt that the supply was inadequate.

The views and experiences of trade school administrators and workers in the occupations are in conformity with those of employers. They indicate that there was a shortage in the four occupations and that it was more severe for tool and die tradesmen than for technicians. In all four occupations, workers were able to find jobs relatively quickly in spite of looseness in the labor market generally and most workers saw their chances for equivalent jobs in other companies as good or excellent.

Pay Levels and Trends

Wage levels for the four occupations at the time of the survey in 1964 and changes since 1959 are shown in Table 7-7, together with other comparative wage data. The trends are not consistent with employer beliefs about a serious shortage. In fact, virtually every phase of employer behavior as contrasted with verbalized beliefs contradicts the notion of serious labor market shortages. Only for the relatively fewer and scarcer metal technicians are wage trends consistent with serious shortages.

For tool and die tradesmen, starting wage rates are relatively high. Tool maker pay rates are at or near the top rates for factory manual workers, but as the BLS data on going rates and the sample-firm data on highest rates paid for the occupations show, the possibilities for pay increases beyond the starting rates are small. Tool makers with long experience receive little more than beginning journeymen. Tool designers, on the other hand, despite the greater training and experience required of them, start at about the same pay rate as

Table 7-5

Time to First Job, Worker and Recent Trainee Samples (Percent Distributions)

	Tool and Die Maker			Tool and Die Designer			Electronic Technician			Metalworking Technician		
	Two Cities	*Chi.*	*St. L.*	*Two Cities*	*Chi.*	*St. L.*	*Two Cities*	*Chi.*	*St. L.*	*Two Cities*	*Chi.*	*St. L.*
						Worker Sample						
Less Than 1 Week	96	96	93	82	80	92	51	48	100	89	88	100
1 - 2 Weeks	4	3	7	5	6	--	21	22	--	5	6	--
3 Weeks to 1 Mo.	--	--	--	2	2	--	6	6	--	5	6	--
Over 1 Month	1	1	--	11	12	8	22	22	--	--	--	--
Total	100	100	100	100	100	100	100	100	100	100	100	100

	Chicago Recent Trainee Sample				
	Tool and Die Maker	Tool and Die Designer	Electronic Technicians From		Metalworking Technician
			Trade Schools	*Correspondence Schools*	
N =	110	24	137	77	11
Has Not Worked	2	13	2	4	9
Less Than 1 Mo.	86	17	4	49	36
1–2 Months	3	8	1	3	--
2–6 Months	3	4	3	5	--
Over 6 Months	--	4	2	1	--
Already had Job (Supplemental Training)	3	54	82	35	45
Unknown	4	--	5	3	9

Source: Worker interviews and trainee questionnaire.

Table 7-6

Perceptions of Mobility Possibilities
(In Percents)

	Tool and Die Maker			Tool and Die Designer		
	Two Cities	*Chicago*	*St. Louis*	*Two Cities*	*Chicago*	*St. Louis*
N =	184	119	65	96	63	33
Horizontal Mobility						
Excellent or Good	81	81	78	80	79	84
Why Fair or Poor:						
Age	54	50	62	21	9	67
Present Job Best	29	35	12	21	27	0
Not Enough Exper.	--	5	12	21	27	0
Why Excellent or Good:						
Experience, etc.	28	25	4	24	29	4
High Demand	64	54	83	67	54	92
Are Enough People Being Trained—No	87	83	94	76	70	88

Electronic Technician			Metalworking Technician		
Two Cities	*Chicago*	*St. Louis*	*Two Cities*	*Chicago*	*St. Louis*
92	76	16	33	23	10
65	62	82	66	79	40
21	22	1	12	0	25
25	26	0	38	75	0
17	4	0	38	0	0
33	29	30	23	11	0
37	32	60	46	33	75
59	55	79	70	74	60

Source: Worker interviews.

Table 7-7

Hourly Wage Levels and Trends, Four Occupations, Chicago and St. Louis, Sample Firms and Other Survey Data

		Tool and Die Maker	
	Two Cities	*Chicago*	*St. Louis*
Number of Cases	53	35	18
Shortage Firms	43	30	13
No Shortage Firms	10	5	5
Median Starting Wage	$3.40	$3.34	$3.63
Shortage Firms	3.39	3.33	3.64
No Shortage Firms	3.45	3.36	3.63
Median Five Year Increase			
Cents per Hour	.40	.39	.49
Percent	13%	13%	7%
Median Highest Wage	$3.77	$3.78	$3.75
Shortage Firms	3.76	3.81	3.75
No Shortage Firms	3.75	3.89	3.75
Percent of Firms Adjusting Wages Due to Shortages	12%	14%	9%

Tool and Die Designer		
Two Cities	*Chicago*	*St. Louis*
30	23	7
25	18	7
5	5	--
$3.75	$3.70	$3.87
3.75	3.75	3.87
3.15	3.18	--
.45	.44	.35
14%	16%	13%
$4.65	$4.51	$5.20
4.60	4.50	5.20
4.45	4.60	--
14%	11%	30%

(continued)

Table 7-7 (*continued*)

	Two Cities	Electronic Technician Chicago	St. Louis
Number of Cases	31	25	6
Shortage Firms	23	20	3
No Shortage Firms	8	5	3
Median Starting Wage	$2.47	$2.49	$2.44
Shortage Firms	2.43	2.53	2.30
No Shortage Firms	2.45	2.33	2.59
Median Five Year Increase			
Cents per Hour	.29	.20	.57
Percent	13%	9%	25%
Median Highest Wage	$3.63	$3.60	$3.72
Shortage Firms	3.71	3.65	4.02
No Shortage Firms	3.30	2.87	3.42
Percent of Firms Adjusting Wages Due to Shortages	20%	25%	0%

Two Cities	Metalworking Technician Chicago	St. Louis
24	16	8
13	10	3
11	6	5
$2.55	$2.95	$2.10
2.62	3.01	2.00
2.31	2.64	2.20
.53	.63	.50
26%	27%	31%
$3.80	$4.27	$3.42
3.98	4.38	3.50
3.15	3.36	3.38
20%	19%	25%

(continued)

Table 7-7 (*continued*)

Bureau of Labor Statistics Occupational Wage Survey Data[1]

	Chicago			
	Average Straight-Time Hourly Earnings		1959-1964 Change	
	1959	*1964*	*Amount*	*Percent*
Tool and Die Maker	$3.16	$3.61	$ .45	14.2%
Senior Draftsman-Mfg.	3.03	3.35	.32	10.6%
All Industries[4]	Index 1961=100	Index 1961=100		
Office Clerical (Women)	95.0	108.2	13.2	13.9%
Industrial Nurses (Women)	93.9	110.2	16.3	17.4%
Skilled Maintenance (Men)	93.9	109.3	15.4	16.4%
Unskilled Plant (Men)	94.1	109.2	15.1	16.0%
Manufacturing[4]				
Office Clerical (Women)	94.5	109.3	14.8	15.7%
Industrial Nurses (Women)	93.5	109.6	16.1	17.2%
Skilled Maintenance (Men)	94.3	108.7	14.4	15.3%
Unskilled Plant (Men)	94.0	107.5	13.5	14.4%

St. Louis[2]			
Average Straight-Time Hourly Earnings		1959-1964 Change	
1959	*1964*	*Amount*	*Percent*
$3.17	$3.69	$ .52	16.4%
3.00	3.44	.44	14.7%
Index 1960=100	Index 1960=100		
97.1	111.4	14.3	14.7%
94.6	113.8	19.2	20.2%
97.2	112.9	15.7	16.1%
95.5	112.4	16.9	17.6%
96.7	111.8	15.1	15.6%
94.6	114.9	20.3	21.4%
97.6	112.0	14.4	14.7%
96.4	113.1	16.7	17.3%

(continued)

Table 7-7 (*continued*)

Some U. S. Wage Trends[3]
(Average Gross Hourly Earnings of Production Workers)

		1959	1964	*Percent Change 1959–1964*
All Manufacturing:	Total	$2.19	$2.53	16%
	Excluding Overtime	2.12	2.44	15%
Nonmanufacturing Total		2.56	2.83	11%
Wholesale and Retail Trade		1.76	2.08	18%
Service Industries:	Hotels, Motels, Etc.	1.06	1.29	19%
	Laundries and Cleaning Establishments	1.19	1.44	21%

[1] Bureau of Labor Statistics, *Occupational Wage Survey,* Bulletin Nos. 1240-18, 1265-5, 1385-66, and 1430-22 (Washington, D. C.: U. S. Government Printing Office). Total designers and technicians are not sampled in the surveys. Senior draftsman was used as an indicator of approximate technician salary levels. Data for April in Chicago and October in St. Louis.

[2] Draftsman definitions were changed in the St. Louis survey for 1964. The 1959 data are for senior draftsman and the 1964 data for Draftsman, Class B.

[3] U. S. Department of Commerce, Office of Business Economics, Business Statistics, 1965 Biennial edition.

[4] Data for these occupations are published in the form of index numbers. Between 1959 and 1964 the base periods for the index numbers were changed. The numbers shown in this table were chained using the base periods shown.

tool makers, but the possibilities for pay increases are much greater. In some companies, the highest paid designers received two to three dollars or more per hour more than beginning designers.

Beginning pay rates for technicians tend to be modest, but there is considerable room for pay increases for those whose training and experience allow them to move to increasingly complex work. On the average, however, even with experience, the technicians are paid less than either tool makers or designers, and their pay ceiling appears to be relatively low.

Wages in firms designated as shortage firms were not related in any consistent way with those in no shortage firms. Starting wages were somewhat higher for tool makers and electronic technicians in no shortage firms, as one would anticipate, but the reverse was true for the other two occupations. The expected relationship; that is, that wages would be higher in no shortage firms, held only for tool designers with respect to the highest wage paid in the occupation. Apparently, wage rates are not particularly potent in these occupations in allocating workers among firms. Other factors presumably intervene to minimize the influence of wages in attracting and holding a work force in the individual firm.

It is probable that quality differences in employees, particularly among technicians, is an offsetting factor that makes wage comparisons difficult. No shortage firms, for example, could well be those that tend to make use of lower level technicians and thus are able to obtain a work force with lower wage rates.

Among tool makers, a factor not reflected in wage rates is the availability of overtime work. The comments of some large employers suggested that many tool makers are attracted more by the amount of overtime work they can be guaranteed than by the wage rate or fringe benefits offered. The survey data did not confirm this phenomenon, however, at least in terms of averages. About half of both shortage and no shortage firms provided more than 40 hours work per week on the average for tool makers. The averages, however, might hide significant differences between the firms.

During the five-year period preceding the survey, wage rates for both tool and die tradesmen and technicians advanced at modest rates. Wage increments, with the exception of those for metal technicians, were about in line with wage increases generally in the economy. Metal technician wages seemed to have advanced more rapidly than wages in the other occupations studied. It should be noted again that relatively few employers were interviewed who employed metal technicians; and those who did employed relatively few such workers. The 26 percent increase in wages, therefore, applies to a small number of workers. It appears clear from the wage data that employers made little effort to adjust to the shortage by increasing relative wages for workers in the four occupations. This conclusion is also confirmed by the statements of employers themselves, very few of whom indicated that adjustments in wage rates were made because of the shortages in the four occupations.

Wage changes, then, offer little indication of a shortage situation. What is suggested is that the shortages during the five years preceding the study were not severe enough to cause undue pressure on wage rates in the four occupations. Employers were generally able to adjust their operations in other ways without jeopardizing the welfare of the firm. One of these was adjustment of hours of work. As the following tabulation shows, substantial numbers of firms had workers in the four occupations working overtime hours, and in general, more of the shortage than the no shortage firms scheduled more than 40 hours work per week. Large amounts of expected overtime increasing in magnitude over a period of time could be defined as a hidden wage increase relative to other occupations. However, although the value of overtime is greater than the average for other pursuits, there is no evidence to suggest that any major increase occurred in overtime hours over the five-year period.

Apparently, the sample firms generally found it more economical to pay premium rates for overtime work than to try to attract more workers to the occupations by offering above average pay increases. Since the training period for the four occupations involves several years of preparation, increasing the supply through the wage rate would also require several years to be effective. There was no evidence that companies had begun to take this step up to the time of the study. Rather, the companies were relying on such techniques as longer hours to meet their short-term needs for personnel. The wage data, therefore, tend to confirm our earlier judgment that the shortages were chronic, but not severe.

Percent of Sample Firms Averaging More Than 40 Hours Work Per Week, Four Occupations

	Tool and Die Maker	*Tool and Die Designer*	*Electronic Technician*	*Metalworking Technician*
Shortage firms	52	36	31	46
No shortage firms	50	40	0	30
Total	50	35	19	38

Some employers also adjusted to the shortages by contracting out some of their tool and die work. This suggests that jobbing shops might have been able to attract tool and die makers more easily than the larger firms, and a reason for this might be that the job shops generally pay higher wages. In 1965, for example, average hourly earnings for tool and die makers in Chicago were $3.99 in job shops and only $3.61 in other firms in the machinery industry. In St. Louis the comparable figures were $3.88 and $3.76, respectively.[1]

Worker Characteristics

Table 7-8 summarizes characteristics of the worker samples for the four occupations. The data are useful both for what they reveal about the nature of the shortages and for background for the chapters that follow.

A number of the worker characteristics are worth particular emphasis. In all four occupations, nonwhite workers comprise only a minute proportion of the total work force. Whatever the explanations for this phenomenon are, it is almost certainly the case that potential candidates for the four occupations from the nonwhite labor force remain virtually untapped. Some efforts have been made since the field work for this study was conducted to begin to introduce nonwhites into training programs. In Chicago, for example, a preapprenticeship MDTA training program was set up for tool and die makers which included a substantial number of black trainees.[2] But the nonwhite labor force has hardly been touched as a source of manpower for these skilled and technical occupations. Thus, although use of minority-group members might be cited as a rational response to a serious shortage, there is no evidence that during the period under study this expedient was resorted to. This, in contrast to the hospital occupations, would indicate that the shortage was not sufficiently serious to induce the employers and unions (where they exist) to make any major adjustments in practices or in norms.

The data on age and tenure with the present employer show relatively large differences between the occupations. Compared with the other occupations, tool makers are much older and have been with their present employers for much longer periods of time, indicating that few young people have entered the trade in recent years. Over 40 percent of the sample tool makers were age 45 and over, and about the same proportion had been employed by their current firm for over 10 years. Only 1 in 20 were under the age of 25. At the other extreme, only about 1 of 10 electronic technicians was age 45 or over, and only slightly more had been with their present employer for over 10 years. Designers and metal technicians fell between the two extremes in both age and length of service, but tended to be closer to the tool makers in their age distribution. Because of the higher age composition, the tool maker occupation will pose a particularly difficult supply problem in the long run unless the future demand turns out to be considerably less than is generally anticipated. The greater extent of the shortage for tool makers thus reflects not expansion, but failure to meet the substantial replacement needs required as a consequence of the skewed age composition of this group.

Employment of electronic technicians differs substantially from the other three occupations in that it tends to be heavily concentrated in large firms. Sixty percent of the sample electronic technicians were employed by firms with 2,000 or more employees. A substantial majority of the workers in the other three occupations were employed by firms with less than 1,000 workers. This fact has particular importance in considering appropriate training policies and programs for the four occupations. It is much more likely that private firms can and will be able to carry a substantial part of the training load for electronic technicians than for the other occupations. It will be much more difficult for the smaller

Table 7-8

Characteristics of Worker Samples, Four Occupations, Chicago and St. Louis (Percent Distributions)

	Two Cities Combined			
	Tool and Die Maker	*Tool & Die De-signer*	*Elec. Tech.*	*Metal Tech.*
N =	184	96	92	33
Recent–Vet. Status				
Recent	12	27	40	24
Veteran	88	73	60	76
Race				
White	98	100	97	97
Nonwhite	2	0	3	3
Marital Status				
Single	8	14	23	24
Married	90	85	74	76
Other	2	2	3	--
Tenure With Co.				
0–1 Year	11	22	28	18
2–5 Years	22	22	35	18
6–10 Years	28	31	24	21
11 Years & Over	39	25	13	42

Chicago				St. Louis			
Tool and Die Maker	*Tool & Die De-signer*	*Elec. Tech.*	*Metal Tech.*	*Tool and Die Maker*	*Tool & Die De-signer*	*Elec. Tech.*	*Metal Tech.*
119	63	76	23	65	33	16	10
9	25	39	22	18	24	44	30
91	75	61	78	82	76	56	70
99	100	96	96	97	97	100	100
1	--	4	4	3	3	--	--
9	17	24	22	6	5	24	30
90	83	74	78	91	94	75	70
1	--	2	--	3	1	1	--
8	16	29	17	17	33	25	20
22	24	34	26	23	18	38	0
34	33	22	9	18	27	1	50
36	27	15	48	42	22	6	30

(continued)

Table 7-8 (*continued*)

	Two Cities Combined			
	Tool and Die Maker	*Tool & Die Designer*	*Elec. Tech.*	*Metal Tech.*
Age				
Under 25	5	12	30	15
25–34	28	35	42	42
35–44	26	28	18	24
45–54	26	21	7	12
55 & Over	15	5	2	6
Size of Employer				
Under 500	57	44	13	24
500–999	10	11	16	52
1000–1999	8	21	11	12
2000–4999	14	11	18	6
5000 & Over	11	14	42	6
Educational Level				
8th or Less	9	--	3	6
Grades 9–11	14	5	4	6
High School	58	38	36	27
Beyond H. S.	20	57	56	61

Chicago: Tool and Die Maker	Chicago: Tool & Die Designer	Chicago: Elec. Tech.	Chicago: Metal Tech.	St. Louis: Tool and Die Maker	St. Louis: Tool & Die Designer	St. Louis: Elec. Tech.	St. Louis: Metal Tech.
4	11	33	17	7	15	19	10
32	37	40	35	22	33	56	60
25	29	20	30	28	24	13	10
24	21	6	13	29	22	6	10
15	2	1	5	14	6	6	10
42	35	1	17	86	56	69	40
16	16	18	57	0	3	6	40
9	10	8	17	7	41	25	0
17	17	22	0	7	0	0	20
16	22	51	9	0	0	0	0
5	0	1	4	15	0	13	10
13	5	4	4	14	6	6	10
61	41	39	26	52	32	19	30
20	55	55	65	19	61	62	50

firms, who hire most of the tool and die tradesmen and metal technicians, to bear the load for the amount of training that will be necessary.

As the educational distribution of the sample workers indicates, almost all of the practitioners have had high school training or beyond as preparation for their fields. And, as Table 7-9 shows, educational requirements have been rising in recent years. For the tool and die trades, much higher proportions of the recent entrants than the veterans of the trades have completed a high school education. And for the technician trades, the recent entrants are more likely to have completed more college work than the veterans. The major exception to the rule is the case of tool designers. Substantially higher proportions of the veterans than the recent entrants to the above occupation had completed some college level work. The difference between the two groups is primarily at the level of college degrees. Seven percent of the designer veterans and none of the recent entrants had completed a college degree. Apparently the occupation is no longer one that finds appeal among college graduages, probably because the college graduate is now more able than in the past to find occupations with higher pay and status.

Although it is not shown in Table 7-8, all of the workers interviewed in the four occupations were men. It is probable that a few women are employed as technicians although none showed up in the worker sample (the sample of recent trainees in Chicago included a few women who had completed technical training courses). However, all occupations are essentially male occupations and there is no indication that industry is turning to women to fill the need for additional personnel.

The evidence on extent of shortages has consisted of employment and wage trends in the four occupations, employer views and experiences in the labor market, trade school administrator opinions of the demand-supply situation, worker experiences in the market and their perceptions of the market situation, and various characteristics of workers who are employed in the four occupations.

The evidence from all of these sources is remarkably consistent. The evidence shows that, in spite of general labor surplus at the time of the study, the market was relatively tight for all four occupations.[b] The tightness existed in spite of the fact that employment of technicians had grown only modestly in the sample firms in the early 1960's, and for tool and die tradesmen had actually declined slightly. Nevertheless, the shortages were clearly most serious for the tool and die tradesmen. For tool and die makers, the shortage was due primarily to a skewed age distribution.

For none of the four occupations, however, could the shortages be described as critical. For the most part, employers were not forced into serious actions to adjust to the shortages. The most typical consequence of the shortages was that considerable time was required to fill vacancies, the results of which were that current employees were worked overtime and sometimes delivery dates for orders had to be extended and other minor changes made in plant practices.

Salary trends did not reflect a serious shortage situation. In the main, wages

[b] A tight labor market is not necessarily one in which shortages prevail. In fact, using the wage evidence as the sole criteria, a shortage in fact did not exist.

Table 7-9

Level of Educational Attainment,
Workers in Four Occupations,
Classified by Recent–Veteran Status
(Percent Distribution)

	Tool and Die Maker		Tool and Die Designer	
	Recent	*Veteran*	*Recent*	*Veteran*
8th or Less	4	10	--	--
9 - 11	9	14	--	7
High School	70	57	52	33
Beyond High School	17	20	48	60

	Electronic Technician		Metalworking Technician	
	Recent	*Veteran*	*Recent*	*Veteran*
8th or Less	--	5	--	8
9 - 11	5	4	--	8
High School	32	38	25	28
Beyond High School	62	52	75	56

Source: Worker interviews.

had advanced in the early 1960's at about the same rate in the four occupations as in the economy generally. Employers tended to choose other mechanisms for adjusting to the shortage, some of which will be examined in more detail in subsequent chapters.

Three major points were made with respect to the characteristics of workers in the four occupations. In all four cases, nonwhites were noticeable primarily by their absence. Among tool makers, advanced age will necessitate relatively high replacement rates unless the demand for tool makers in the future declines. And, except for electronic technicians, the majority of workers in the occupations studied are employed by relatively small firms, which has important implications for training programs.

The major conclusion of the chapter is that the labor market was tight in all four occupations. If this tightness, which according to dynamic shortage model definitions which prevail in the literature could not be defined as a shortage in economic terms, had any impact it was not of a serious nature. Thus, the extent of the shortage was in all four cases not critical. This continued use of the term shortage to describe the over-all situation in the face of the conflicting wage movements (i.e., not more rapid than for other activities) would imply that use of wage movements as a single criterion for classification even for an economic definition leaves something to be desired. It is likely, but far from certain, that since there was no labor reserve, the shortage might have become serious after mid-1965 when the economy was at or above the so-called full employment level. The examination of barriers to expansion of supply, which follows in subsequent chapters, therefore, is of relevance to meeting the long-term needs of the four occupations.

8 Factors Affecting Supply: Information, Counseling, Guidance, and Recruitment

Analysis which results in the identification of factors affecting entry to training and to employment in the four technical occupations is crucial to any evaluation of measures aimed at reducing or minimizing shortages in the given occupations.

Sources of Information and Knowledge

Virtually all who have studied career choices would agree that choosing an occupation is not a step taken by an individual at a particular point in time, but is rather a process that begins relatively early in life and gradually terminates with a more or less specific decision to follow a particular career pattern. Decisions made along the way generally tend to narrow the possible choices for an individual as he selects fields or is forced by circumstances to engage in particular educational, training, or work experiences. The four occupations under consideration here all require an individual to have some specialized training, either of a classroom or on-the-job type, or some combination thereof, to qualify for employment. Individuals contemplating entry into these occupations generally must be informed of the educational and training requirements and opportunities in order to properly prepare for possible entry. In this study, therefore, effort was made to identify the factors that influenced practitioners of the occupations to enter training for the occupations. The extent to which various factors are related to their choices are summarized in Table 8-1.

In all four occupations, only a minority of practitioners indicated that they had received any authoritative counseling concerning training possibilities and opportunities. For the majority, obtaining information about the occupations and training opportunities was a matter of their own initiative in seeking out information or the happenstance of receiving information from persons with whom they were associated.

Formal counseling, however, was a greater factor in occupational choice for electronic technicians than in the other three occupations. Nearly half of the practitioners in this group said they had been counseled about training opportunities, most of them by high school, trade school, or college counselors. The reasons for the greater role of counseling for electronic technicians are not readily apparent, but the sources of counseling give some clues. It is clear, first of all, that the counseling did not come from the high schools; only 6 percent of the technicians indicated they received information about the occupation from high school counselors. Twenty-five percent indicated their information came from college or trade school counselors, and 16 percent said their information came from employers (8 percent) or military counselors (8 percent). Thus, greater exposure to college education and to training opportunities in the military service would appear to mark the difference between the electronic technicians and the other occupations.

It is significant that the two occupations for which counseling was of the most importance – tool makers and electronic technicians – are the best delineated of the four occupations. The fact that they are better known and delineated occupational careers undoubtedly improves the chances that counselors will be informed about them and prepared to offer guidance and counseling.

For all four occupations, high school, trade school, or college personnel were the most important sources of occupational information. Employers or supervisors were also important sources, particularly for the tool and die tradesmen. Unlike the medical occupations, personal friends and relatives appear to be unimportant sources of occupational information.

The data give some indication that the role of formal counseling is expanding. In all four occupations higher proportions of recent entrants than of veterans said they had received information about training through formal counseling, and the differences between the two groups were quite substantial. It is apparent that many of the veterans were exposed to formal counseling somewhat before the various technical fields were either recognized or were of any universal significance in terms of employment opportunity. It is not so clear, however, that the result is better information. A majority (about two-thirds) of all of the practitioners said that they had sufficient information about the occupations prior to entry into training. Recent entrants, however, were not significantly more satisfied with the information they had received; in fact, smaller proportions of recent entrants than veterans among tool designers and metal technicians felt they had received adequate or sufficient information prior to entry into training. A plausible explanation is that as the entire technical area grows in complexity the amount of information which the counselor can provide becomes less adequate relative to the totality of knowledge. The evidence in regard to satisfaction with counseling does not suggest that the quality of counseling has improved. For those who had received counseling from some source there was generally little difference between recent entrants and veterans concerning the adequacy of the counseling they received. Among metal technicians, the recent entrants were less well satisfied than the veterans.[a] In general, somewhat more than a majority of those who had been counseled indicated the counseling was adequate.

Formal counseling aside, what did the practitioners feel was the major factor that stimulated their decision to enter into training? The largest proportion of

[a] The data on the adequacy of counseling received are for all those who said they had received counseling. There is no basis for judging the adequacy of the various sources of counseling. The responses, in other words, do not distinguish among high school, employers, friends, or other sources.

Table 8-1

Factors Related to Entry into Training, Four Occupations, Chicago and St. Louis (Percent Distributions)

	Tool and Die Maker				
		Two Cities		*Chicago*	*St. Louis*
	Total	*Recent*	*Veteran*	*Total*	*Total*
Counseling Received on Training Available:					
None	58	45	60	60	55
High School, Trade School or College	12	25	10	9	18
Personal Friend in Occupation	6	5	7	6	7
Employer or Supervisor	15	15	15	20	4
Other (e.g., SES, Union, Military)	8	10	8	5	17
Whether had Sufficient Information–Yes	70	76	69	70	75
Whether Counseling Adequate–Yes (Those Who Had Received Counseling)	66	67	65	74	49
How Got Into Training					
Always Interested, Sought Out	30	7	33	35	10
Father's Work the Same	11	20	10	11	10
Suggestion of Friend or Relative	14	13	14	15	10
Military Training or Previous Experience	4	--	5	4	3

Table 8-1 (*continued*)

	Tool and Die Maker				
		Two Cities		*Chicago*	*St. Louis*
	Total	*Recent*	*Veteran*	*Total*	*Total*
How Got Into Training (continued)					
Co. Initiated Training Program	18	20	18	21	7
E. S., School or Other Counseling	16	20	15	11	34
Other and Unknown	7	20	6	3	24
Parent in Same Occupation					
Identical, or Nearly so	8	9	8	12	--
Similar, but Higher or Lower Skill	6	--	7	6	7
	Tool and Die Designer				
Counseling Received on Training Available:					
None	64	45	70	58	75
High School, Trade School or College	22	23	21	25	15
Personal Friend in Occupation	1	5	--	2	--
Employer or Supervisor	11	27	6	15	4
Other (e.g., SES, Union, Military)	2	--	3	--	7

(*continued*)

Table 8-1 (*continued*)

	Tool and Die Designer				
		Two Cities		*Chicago*	*St. Louis*
	Total	*Recent*	*Veteran*	*Total*	*Total*
Whether had Sufficient Information–Yes	66	54	71	73	53
Whether Counseling Adequate–Yes (Those Who Had Received Counseling)	58	72	52	72	35
How Got Into Training					
Always Interested, Sought Out	41	35	43	38	43
Father's Work the Same	3	6	2	4	--
Suggestion of Friend or Relative	6	6	7	7	--
Military Training or Previous Experience	8	6	9	9	--
Co. Initiated Training Program	30	35	27	31	14
E. S., School or Other Counseling	6	6	7	6	14
Other and Unknown	5	6	5	2	29
Parent in Same Occupation					
Identical, or Nearly so	3	--	4	5	--
Similar, but Higher or Lower Skill	7	8	7	9	3

Table 8-1 (*continued*)

	Electronic Technician				
		Two Cities		*Chicago*	*St. Louis*
	Total	*Recent*	*Veteran*	*Total*	*Total*
Counseling Received on Training Available:					
None	51	38	59	46	75
High School, Trade School or College	31	41	24	36	8
Personal Friend in Occupation	--	--	--	--	--
Employer or Supervisor	8	12	6	7	17
Other (e.g., SES, Union, Military)	10	9	10	11	--
Whether Had Sufficient Information–Yes	64	68	62	65	62
Whether Counseling Adequate–Yes (Those Who Had Received Counseling)	63	62	64	69	36
How Got into Training					
Always Interested, Sought Out	28	23	32	30	14
Father's Work the Same	3	3	2	3	--
Suggestion of Friend or Relative	10	16	5	8	29
Military Training or Previous Experience	25	13	35	23	43

(continued)

Table 8-1 (*continued*)

		Electronic Technician			
	Total	Two Cities *Recent*	*Veteran*	*Chicago Total*	*St. Louis Total*
How Got into Training					
Co. Initiated Training Program	14	16	12	14	14
E. S., School or Other Counseling	13	19	8	14	--
Other and Unknown	7	10	5	8	--
Parent in Same Occupation					
Identical, or Nearly so	1	--	2	1	--
Similar, but Higher or Lower Skill	8	9	8	8	7
		Metal Working Technician			
Counseling Received on Training Available:					
None	69	57	72	65	78
High School, Trade School or College	12	43	4	18	--
Personal Friend in Occupation	6	--	8	4	11
Employer or Supervisor	6	--	8	9	--
Other (e.g., SES, Union, Military)	6	--	8	4	11

Table 8-1 (*continued*)

	Metal Working Technician				
		Two Cities		*Chicago*	*St. Louis*
	Total	*Recent*	*Veteran*	*Total*	*Total*
Whether had Sufficient Information—Yes	66	50	70	82	14
Whether Counseling Adequate—Yes (Those Who had Received Counseling)	50	33	58	70	25
How Got into Training					
Always Interested, Sought Out	48	50	47	52	*
Father's Work the Same	--	--	--	--	*
Suggestion of Friend or Relative	9	--	11	5	*
Military Training or Previous Experience	9	25	5	10	*
Co. Initiated Training Program	22	--	26	19	*
E. S., School or Other Counseling	8	25	5	10	*
Other and Unknown	4	--	5	5	*
Parent in Same Occupation					
Identical, or Nearly so	3	--	5	4	*
Similar, but Higher or Lower Skill	7	--	9	9	*

*Too few cases responding for analysis.

Source: Worker interview.

workers in each occupation were unable to identify a single factor; the type of work was just something they had always been interested in and they sought out the appropriate training program. This type of response, together with replies indicating entry to training was the result of a suggestion of a friend or relative, account for 38 percent (electronic technicians) to 57 percent (metal technicians) of the total. With the exception of the electronic technicians, the single most specific stimulus to entry into training was the suggestion to enter a training program by someone in the company for which the individual worked. Substantial numbers, in other words, had started a work career with no intention of entering one of the four occupations, but had been picked out by employers as likely candidates for upgrading and encouraged to enter training. For electronic technicians previous work or military experience in similar lines of work was the most frequent specific stimulus leading to entry into a training program. Formal counseling was viewed by relatively small proportions in each occupation as the determining factor leading to entry, and the influence of a parent engaged in the same line of work was of significance only in the case of tool makers.

The attempt to trace the route by which practitioners entered their trades does not produce a particularly clear picture. However, formal counseling and guidance had a comparatively minor role in directing people to these occupations. The single most specific factor is the identification of workers by employers as potential trainees and their encouragement to enter into appropriate training programs. In spite of the absence of powerful stimuli directing people to the occupations, about two-thirds of the practitioners were satisfied that they had sufficient information to make intelligent decisions regarding their entry into training. Apparently the general environment of education and association with family and friends, plus employer advice, produced enough occupational information at least to get the individual started in the right direction. In part, the reason for this is that the occupations and the appropriate training programs are commonly known.

Would increased emphasis on counseling, guidance, and the dissemination of occupational information be effective in attracting more people into training for the four occupations? It would seem, on the face of it, that the answer would have to be yes. The fact that so many of those in the occupation entered it without the benefit of formal counseling would suggest that many others, who might not have had an equivalent access to information in their environment and associations, would have entered these occupations had they been provided with the appropriate information and guidance through other means. Also, at least a majority of those who had been exposed to formal counseling judged it effective. And those who felt there was a shortage of workers in their occupation were asked what they thought was the most important thing that could be done to attract more workers into the field. As in the case of the medical practitioners, the most frequently cited suggestion was for more adequate information, guidance, and counseling. These were the major suggestions of 33 percent of the tool makers, 42 percent of the tool designers, and 57 percent and

50 percent of the electronic and metal technicians, respectively. The second most frequent suggestion in each case was higher pay, mentioned by 25, 13, 20, and 18 percent of the practitioners in the four occupations, respectively.

In addition to those of the practitioners, the opinions of the trade school administrators were also sought regarding the adequacy of information and counseling. On the question of the adequacy of information, the administrators were about evenly split. Forty-two percent of the skilled trades school administrators and 55 percent of the technical school officials thought adequate information was available. There was more unanimity, however, in their evaluation of occupational counseling. Of the school officials interviewed, only a third from the trade schools and 18 percent from the technical schools felt that high school counseling was adequate. The most frequent complaints were that counselors were poorly qualified or knew little about the occupations in question and that counselors placed too much emphasis on college careers. The complaint about the emphasis on going to college was also heard from other sources. Many supervisors, particularly in tool and die shops or departments, mentioned it as a factor which limited the supply of high quality candidates for tool and die apprenticeships. Informal interviews conducted with counselors in Chicago high schools indicated the possibility of the same sort of emphasis. Counselors in innercity schools, for example, often pointed out that these occupations all required students of at least average ability. They would then go on to point out that only a small proportion of students in their schools tested out to the average for the whole city school system; those that did were usually encouraged to go on to college. Counselors in suburban schools, on the other hand, often complained that parental pressure made it almost impossible to counsel students about occupations or careers other than those which required a college education. Parents were so set on their children going to college that they would not tolerate counselors suggesting that their children consider skilled or technical occupations.[b]

The data strongly suggest that more effective counseling, guidance, and dissemination of occupational information would be an effective influence on the supply of candidates for the four occupations. The suggestions regarding improvement of occupational information made in the discussion of medical occupations apply equally well here (see Chapter 4).

[b]It is not only parents and counselors who put a heavy emphasis on the desirability of college education for everybody. Spot announcements on radio, sponsored by the U. S. Employment Service, are run daily urging all young people to get as much education as they can absorb. Even the official line, therefore, while not specifically recommending college for everyone, is highly suggestive that it's the thing to do if you want a good job. Perhaps such announcements would be more useful and effective if they were oriented to specific training opportunities.

Recruitment – Efforts to Tap Potential Supply

How is the supply of labor in the four occupations related to the efforts of employers and training schools to attract workers to employment and training? This question is approached through an examination of employer hiring policies and recruitment efforts, trade school efforts to attract students, and the factors that seemed to be effective and helpful in the workers' search for a job following the completion of their training.

Minimum Hiring Standards

An obvious place to look for a barrier to an adequate supply of labor in a shortage situation is the minimum hiring standards imposed by employers. These requirements may be related to educational and training prerequisites or to certain worker characteristics such as age and race. One source for discovering these requirements is the statements of employers on the policies and practices they follow in hiring. Since these statements cannot always be taken at face value, particularly with reference to such matters as age and racial requirements, it is helpful to check them to some extent by examination of the characteristics of workers employed in the occupations. It was noted in the previous chapter, for example, that virtually no nonwhites were employed in any of the four occupations, indicating clearly that barriers have stood in the way of access by nonwhites to these occupations.

Statements of employers on their minimum hiring requirements are summarized in Table 8-2.

Most employers had no minimum formal educational requirements for tool and die tradesmen, although substantially greater numbers did for designers than for tool makers. Even for technicians, who presumably require a certain amount of basic scientific and other knowledge, a large majority of employers had no specific educational standards that applicants were required to have. However, educational requirements for technicians were generally more strict than for tool and die tradesmen. The essential point is, however, that for all four occupations the lack of completion of a specific educational requirement does not, for the most part, preclude one from entry to the occupations.

The picture on training requirements is somewhat different. For designers and metal technicians it is again unnecessary in a large proportion of cases to have met specific training requirements. In general, tool and die makers must have met an apprenticeship requirement or its equivalent. For somewhat more than half of the designers, some sort of formal training requirement is necessary, either in an apprenticeship or in a technical school, and experience in related employment is invariably required. In neither of these occupations is journeyman status possible without working experience as machinist or draftsman or other shop and design experience. In the case of electronic technicians the entry route through training is reasonably clear. About two-thirds of the employers required some technical school training; most of the rest, however, imposed no specific training standard. And in the case of metal technicians, only a small

Table 8-2

Employer Hiring Requirements, Four Occupations, Chicago and St. Louis Combined (Percent Distributions)

	Tool & Die Maker		*Tool & Die Designer*		*Electronic Technician*		*Metal Technician*	
N =	57		31		26		24	
Minimum Education Requirements								
No Specific Requirements	91		71		38		37	
Some High School	2		6		8		--	
High School Graduate	7		10		31		25	
One Year of College	--		6		--		17	
Two Years of College	--		6		23		21	
Three or More Years of College	--		--		--		--	
Minimum Training Requirements								
No Specific Requirements	21		48		31		71	
Formal Apprenticeship	42		3		--		--	
Apprenticeship, not Formal Req'd.	30		26		4		4	
Technical School Graduate	4		6		27		12	
Some Technical School Training	4		16		38		12	
Other Hiring Requirements	1st	2nd	1st	2nd	1st	2nd	1st	2nd
None	54	56	26	45	54	54	62	58
Some Experience	16	7	52	6	35	8	21	8
1–5 Year Experience	12	12	6	23	4	23	4	12

(continued)

Table 8-2 (*continued*)

	Tool & Die Maker		*Tool & Die Designer*		*Electronic Technician*		*Metal Technician*	
Other Hiring Requirements (*cont.*)	1st	2nd	1st	2nd	1st	2nd	1st	2nd
Over 5 Years Experience	9	5	10	19	--	4	8	--
Maximum Age Limit	2	--	--	--	--	--	--	--
Good Work Record	2	9	3	3	--	--	--	8
Various Personal Characteristics	5	11	3	3	8	11	4	12
Whether Requirements are Too High—Yes	4		4		4		5	
Whether Requirements are Too Low—Yes	2		11		17		23	
Have Hiring Requirements Changed Last 5 Years?								
No	88		70		67		82	
Yes, Raised	6		15		33		14	
Yes, Lowered	6		15		--		--	
Yes, Unspecified	--		--		--		5	
Optimum Training Requirement								
Can't be Specified	21		48		15		50	
Apprenticeship Training	68		22		--		4	
Some Technical or Advanced Training	5		16		27		4	

Table 8-2 (*continued*)

	Tool & Die Maker	*Tool & Die Designer*	*Electronic Technician*	*Metal Technician*
Optimum Training Requirements (*cont.*)				
Technical School Graduate or Two Years College	5	6	58	42
Drafting Training	--	6	--	--
Are the Co's, Hires Far From Optimum? No	74	54	75	55

Source: Employer interviews.

minority of employees identified a specific training route to the occupation, usually through a technical school. Nor did most employers seem to have an experience requirement for the occupation.

Few employers named any personal characteristics as requirements for hiring. A few indicated they had imposed maximum hiring ages for tool and die makers, none mentioned any racial barriers, and when other characteristics were mentioned they were usually of such vague character as initiative, motivation, or a good work record.

Employers were nearly unanimous in their judgment that the hiring policies they were following were the correct ones. Where there was dissatisfaction it was generally in the direction of feeling that the requirements were not high enough. Employers of technicians were more likely to feel this way than employers of tool and die tradesmen. Those who thought standards should be more rigorous felt precluded from raising them for fear they would be unable to staff their plants.

Among a large majority of the sample firms, minimum hiring standards for the four occupations had not changed during the five years preceding the study. In those firms where changes had been made it was more likely that hiring standards had been raised than lowered, in spite of the alleged scarcity of labor. This tendency was particularly strong for the case of electronic technicians; one-third of the sample companies claimed that hiring standards were more rigorous than five years earlier. The general situation, however, was that little adjustment to the shortage occurred through relaxation of hiring standards.

However, official standards are not the only element which must be considered. How they applied standards in the face of shortages is another matter and in this context recent entrants were probably screened with greater exactitude and had to meet higher standards than their veteran counterparts. Thus the answer must be that the shortage was not perceived to be critical enough to dilute entry requirements. In fact, employers acted as if there were no shortages.

Minimum hiring standards imposed by employers fit very closely their ideas of what the optimum preparation for the four occupations entails. Particularly for the tool and die tradesmen the distribution of employer responses concerning their minimum and optimum hiring requirements match very closely. The proportion, for example, who were unable to identify specific hiring requirements was the same in both cases. And the proportions citing apprenticeship and technical school requirements were approximately the same. In the case of the technician occupations, the minimum qualifications being applied fell somewhat short of the stated optimum requirements; that is, in discussing optimum standards fewer employers left the requirements open ended and flexible; greater numbers expressed a preference for technical school or junior college preparation. Most employers felt that the people they were hiring at the time came very close to meeting their current ideas of optimum preparation. Employers expressed the least satisfaction with the quality of their hires for tool designers and metal technicians. For designers, most of the dissatisfaction expressed was with reference to the inadequate work experience of some of the people they found it necessary to hire. For metal technicians, as with the other two occupations, dissatisfaction was expressed with respect to a variety of worker qualifications, including education, training, and experience.

The analysis of hiring standards imposed by employers in their recruitment efforts reveals a difficulty in assessing the problem of shortages among the four occupations. Specific educational criteria are not ordinarily applied by employers in the hiring process and to a considerable extent, particularly for technicians, the same is true of training requirements. The education, training, and experience that qualify one for entry to the occupations are numerous and flexible. On the whole, employers seem to be satisfied with the recruits that come through the various routes to the occupations. This being the case, it is difficult to pinpoint what labor market institutions need particular attention in efforts to reduce or eliminate shortages. The most obvious untapped source of potential manpower for all four occupations is the nonwhite sector of the labor force.

Employer Recruitment Efforts

Most employers in the Chicago and St. Louis areas confined their recruitment efforts for the four occupations to the local labor market area (see Table 8-3). Significant numbers, in fact, indicated that their recruitment was confined to selecting workers for these occupations from their own work force; between 14 and 24 percent claimed that they did not go to the external labor market to fill vacancies.

Dependence upon internal sources (i.e., through company training programs or upgrading) was most marked for tool and die makers and was also the most important source for metal technicians. Advertising in the mass media was the most effective source of tool designers and was important in recruitment efforts for all four occupations. Training schools were a prime source of labor supply for technicians, particularly electronic technicians. And public and private employment agencies were an important secondary source of recruits for all four occupations. The latter is not surprising since shortages of labor existed in all four occupations and it would be expected that employers would turn to outside help in their efforts to recruit an adequate supply of labor.

Turning again to internal sources, however, a large majority of firms found employees engaged in other functions within the firm a source of workers for filling vacancies in the four occupations. Most firms filled less than half their vacancies from the ranks of present employees, but a fourth or more of the firms, excepting the case of electronic technicians, ordinarily managed to staff more than half of their openings with their own employees. The reliance on internal sources is also revealed in the responses of the practitioners specifying how they found their first job upon completion of training (see Table 8-4). Fully four out of five tool makers stayed on for employment at the firm where they

Table 8-3

Employer Recruitment Practices, Four Occupations, Chicago and St. Louis Combined (Percent Distributions)

	Tool & Die Maker		*Tool & Die Designer*		*Electronic Technician*		*Metal Technician*	
N =	57		31		26		24	
Where Recruit								
Within Co. Only	24		14		15		21	
Within Metro Area	67		68		73		79	
All Over	9		18		12		--	
Primary & Secondary Recruitment Sources	Prim.	Sec.	Prim.	Sec.	Prim.	Sec.	Prim.	Sec.
Our Training Program or Upgrade	46	9	28	9	12	9	29	15
Schools	--	12	4	13	23	36	13	20
State & Private E. S.	11	21	14	35	27	14	17	20
Walk-Ins	--	--	--	--	--	--	4	--
Employee Referrals	4	14	11	9	4	18	4	10
Advertising	30	32	39	30	35	23	25	35
Other Employers	4	2	--	4	--	--	4	--
Union	5	9	4	--	---	--	4	--
Proportion from Other Occupations Within the Company								
None	28		32		20		27	

Table 8-3 (*continued*)

	Tool & Die Maker	*Tool & Die Designer*	*Electronic Technician*	*Metal Technician*
Proportion from Other Occupations Within the Company (*cont.*)				
1–25%	26	25	28	32
26–50%	16	18	40	9
51–75%	8	11	8	14
76–100%	20	14	4	18
Success of Recruitment Practices				
Excellent	31	23	42	17
Good	40	50	54	61
Fair	19	15	4	13
Poor	10	12	--	9
If Dissatisfied, Why?				
Can't get Qualified People	62	60	N.A.	57
Too Long to Fill Vacancies	23	30	N.A.	43
Would like to Train Own	8	--	N.A.	--
Pay Rate Too Low to Compete	8	10	N.A.	--

Source: Employer interviews.

were trained, reflecting the large role of on-the-job training in the preparation of tool makers, and substantial proportions of tool designers and metal technicians also accepted employment where they were trained. The fact that the person was trained in a particular firm was also frequently given as the primary reason why he accepted his first job, particularly by the tool makers. This point, of particular importance in considering the relationship between company training program costs and turnover among workers who have completed training, will be analyzed further in the next chapter.

Most of the companies were at least moderately well satisfied with the results of their recruiting efforts. Of those who were dissatisfied, nearly all indicated that they were unable to get the number of well-qualified people they needed or that the time required to fill vacancies was too long. A large majority of all firms, both satisfied and dissatisfied, had no suggestions or recommendations for more effective recruitment methods. The few making suggestions spread them among improving pay (for tool and die tradesmen only), setting up training programs, hiring more inexperienced and younger workers, more intensive recruitment from training schools, and better screening or testing of applicants. No employers suggested such things as greater utilization of minority groups, joint training efforts by employers, or special efforts to develop more or improved training in the schools.

Furthermore, very few companies had made changes in their recruitment efforts in the previous five years or had any plans to alter their recruitment in the future. This is shown in the following tabulation.

Proportion of Sample Firms

	Tool and Die Maker	*Tool and Die Designer*	*Electronic Technician*	*Metal Technician*
Making no recruitment changes past 5 years	81%	81%	74%	78%
With no plans for changes in recruitment in the future	89%	90%	85%	75%

The minority of firms which had made or were planning changes in recruitment had generally confined their changes to relatively minor and standard forms. Typical changes or plans for change were more recruitment from within, more contact with training schools, greater use of employment agencies, expansion of training programs, or expanding the recruitment area. A very few planned to institute new training programs.

In general, the evidence on recruitment by employers shows a high reliance on established institutions and methods for recruitment and considerable dependence on internal sources of labor for the four occupations. Up to the time of the study, there was little response to the shortage situations through new

Table 8-4

First Post Training Job, Four Occupations, Chicago and St. Louis Combined
(Percent Distributions)

	Tool & Die Maker	*Tool & Die Designer*	*Electronic Technician*	*Metal Technician*
How Found First Job After Training				
Friend or Relative Referred	9	7	15	22
Stayed Where Trained	79	57	23	44
Direct Application	8	13	29	6
State Employ. Serv.	--	--	--	--
Private Employment Service	--	4	1	--
Answered Advertisement	2	6	11	17
School Placement Bureau	1	13	15	6
Military Employment	1	--	5	6
Why Took First Job				
To Stay Where Trained	65	49	24	42
Highest Pay Available	11	5	10	17
Other	24	46	66	41

Source: Worker interviews.

recruitment programs, nor were the sampled firms anticipating major changes. Most of the change that had occurred was in the form of more intensification or expansion of existing recruiting programs. There was virtually no evidence of plans put into effect or even discussed for meeting what was a long-term and continuing labor shortage problem. The impression is left that the companies had settled into long-established methods of conducting their recruitment efforts and they were not likely to move out of them in the absence of a much more critical situation than existed at the time of the study. The evidence suggests that most employers are not likely to be the source of innovation in developing new approaches to attracting greater numbers of people to the four occupations. Outside stimulation is likely to be necessary if there is to be a breaking-out of the chronic labor shortage situation.

Recruitment by Training Schools

Recruitment efforts of the training schools are summarized in Table 8-5. The data indicate both considerable variety in techniques used to attract students and considerable differences among individual schools. The most commonly used device for both trade and technical schools is advertising in brochures and other media. However, industry contacts, participation in career days at high schools, direct mail contacts with potential students, and contacts with school counselors are all methods used by substantial numbers of schools. How intensively and effectively these methods are used cannot be determined from the data. In the judgment and experiences of the school administrators, advertising the school curriculum and work with high school counselors are the most successful in obtaining students.

Practitioners in the four occupations were asked whether they were actively recruited by training schools, and if so, through what means. As Table 8-6 shows, only a minority of practitioners indicated they were the subject of active recruiting, but except for tool makers the minorities were substantial. Nearly half of the electronic technicians said they were approached directly by training schools. By far the most important method of contact was through the mail (on what basis the schools selected them to receive mail communication was not determined), and in-person contact by representatives of the schools was also important.

As was the case with training schools for the medical occupations, most schools had made little change in their recruitment methods over the past ten years and anticipated few changes in the future. Changes that had occurred or were anticipated were mainly intensification of already existing recruiting programs. There was no evidence of joint planning or efforts by the various schools to promote interest in the occupations for which they provided training; the schools tended to go their own way trying to attract students to their own programs. Since many of the schools were private, this procedure is understandable.

Despite the fact that most of the schools were operating at less than their maximum capacity, the school administrators tended to feel that the recruitment of students was becoming easier. Reasons cited for the easing of recruitment difficulties included rising educational levels of the population (more students with high school educations), more interest in the occupations (particularly in technical work), improved high school training in mathematics and science, and the success of some shifts in recruitment methods. The few schools for which recruitment was more difficult than in the past, all of them skilled trades schools, cited the growing propensities for college attendance and rising employer standards as reasons for the greater difficulty.

The general picture of school recruitment is one of fairly active effort. The schools seem to have generally arranged contacts with appropriate labor market institutions such as school counselors and industrial firms. The major gap in recruitment programs is probably the lack of a systemic approach to schools to jointly bring training and employment opportunities to the attention of potential students. Each school tends to operate individually, thereby producing overlapping efforts with no assurance that the potential field of applicants is being covered. Although this approach is no doubt common to most types of training schools, it can leave a gap in coverage. How serious the gap is depends upon the extent to which adequate information about training opportunities is brought to the attention of students through other means.

The role of information, counseling, guidance, and recruitment as factors related to the shortages of tool and die makers, tool and die designers, and electronic and metalworking engineering technicians has been analyzed in this chapter. The results of the analysis can be briefly summarized as follows:

1. It was not possible to identify any sources of occupational information that were of either dominant or decisive importance in stimulating interest in the four occupations. Formal guidance and counseling were influential in decisions to enter training programs for the occupations in only a small minority of cases. Most practitioners could not point to the specific factors that motivated them to enter training. Of those who could, the single most important factor was the suggestion of an employer or supervisor. An exception was the electronic technicians, among whom related military or work experience was most often cited as the decisive factor in their decision to enter the occupation. It was concluded that more systematic dissemination of occupational information is a prerequisite to attracting greater numbers of people to the four occupations. The high school curriculum would seem to be a prime choice as a setting for developing such a program of occupational information.

2. In none of the four occupations is there a single, well-identified preparatory route to entry. A number of possible combinations of education, training, and work experience are satisfactory to employers for qualifying for the four occupations. This flexibility has both advantages and disadvantages. On the positive side, workers are not precluded from entry because they did not follow specific preparatory programs and the resulting flexibility widens the possibilities for entry. On the negative side, however, the entry route is not

Table 8-5

Training School Recruitment, Four Occupations, Chicago and St. Louis Combined (Percent Distributions)

	Skilled Trades	*Technical Schools*	*Electronic Correspondence*
N =	12	11	2
Where Recruit Students			
All Over Country	42	27	100
Immediate Metropolitan Area	58	64	--
200-Mile Radius	--	9	--
Recruitment Methods			
Advertising	66	55	100
Industry Contacts	42	27	--
Career Days	25	54	--
Personal Representatives	16	9	50
Direct Mail	42	36	50
Contacts with Counselors	33	54	--
College Contacts	--	9	--
Employment Service	8	9	--
Where Most Students Come From			
High Schools	58	64	--
Industry	25	18	--
Student Referrals	8	--	--

Table 8-5 (*continued*)

	Skilled Trades	*Technical Schools*	*Electronic Correspondence*
Where Most Students Come From			
College	--	9	--
Mailing Lists	--	--	50
Rural Areas	8	--	50
No Answer	--	9	--
How Recruit Most Students			
Advertising	25	27	50
Industry Contacts	17	9	--
Career Days	8	9	--
Personal Representatives	8	--	--
Counselors	17	36	--
Direct Mail	--	--	50
Referrals	8	9	--
Employment Service	8	--	--
No Answer	8	9	--
Any Recruitment Changes Last 10 Years			
No	75	45	50
More Advertising	8	9	--

(*continued*)

Table 8-5 (*continued*)

	Skilled Trade	*Technical Schools*	*Electronic Correspondence*
N =	12	11	2
Any Recruitment Changes Last 10 Years			
Less Advertising	17	9	--
Phone Contacts	--	9	--
More Work with High School Counselors	--	18	--
Recruit at Colleges	--	9	--
Changes in Brochures	--	--	50
What Changes Anticipated			
None	67	64	50
More H. S. Contacts	8	9	--
More Industry Contact	17	9	--
Direct Mail	8	--	--
Advertising, Scholarships & Personal Representatives	--	9	--
More Active Recruitment	--	9	--
More Newspaper Advertising	--	--	50
Recruiting Trends			
Easier	42	55	50

Table 8-5 (*continued*)

	Skilled Trades	*Technical Schools*	*Electronic Correspondence*
N =	12	11	2
Recruiting Trends			
Harder	17	--	--
About Same	25	36	50
Don't Know	17	9	--

Source: Training school interviews.

Table 8-6

Extent of Active Recruitment by Training Schools, Four Occupations, Chicago and St. Louis Combined (Percent Distributions)

	Tool & Die Maker	*Tool & Die Designer*	*Electronic Technician*	*Metal Technician*
Whether Worker Actively Recruited by Training School? Yes	14	25	45	33
Method of Contact Used				
Mail	65	74	54	100
Telephone	--	5	3	--
Personal Representative	24	16	37	--
Friend or Relative	--	--	--	--
Visual Aids	6	--	3	--
Mail and Personal Contact	6	5	3	--

Source: Worker interview.

always obvious and sure, and this absence of delineated channels of entry probably increases the difficulty of attracting persons into appropriate programs, thereby making it more difficult to define the occupation and the specific labor market. A licensed practical nurse knows that the completion of the one-year approved training program will qualify her as a licensed practical nurse, and this fact is a positive influence in attracting people to the field. Completion of a two-year trade school program for tool makers, however, does not qualify the student to be a journeyman tool maker; in addition there is the alternative of on-the-job experience in a machine shop as a possible route to the occupation. This lack of definition of what various types of training and experience might lead to is probably a negative factor in bringing about specific commitments to enter the occupation. In all four occupations there is considerable emphasis on recruiting candidates for training from the internal labor force of the firm. On balance, it is probably better to leave the training routes flexible as they now are, rather than to try to prescribe strict requirements for qualifying for the occupations. Possibilities for encouraging more students and workers to take appropriate training will be discussed in the next chapter.

3. In general, the data did not reveal undue restrictions on entry into the four occupations. The major exception is that nonwhites have failed almost completely to find their way into any of the four occupations. This failure is undoubtedly due to a combination of discriminatory treatment by employers and unions, the self-determined work norms of the practitioners in the field, economic inability to finance the training, and inadequate educational preparation to qualify for training.[1] Although overcoming these problems is not simple, there is surely a large reserve of untapped manpower among minority groups which can be a prime source of increased labor for these occupations. In addition to the lack of participation by nonwhites, attracting an adequate supply of manpower, particularly in the tool and die trades, appears to be hampered by an overemphasis on the value of college level education. Although this emphasis is strong and not likely to be easily changed (nor should the value of college education be generally downgraded), some reorientation in educational publicity towards alternative types of training and employment opportunities would be helpful in directing attention to opportunities in skilled and technical occupations.

4. Hiring standards and recruitment efforts for the four occupations have been relatively stable over time. There was little evidence that the shortages were deemed sufficiently serious to have necessitated significant adjustment of hiring or entry standards or changes in recruitment programs by employers or training schools.

Hiring standards, however, are relatively flexible in any event and, therefore, are suited to varying labor market conditions. Recruitment programs tend to be rather highly routinized, although intensification of established practices do occur when the market is tight. It seems likely that innovation in recruitment efforts (e.g., in attempting to increase nonwhite participation) will have to come from, or at least be stimulated by, educational and governmental institutions.

9 Factors Affecting Supply: Training and Placement

Availability of training facilities and access to them are crucial factors in appraising the problem of shortages in the supply of labor for particular occupations. Also, the effectiveness of the labor market in matching the available supply with employer needs is an important determinant of the nature and extent of labor market imbalance. The focus of this chapter is on the preparation and placement of tool and die tradesmen and engineering technicians.

The Nature of Training Schools

Twenty-five training school programs offering instruction and/or training in subjects which prepared students for employment as tool and die tradesmen or technicians were examined for this study.[a] The sample, which included all schools (other than four-year colleges) in the two metropolitan areas offering substantial programs of instruction that focused directly on preparing students for the occupations under consideration, was as follows:

Type of School	*Chicago*	*St. Louis*	*Total*
Skilled trades	8	4	12
Technical	10	1	11
Correspondence (electronics)	2	0	2
Total	20	5	25

In addition, the role of training by individual industrial firms was examined.

The schools designated as skilled trades schools do not, in general, specialize in the training of tool and die tradesmen. Some of them offer classroom and practical training in a variety of trades, such as welding, automotive mechanics, automobile body repair, diesel mechanics, refrigeration and air conditioning, and engineering drawing, as well as tool and die making. One school of this type offered two 18-week courses, one in primary machine shop and the other in advanced machine shop (tool and die). This type of school, which is usually privately operated for profit, appears to prepare youngsters for beginning machine shop work as machine operators or, perhaps, machinists. Five of the

[a]The analysis presumes that the labor market is essentially a local one rather than a regional or national one.

nine schools offering a curriculum in tool and die maker work were of this type, and their programs varied in length from about six months to two years.

The sample of skilled trades schools also included, however, four publicly sponsored schools that offered more extensive training in preparation for tool and die making work. One of these, co-sponsored by the Tool and Die Institute of Chicago, was concerned exclusively with tool and die training. Another provided training only for workers in formal apprenticeship programs, including tool and die making. Both of these programs entailed four years of on-the-job and related classroom instruction. A third program was an 18-month MDTA program in tool and die making, also conducted in conjunction with a public trade school.

For the prospective tool and die maker then, there are two general choices possible for formal, specialized training. One is the private trade school which offers a relatively short period of training that probably prepares the student in the rudiments of the trade. The other is the longer formal apprenticeship, at the end of which the student attains journeyman status as a tool and die maker. In addition, the tradesman, in some cases one who has had the rudimentary type of machinist training, may attain tool and die maker positions through informal on-the-job training provided in the shop by the employer.

The category of skilled trades schools also includes three schools which offered two-year programs preparing students to take positions as tool and die designers. All three schools were private profit organizations which identified themselves as technical institutes or schools of engineering and technology. They offered a variety of curricula in mechanical, electrical, civil, and architectural engineering and technology as well as in tool and die design. The design curricula tended to be very practically oriented and very light on mathematics and sciences. In addition to these programs, preparation for tool and die design work is available in public junior colleges, where the preparation more heavily emphasizes work in the sciences, mathematics, English, and other general subjects.

The sample of eleven schools offering training leading to positions as engineering technicians included four public schools (three programs in junior colleges and one in a high school) and seven private schools (two of which were nonprofit institutions). Three major and distinct types of education and training programs can be identified. One is that offered by the junior college. In this instance the student, in a two-year period, pursues a course of study that includes a general education core and a specialty in applied sciences. The general education section, which might comprise from one-quarter to one-third of the program, consists of basic and general courses in English, social science, physical or biological science, and humanities. The applied section, comprising a majority of the course work, might allow the choice of such specialties as drafting design, electronics, and mechanical technology. The technical courses in these curricula include both class and laboratory work. The applied curricula might also allow electives in related fields such as mathematics, report writing, business management or general business, and psychology. The junior college program, in other words, provides a combination of general and technical education. The programs offered can serve as preparation for careers as engineering technicians in either electronics or metalworking.

A second type of institution offering technical training is the private technical institute which provides training in a variety of technical specialties. These schools grant certificates, diplomas, and associate degrees, depending on the program followed, in engineering and technical fields, including various design curricula such as tool and die design. In general, their programs are more technically oriented than those of the junior college; less emphasis is placed on general education. Although these schools are not approved by academic accrediting associations, they do include in their programs courses in the basic mathematical and scientific fields necessary for advanced technical work and few nontechnical courses in such areas as economics and psychology.

A third type, similar to that just discussed, is the private technical institute which specializes in a certain area of technology. In our sample, four schools were of this type, three of which specialized exclusively in electronics technology and one in aerospace technology. These institutes are similar to the general technical institute in that their emphasis is very strongly on the technical and applied as contrasted with general education. Two types of electronics programs are offered. One, which runs for approximately two years, is designed to prepare students for positions as engineering technicians in electronics. This program stresses the scientific and mathematical basis and the applied training necessary for work in engineering technology. The other program, approximately one year in length, is designed to prepare students for a lower level and narrower field of work as electronic technicians and contains less emphasis on basic science and mathematics. In addition, schools of this type in some cases also offer shorter programs (8 to 48 weeks) in specialized areas of electronics such as TV-radio electronics and electrical appliance repair. In general, this latter type of training does not directly prepare workers for positions as engineering technicians, in the sense the term is used in this study.

In addition to the three major types of training schools discussed above, the sample included two private correspondence schools, both of which specialized in training in the electronics field. In both cases, the schools provide the students with instructional materials and training kits. The training kits consist of various types of electronic equipment and instruments and are a substitute for the laboratory of the resident school. The emphasis in these schools is almost entirely on applied work. The absence of basic offerings in mathematics and science means that those who complete these schools are generally not qualified for positions as engineering technicians and are prepared only for more routine and simple technical work, such as TV or radio repair work.

All of the training schools, both for skilled trades and technical training, offered programs on both day and night schedules. Most of the schools had been in operation for many years, a majority for more than twenty years. Most of the programs for the occupations under study here, however, had been instituted within the past ten years, and a few had been operative for only one or two years. Enrollment in the programs under consideration was difficult to determine because of the multiprogram offerings of most schools. Total enrollment in all programs offered by the schools, however, varied from less than 100 to well over 1,000. Most seemed to be very flexible as to the number that could be admitted to any particular program of study. Sources of finance for the schools, of course, depended greatly on the sponsorship. The private schools were all supported primarily by tuition paid by the student. The public schools were supported primarily by tax revenues from local, state, and federal sources. Costs to students are discussed in the following section.

To show that none of these types of schools is the primary provider of training, the types of training secured by the sample of practitioners interviewed in this study are shown in Table 9-1. As the data in the table show, there is no single type of specialized training that predominates in any of the four occupations. None of the listed types of specialized training – on-the-job, technical school, military school, trade school, or apprenticeship – provided the major training for as much as a majority of the practitioners.

Tool and die makers come closest to a standard form of training; 47 percent of the sample completed an apprenticeship. Also of note is that close to a majority of designers (45 percent) had attended a private or public trade school, generally for two or more years. For electronic technicians more than for the other three occupations, training in the military was an important preparatory path.

Of more general importance is the fact that nearly all of the practitioners in all four occupations had obtained some form of formal specialized training. Of the few who had not, largely designers, most had completed some college level work. Some college education, in fact, was in the educational background of a majority of all of the practitioners, tool and die makers excepted. As noted in Table 9-2, many of those with college training had begun their college work in engineering curriculums (as well as other curriculums) and had then dropped out for a variety of reasons, including pursuing a career demanding less formal educational requirements. Others, however, obtained college training as a supplement to other training or on-the-job experience after having entered the occupation, or in anticipation of moving into the occupation out of other related types of employment. For tool and die makers, college work is not an integral part of their preparation for the occupation. Those with some college background had usually tried college work and abandoned it in favor of preparing for a career as tool and die makers.

The main points regarding the educational and training preparation of the

Table 9-1

Level of Education and Training of Workers, St. Louis and Chicago, Four Occupations

	Tool and Die Makers				Tool and Die Designers			
	No. Chi.	*No. St. L.*	*Tot. No.*	*% Tot.*	*No. Chi.*	*No. St. L.*	*Tot. No.*	*% Tot.*
	116	63	179	100%	51	33	84	100%
No Specialized Training Identified	3	12	15	8	6	9	15	18
H. S. Diploma or Less	3	9	12		1	2	3	
Junior College Work	0	0	0		0	2	2	
Other College Work								
1, Less Than 2 Yrs.	0	2	2		0	2	2	
2, Less Than 3 Yrs.	0	1	1		0	2	2	
3 or More Yrs.	0	0	0		5	1	6	
On-the-Job Training Only	15	8	23	13	4	7	11	13
H. S. Diploma or Less	12	6	18		3	3	6	
College Work								
1 to 2 Yrs.	0	0	0		1	3	4	
Over 2 Yrs.	3	2	5		0	1	1	
Specialized Training	98	43	141	79	41	17	58	69
Trade School or Technical Institute	22	34	56	40	29	13	42	50
High School Diploma Less Than 1 Yr. of Specialized Training	3	2	5		2	0	2	

Table 9-1 *(continued)*

	Tool and Die Makers				Tool and Die Designers			
	No. Chi.	*No. St. L.*	*Tot. No.*	*% Tot.*	*No. Chi.*	*No. St. L.*	*Tot. No.*	*% Tot.*
1 to 2 Yrs. of Training	2	5	7		2	1	3	
Above 2 Yrs.	14	19	33		8	6	14	
Some College Work								
0 to 2 Yrs. of Training	1	2	3		0	1	1	
Above 2 Yrs.	2	6	8		17	5	22	
Military Training	0	1	1		1	0	1	1
H. S. Diploma or Less	0	1	1		0	0	0	
Some College Work	0	0	0		1	0	1	
2 Yrs. of Trade School	0	0	0		0	0	0	
Apprenticeship	76	9	85	60	11	4	15	19
No Other Special Training								
H. S. Diploma or Less								
2 Yrs. Appren.	3	0	3		0	0	0	
3 Yrs. Appren.	3	1	4		1	0	1	
4 Yrs. Appren.	38	2	40		3	1	4	
5 Yrs. or More	11	0	11		0	0	0	
Some College								
3 Yrs. Appren.	1	0	1		0	1	1	
4 Yrs. Appren.	11	1	12		4	1	5	
5 Yrs. or More	4	1	4		0	1	1	

(continued)

Table 9-1 (*continued*)

	Tool and Die Makers				Tool and Die Designers			
	No. Chi.	*No. St. L.*	*Tot. No.*	*% Tot.*	*No. Chi.*	*No. St. L.*	*Tot. No.*	*% Tot.*
Technical and Trade Training								
1 to 2 Yrs. Trade Training								
4 Yrs. Appren.	1	2	3		2	0	2	
5 Yrs. Appren.	2	0	2		0	0	0	
2 or More Yrs.								
4 Yrs. Appren.	1	0	1		1	0	1	
5 Yrs. Appren.	1	0	1		0	0	0	
Apprentice in Training	0	2	2		0	0	0	
Total Cases in Sample With Some College Education	22	14	36	20	25	20	45	54

	Electronic Technicians				Metal Technicians			
	No. Chi.	*No. St. L.*	*Tot. No.*	*% Tot.*	*No. Chi.*	*No. St. L.*	*Tot. No.*	*% Tot.*
	76	14	90	100%	23	10	33	100%
No Specialized Training Identified	4	3	7	8	0	1	1	3
H. S. Diploma or Less	0	0	0		0	0	0	
Junior College Work	0	0	0		0	0	0	
Other College Work								
1, Less than 2 Yrs.	0	0	0		0	1	1	
2, Less than 3 Yrs.	1	1	2		0	0	0	
3 or More Yrs.	3	2	5		0	0	0	

Table 9-1 (*continued*)

	Electronic Technicians				Metal Technicians			
	No. Chi.	*No. St. L.*	*Tot. No.*	*% Tot.*	*No. Chi.*	*No. St. L.*	*Tot. No.*	*% Tot.*
On-the-Job Training Only	18	1	19	21	12	2	14	42
H. S. Diploma or Less	3	1	4		1	0	1	
College Work 1 to 2 Yrs.	2	0	2		11	1	12	
Over 2 Yrs.	13	0	13		0	1	1	
Specialized Training	54	10	64	71	11	7	18	54
Trade School or Technical Institute	32	6	38	42	5	5	10	30
H. S. Diploma Less than 1 Yr. of Specialized Training	0	0	0		1	0	1	
1 to 2 Yrs. of Training	4	5	9		2	2	4	
Above 2 Yrs.	9	0	9		2	1	3	
Some College Work 0 to 2 Yrs. of Training	18	1	19		0	1	1	
Above 2 Yrs.	1	0	1		0	1	1	
Military Training	20	4	24	27	1	2	3	9
H. S. Diploma or Less	9	2	11		0	2	2	
Some College Work	5	2	7		0	0	0	
2 Yrs. of Trade School	6	0	6		1	0	1	

(*continued*)

Table 9-1 (*continued*)

	Electronic Technicians				Metal Technicians			
	No. Chi.	*No. St. L.*	*Tot. No.*	*% No.*	*No. Chi.*	*No. St. L.*	*Tot. No.*	*% No.*
Apprenticeship	2	0	2	2	5	0	5	15
No Other Special Training								
H. S. Diploma or Less								
2 Yrs. Appren.	0	0	0		0	0	0	
3 Yrs. Appren.	0	0	0		0	0	0	
4 Yrs. Appren.	0	0	0		1	0	1	
5 Yrs. or More	0	0	0		0	0	0	
Some College								
3 Yrs. Appren.	0	0	0		0	0	0	
4 Yrs. Appren.	2	0	2		3	0	3	
5 Yrs. Appren.	0	0	0		0	0	0	
Technical and Trade Training								
1 to 2 Yrs. Trade Training								
4 Yrs. Appren.	0	0	0		0	0	0	
5 Yrs. Appren.	0	0	0		0	0	0	
2 or More Yrs.								
4 Yrs. Appren.	0	0	0		0	0	0	
5 Yrs. Appren.	0	0	0		0	0	0	
Apprentice in Training	0	0	0		1	0	1	
Total Cases in Sample With Some College Education	44	11	55	61	14	5	19	58

Source: Worker interviews.

Table 9-2

General Educational Factors in Practitioners' Backgrounds, Four Occupations, Chicago and St. Louis Combined (In percents)

		Tool & Die Makers (184 cases)	*Tool & Die Designers (96 cases)*	*Electronic Technicians (92 cases)*	*Metal Technicians (33 cases)*
	N =				
Type of High School Education	N =	161	93	89	30
Academic		26%	39%	39%	37%
Vocational and Technical		45	35	25	36
Commerical		3	2	--	--
General		24	22	32	27
Academic-Technical		2	2	3	--
Field of Study in College	N =	42	58	55	19
Technical		12%	5%	4%	--
Electrical Engineering		2	9	42	--
Mechanical Engineering		26	43	13	37
Other Engineering		19	14	13	32
Other Curriculum		41	29	30	32
Why Left College	N =	37	52	49	18
Finances		8%	13%	33%	22%

(continued)

Table 9-2 (*continued*)

	N =	*Tool & Die Makers (184 cases)*	*Tool & Die Designers (96 cases)*	*Electronic Technicians (92 cases)*	*Metal Technicians (33 cases)*
Why Left College	N =	37	52	49	18
Marriage or Domestic Pressures		8	6	6	22
Lost Interest or Poor Grades		22	10	20	--
For Vocational Training		30	29	8	17
Other		27	36	28	39
Completed Junior College		5	6	4	--

Source: Worker interviews.

practitioners can be summarized as follows. For none of the occupations do practitioners tend to qualify for the occupation through a common training format. The preparation of tool and die makers through apprenticeship comes closest to being a standard training program. Second, many practitioners have prepared for their work with a variety of types of training experiences. Third, for all of the occupations, on-the-job training or experience is an important part of the requirement for attaining journeyman status. This experience, however, may be obtained through informal as well as formal training. Finally, except for tool and die makers, college level work has been a very important channel of entry into each of the occupations. This may all be summarized by saying that the prerequisites for qualifying for the occupation are very flexible. In part, at least, the path chosen by the student depends upon the types of training institutions available in his locality. There were some substantial differences in the specialized training backgrounds of St. Louis and Chicago practitioners, presumably the result of differences between the two cities in the types of training institutions and programs that had been developed.

The diversity of backgrounds of practitioners in the four occupations is also shown in the variety of types of general education preparation (see Table 9-2). Substantial proportions in each occupation followed academic, vocational and/or technical, and general programs in high school, although somewhat fewer tool and die makers than practitioners in the other three occupations followed an academic curriculum. A quarter or more of the practitioners in each occupation (nearly half of the tool and die makers) attended vocational or technical high schools. Most of those who had attended college did not complete work for a bachelor's degree. About two-thirds of those who had attended college, with the exception of tool and die makers, did their work in an engineering curriculum. Substantial numbers, however, had been in nonengineering programs, mainly liberal arts and science.

A variety of factors influenced their decisions to terminate their college work. For the technicians, financial difficulties were a factor for a good many. Close to a third of the tool and die tradesmen left college to take more specific vocational training. For none of the occupations, however, did any one reason predominate as the major factor influencing termination of college education. In any event, the college drop-outs, particularly from engineering schools, are an important manpower source for both specialized training programs and employment. Data in the previous chapter seem to indicate, however, that active recruitment on the college campus is relatively rare. The college dropout must generally find his way to the four occupations by himself or, in some cases, through the advice of a college counselor. Counselors might play a role in the process for those who leave college for reasons of poor grades; namely by recommending technician careers for those whose conceptual abilities might be marginal for successful work as engineers but who possess qualities as potential technicians.

The Role of Employers in Training

With the great variety of possible training routes into the four occupations, it is difficult to deal concretely with the relationship between training opportunities and the supply of labor. The existence of several alternative types or combinations of training programs, in fact, is undoubtedly an important factor in our finding that there were not severe shortages of manpower in any of the four occupations at the time of the study. The greater the extent of flexibility, even if over-all standards of competence and intellectual ability are high, the greater the opportunity for recruitment from generally educated persons. This means that a large potential supply of technicians exist for which there are multiple ports of entry. The effect of formalizing minimum training requirements and limiting entry, while creating homogeneity and occupational identifiability, is the reduction of potential supply.

The shortage was most severe for tool and die makers, the occupation for which there is the least flexibility in meeting minimum training requirements. In this occupation, a great deal of the training is on-the-job and must therefore be tied to a training program, formal or informal, provided by the employer. In the others, workers may qualify to a greater or less extent through high school, night school, trade school, technical school, junior or four-year college, none of which is training necessarily tied to an employment relationship. The resulting flexibility increases the probabilities that an adequate supply of labor for the occupations will be trained. However, the absence of definite, clear-cut qualification standards makes it difficult to assess aspects of training that might interfere with turning out a satisfactory flow of trained personnel.

Responses to questions asked in the interviews with employers concerning their training programs are summarized in Table 9-3.

Company involvement in training programs is more extensive and more intensive for tool and die makers than for workers in the other three occupations.[b] About two-thirds of the companies employing tool and die makers conducted some type of formal training program for these workers; well below half of the companies employing workers in the other three occupations did so. As the tabulations in Table 9-3 indicate, larger firms were more likely to have training programs for tool and die makers and metal technicians than smaller firms. For the other two occupations this relationship did not hold. Except for metal technicians, firms classified as shortage firms participated more often in training programs than firms which indicated they were not experiencing a labor shortage. One might have anticipated that the no shortage firms would more often have had their own training programs, on the assumption that having a training program would reduce the likelihood that a firm would find itself short of labor. Apparently the opposite is more likely; that is, that one of the reasons one has a training program is that labor available on the market is in short supply and one must, therefore, train his own workers. It is also conceivable that companies which had special requirements and more narrowly defined but more highly specialized personnel were almost compelled to formulate their own training programs. These are the subspecialties which are most likely to be in shortest supply.

Tool and Die Maker Programs

Nearly all of the 39 firms in the sample conducting training programs for tool and die makers were participating in a formal apprenticeship program. Thirty-three of the training programs were of this type, in a majority of cases set up under the joint auspices of a labor-management committee and approved by the Bureau of Apprenticeship and Training. Completion of the apprenticeship training program required either four or five years of on-the-job training and related classroom instruction, the latter usually provided by a high school or public trade school. The other six programs did not involve formal apprenticeship arrangements and in most cases consisted entirely of on-the-job training in the plant. One company in this group conducted its own classes of related instruction. Some of these programs required shorter periods of training to attain journeyman status than the formal apprenticeship programs. In most cases, the firms with apprenticeship programs hired trainees directly into the program from high school (though high school graduation was not always essential) or from a trade school. Firms which recruited training candidates from

[b]The extent of formality in training programs, as well as their apparent greater magnitude, is related to union–management relationships and the traditional nature of this occupation.

Table 9-3

Aspects of Company Training Programs, Chicago and St. Louis Combined, Four Occupations
(In percents)

		Tool & Die Maker	*Tool & Die Designer*	*Electronic Technician*	*Metal Technician*
Have Formal Training Programs	N =	57	31	26	24
Percent Yes:					
Total		68%	43%	19%	38%
Shortage Firms		70	52	25	38
No Shortage Firms		60	--	10	40
Under 2000 Employees		62	50	19	24
2000 Employees or More		87	33	20	67
Minimum Requirements for Entry to Training	N =	34	11	*	6
High School Graduates		65%	73%	*	50%
Technical School Background		29	--	*	17
Formal Apprenticeship in Related Field		3	9	*	--
Two Years of College or Technical School		3	18	*	17
One Year of College		--	--	*	17
Occupational Groups From Which Trainees Selected	N =	29	9	3	5

(continued)

Table 9-3 (*continued*)

		Tool & Die Maker	*Tool & Die Designer*	*Electronic Technician*	*Metal Technician*
Machine Operators		55%	33%	--	--
Production & Assembly		14	11	33%	--
Draftsman and Other Semitechnical Jobs		7	22	--	40
Tool and Die Workers		--	22	--	--
Combination of 1 and 2		7	--	--	--
Technicians		--	--	--	--
All, No One in Particular		10	--	67	60
Machinist		7	11	--	--
Number in Training Program	N =	35	10	3	7
1		11%	20%	--	14%
2–5		46	60	67	29
6–10		14	10	33	29
11–15		20	--	--	14
16–20		6	--	--	14
21–25		--	--	--	--
26–50		3	10	--	--
51–98		--	--	--	--

Table 9-3 (*continued*)

		Tool & Die Maker	*Tool & Die Designer*	*Electronic Technician*	*Metal Technician*
Number Compared with Five Years Earlier	N =	36	12	4	7
Higher Now		36%	8%	50%	29%
Lower Now		19	17	--	14
Same		42	75	50	57
New Company		3	--	--	--
Length of Training Program	N =	41	9	4	7
Four Years		46%	33%	-	--
Five Years		37	33	50%	14%
Three or Four Years		10	--	--	29
Less than Three Years		7	33	--	57
One Year		--	--	50	--
Automatic Pay Increases for Promotions	N =	42	13	4	7
Yes		69%	77%	100%	57%
Yes, Gradually Through Apprenticeship		26	8	--	--
Award Certificate After Training	N =	41	13	4	8
Yes		80%	46%	0%	0%

(*continued*)

Table 9-3 (*continued*)

		Tool & Die Maker	*Tool & Die Designer*	*Electronic Technician*	*Metal Technician*
Company Has Complete Control	N =	15	14	4	8
Yes		36%	86%	100%	88%
Evaluation of Their Training Program	N =	36	13	2	9
Excellent or Good		95%	84%	50%	100%
Are Enough People Attracted?	N =	41	13	4	9
Yes		85%	85%	100%	100%
Whether Would Like to Train More People	N =	41	6	4	9
Yes, Restricted by Ratio		27%	--	--	--
Yes		17	46%	50%	22%
Yes, Shortage Firms		44	55	67	40
Yes, No Shortage Firms		67	--	--	--
Place Where Most Non Company-Trained Workers are Trained	N =	39	31	26	24
All Trained at Co.		32%	16%	4%	21%
At Other Companies		56	48	12	33
At Technical Schools		2	13	38	4

Table 9-3 (*continued*)

		Tool & Die Maker	*Tool & Die Designer*	*Electronic Technician*	*Metal Technician*
At Colleges		--	6	8	17
At Technical Schools and Colleges		--	10	23	8
Various; No Particular Place		9	6	15	8
In Europe		2	--	--	4
Armed Forces		--	--	--	4
How Evaluated Other Training	N =	30	17	23	18
Excellent–Good		39%	35%	47%	39%
Varies		46	31	43	44
Whether Own Company Better Qualified to do the Training Than Others	N =	45	23	6	16
Yes		73%	52%	26%	44%
Whether Plan to Initiate Training Programs	N =	48	25	23	17
Yes, or Maybe		6%	0%	4%	6%

(continued)

Table 9-3 (*continued*)

	Tool & Die Maker		Tool & Die Designer		Electronic Technician		Metal Technician	
	First Choice	*Second Choice*	*First Choice*	*Second Choice*	*First Choice*	*Second Choice*	*First Choice*	*Second Choice*
Best Training Schools N =	27	14	16	8	22	18	9	10
H. S.	15%	14%	--	--	--	6%	--	10%
Jr. Colleges	--	--	--	--	5%	6	--	--
Colleges	--	7	56%	50%	14	39	67%	70
Technical or Trade Schools	81	57	46	50	77	39	33	20
Armed Forces School	--	--	--	--	5	11	--	--
Tool & Die Institute	4	21	--	--	--	--	--	--
M. D. T. A.	--	--	--	--	--	--	--	--

*No data available.

Source: Employer interviews.

their own work forces most often found them among their machine operators. Although a majority of firms specified a high school education as a minimum qualification for entry into the training program, formal educational background is not the crucial factor in entry. Most important is aptitude for the work and interest and motivation to engage in the lengthy training period required for journeyman status.

A number of points can be made regarding the role of employer training programs as they relate to the supply of tool and die makers. It is, first of all, reasonably clear that on-the-job training of a substantial order is an essential ingredient in the preparation of tool and die makers. At present this training is provided almost exclusively through the employment by private firms of tool and die trainees. Companies conducting such training programs generally train only to the extent required to meet their own needs, and some firms do no training at all.[c] Some of the training firms indicated that they would like to be training more tool and die makers. About one-fourth of all the firms with training programs said their desire to train more people was frustrated because they were already training the maximum allowed by the journeyman-apprentice ratio agreed to in the collective bargaining agreement. Others, however, indicated that, although they would like to expand their training program, their ability to do so was limited by facilities (machines for training, instructors, or the volume of work available for trainees to work on). A majority of firms, though, said they did not wish to train beyond their present volume because they had no need for more trained people.

The fact that most firms train tool and die makers only to the extent of their own need, together with the fact that some firms do no training at all, means that it is almost inevitable that the number of tool and die makers trained will be insufficient to meet the needs of the market. At the same time the high opportunity costs involved, if more formalized training through the public or private educational system were the alternative, would effectively limit supply from this source.

Attitudes of employers toward conducting their own training programs fall into two general groups. One group refuses to conduct training programs at all or strictly limits the extent of its training because it feels that training programs do not pay off. They fear that their investment in training will be lost by turnover among tool makers shortly after, or even before, the worker has completed his training, and that the benefits of training will therefore accrue to other employers. The extreme of this viewpoint was exemplified in the statement of one personnel director that it was the policy of his firm to "buy tool and die makers at the cheapest price possible and have someone else train them."

The viewpoint of the other general group of employers is that it is the responsibility of companies to provide the necessary training of tool and die makers, at least for their own needs. One view expressed, perhaps not a typical one, was that "his company has an obligation to train and it gets its money's worth in the first year following training."

In effect, companies in the first group are willing to have training costs

[c] The number not engaged in training is probably greater than that suggested by the data in this study. The employer sample over-represents larger firms, and the larger firms more often have training programs.

subsidized by other firms. In part this attitude seems to flow from a desire to take advantage of the willingness of a majority of companies to meet their obligation (and need) to provide training opportunities. In part, also, it reflects differences in the efficiency and profitability among firms. Some firms feel they cannot afford to meet the costs of training and the risks of loss of investment in training through labor turnover. With respect to labor turnover, it is true, of course, that many tool and die makers do leave the companies where they were trained for other employment. Among tool and die makers included in the worker sample for this study, only 38 percent were still working at the time of the study on their first job following completion of their training. The figure was much higher for workers in firms with over 2,000 employees (56 percent) than for workers in smaller firms (32 percent).[d] The variation by size of firm suggests that wages and other benefits in larger firms probably result in lower turnover and therefore lower costs in training programs. A number of larger firms said, in fact, that turnover among their tool and die makers was very low and there was little risk of losing these trained workers.[e] Perhaps the greater degree of specialization which generally characterizes the activities of large firms makes mobility less attractive and less possible.

In any event, the differences in attitudes toward training programs and the ability to conduct them means that qualified tool and die makers are likely to be in short supply regularly (assuming no important declines in demand). This phenomenon can be eliminated only if the responsibility for training can be transferred, at least in part, to the public, or mechanisms can be found to share the training responsibility and training costs more equitably among all employers, or if programs can be developed that would serve as an incentive for some employers to train beyond their own needs. The preapprenticeship training programs for tool and die makers developed under MDTA would appear to be a step in the direction of accomplishing the latter objective. For some firms with a particularly aged labor force, however, limitations in the apprentice-journeyman ratio make it impossible to train sufficient numbers to meet immediate replacement needs.

As an institutional arrangement for encouraging quality training of tool and die makers, the Chicago Tool and Die Institute is worthy of note. This organization of Chicago firms co-sponsors apprenticeship training for tool and die

[d] The remainder, however, does not reflect only voluntary quits. Some left their first jobs because of layoff, the closing of a department or plant, or other involuntary reasons.

[e] On the contrary, some firms explained the absence of a training program in their firm on the basis of their experience with high turnover among tool makers. A couple of firms expressed the problem in terms of what they saw as a general characteristic of tool makers; namely, that they were only interested in money. They would, therefore, leave a firm whenever there was an opportunity to make a few cents an hour more in another job, even if it meant giving up security and fringe benefits rights. From these observations, it should be apparent that tool and die makers are much more strongly attached to a career pattern in the occupation than they are to firms. For an historical examination of tool maker career attachment, see Carol P. Brainerd, "Trends in the Character of Work Attachments Among Philadelphia Toolmakers," in Gladys L. Palmer, *et al.*, *The Reluctant Job Changer* (Philadelphia: University of Pennsylvania Press, 1962), pp. 81-114.

makers with the Chicago Board of Education. Its major contribution to training is the establishment of acceptable training standards for employers and the involvement it gives employers in the planning of classroom instruction provided by the cooperating vocational school. In addition, the institute makes a small contribution toward the sharing of training costs among a large number of companies in that it pays part of the instructional costs from member fees (see Chapter 2). The institute also provides a central organization of employers through which plans for new or expanded training programs could be formulated.

A second point regarding the role of employer training programs is that most employers at the time of the study were having no difficulty finding qualified candidates for their training programs. As Table 9-3 indicates, 85 percent of the firms with training programs said enough persons were available to fill all of their training slots. Most of them, in fact, said they had many more applicants than training positions and had qualified candidates on waiting lists to get into the training programs. In general then, in spite of some belief that everybody wants to go to college or nobody wants to work with his hands anymore, the evidence is that the trade is still attractive to a sufficient number of people and the shortage cannot be attributed to a lack of willing candidates.

Clearly for the case of tool and die makers, the role of the employer in training is crucial. The major problem is that of finding ways to encourage more employers to undertake training programs and/or to develop incentives for employers presently engaged in training to expand training beyond the needs of their own companies. The high age of tool and die makers undoubtedly means that a large number of training programs are designed at best to maintain, not increase, supply. Additional evidence that the amount of training that takes place is closely tied to the immediate manpower needs of the employer is the fact that seven firms in the sample had formal apprenticeship programs "on the books" or at one time did have. In all of these cases the training program was either inactive or terminated because the company had no current need for apprentices. As a matter of public policy, if training incentives are provided they should be designed and administered to increase training opportunities for minority groups.

Tool and Die Designers

In general, the role of the employer in the training of tool and die designers is quite different from that of tool and die makers. In a few instances, employers have apprenticeship programs for designers and the training problem is very similar to that for tool makers. In most cases, however, the role of the employer is that of providing on-the-job training for people who have already obtained a specialized educational background, usually in a college or trade school, in design work or a closely related field.

As is shown in Table 9-3, somewhat less than half of the sample firms had what they would identify as a formal training program for tool and die designers. Of the fourteen firms with such programs, eight sponsored programs that entailed only on-the-job training, four had apprenticeship programs, and two had programs that coupled on-the-job training with the company's own classes for designers. In addition, two firms had tuition rebate programs for designers or other employees who took approved course work in subjects related to design work. Other firms involved their designers or potential designers in informal training on the job; that is, the persons worked under the supervision of designers who were responsible for assisting in the development of workers interested in becoming qualified designers. Generally, designers tend to *work into* their jobs as designers, starting in lower level design, drafting, or tool and die maker positions and working into more responsible design positions as their experience and progress merit. Commonly, during this working-in period the worker will take related college or technical work on his own in preparation for advancement to designer positions. The training process, in other words, is continuous rather than discrete.

As in the case of tool and die maker, 85 percent of the companies interviewed said that they were able to attract a sufficient number of people to fill available training slots. Also, as with the tool and die makers, the typical company had a relatively small number of persons in training at any given time, between two and five people. In part, this reflects the fact that companies, even large ones, often need only small numbers of designers. Although about half of the companies with training programs would have liked to increase the number of trainees, they were precluded from doing so because of limitations in the instructional capacity of the design department; that is, additional trainees would interfere with the regular work of designers who served as instructors. The fact that training is very closely tied to the employer's manpower needs is indicated by the fact that all of the training programs were in firms in the shortage category.

The designer case differs substantially from the tool maker case in that a much smaller proportion of firms conducted training programs. Those without training programs, and to some extent those with training programs, filled their needs for designers by hiring designers with experience and/or training at other companies or by hiring inexperienced people from technical schools or colleges and having them learn their work on the job. As a result, the employer depends less upon the productivity of his own training program for meeting designer needs than he does for meeting his needs for toolmakers. On the other hand, he is highly dependent upon a flow of well-trained people from technical schools and colleges. As noted earlier, most designers have had a couple of years of training in a technical or trade school, or college.

To summarize, the major role of the employer in training designers is to provide training and experience on the job for people who either already have a good technical training in technical or trade schools or college or who are obtaining such training on their own time while they are employed in jobs that could lead to designer positions. These programs generally attempt to apply the general technical knowledge candidates may have to the specific design needs of the employer. Companies which have formal training programs for designers, and they are in the minority, have little difficulty finding qualified persons for available training slots. To the extent that shortages occur they are for experienced people, those who already have the requisite education, training, and experience. Employer training programs are mainly of the on-the-job type and tend not to be discrete in the sense of prescribed starting and ending times and specific training content. Also, the number of people that can be trained by an employer at any one time appears to be severely limited by the instructional capacity of the design department as well as by the volume of work available to which the trainee can be assigned.

This set of circumstances is not one for which it is easy to prescribe a remedy. Additional training effort probably is not the primary answer to the problem. It may be, for example, that in times of substantial shortage of qualified designers, a more effective solution is job redesign or reassignment of technical and professional personnel, matters discussed more fully in the next chapter. With respect to training, however, perhaps consideration should be given to the possibilities for providing the equivalent of some of the necessary on-the-job training outside the employment relationship. It may be possible, for example, to incorporate a larger practical or applied element into the technical curricula of junior colleges. Alternatively, it might also be possible to encourage broader participation by employers in training programs through economic incentives. One possibility might be the subsidization of instructor costs since one constraint on the expansion of training programs seems to be the reluctance to use the time of journeymen designers for instructional purposes. As in the tool and die maker case, an incentive program might be coupled with a policy encouraging increased utilization of minority groups in training programs.

Engineering Technicians

Employer participation in the training of engineering technicians is less common than for tool and die tradesmen. Only about one in five of the sample firms conducted training programs for electronic technicians; 38 percent participated in the training of metalworking technicians (see Table 9-3). Almost all of the training given by employers in both occupations was of the on-the-job variety. Three of the five employer training programs for electronic technicians were of this type. The other two programs combined on-the-job training with some classroom instruction provided by the employer. In one case, the class work was of 12-week duration; in the other, class work extended over a two or three year period and involved advanced training for technicians. In addition, five firms gave informal on-the-job training for electronics technicians and four firms offered tuition rebate programs for workers taking formal training at a college or technical school. The picture is very similar for the metalworking technicians. Six of the eight formal company training programs were limited to on-the-job training and the other two combined on-the-job training with limited classroom work provided by the company. Additionally, three firms had informal on-the-job training programs and two sponsored tuition rebate programs.

All of the firms with training programs said they were able to attract all of the people they needed to their training programs. Those without training programs rely on the backgrounds of potential workers trained in other companies, technical and trade schools, and colleges. For electronic technicians, companies generally prefer workers with backgrounds in technical or trade schools; companies prefer workers with some college preparation for their metalworking technician positions. As was shown in Table 9-2, many engineering technicians, particularly electronics technicians, have had a training background combining technical or trade school training and college. About 60 percent of all of the sample engineering technicians had had some college education.

The most crucial aspect of training for engineering technicians is the post-high school specialized training received in technical or trade schools and college, not the training provided by the employer. The employer training is largely on the job and is given to the new worker in the form of formal, informal, or orientation training on the job. If a sufficient supply of persons with appropriate backgrounds is available, there is little difficulty for employers to supply what is required for specific job training. The definition of appropriate background seems to be quite flexible both as to type and time. If persons with appropriate backgrounds are not available, others can be hired and then encouraged or required to obtain additional training in night school programs offered by trade and technical schools or colleges, as well as on-the-job training provided by employers. The key for ensuring an adequate supply of engineering technicians, therefore, would appear to be at the point of recruiting adequate numbers of students into technical and trade schools and into the technical and engineering curricula of junior and four-year colleges.

Training Capacity

The relationship between the training capacity of industrial firms and the supply of workers in the four occupations was discussed in the previous section. It was noted that the ability (or willingness) of employers to take on trainees was extremely important in determining the supply of tool and die makers and of some importance in the case of tool and die designers. On the other hand, the extent to which employers engage in the training of engineering technicians is of secondary importance in determining the adequacy of the supply of labor. In this section we consider the availability of training capacity in trade and technical schools as a factor in the supply situation.

It has already been noted that most of the sample training schools were operating at less than their full capacity at the time of the study. Only three of the twelve trade school programs were filled to capacity, and the same was true of only one of the eleven technical schools. It may be generally concluded, therefore, that it was not a lack of training capacity in the relevant training institutions that was causing a shortage of personnel in any of the four occupations. It may also be said that the ability of the schools to expand in the event of increased demands for training was quite flexible in two respects. In the first place, the schools, most of which were privately operated, were generally very flexible in adjusting their programs to the nature of the demand for training at a particular time. The schools were able and willing to offer programs of various durations and content, depending upon the desires of their clients. Secondly, many of the schools indicated they would be able to expand their capacity rather quickly should the demand warrant it. Many of them were in business for the purpose of making a profit, and they indicated that they would rather quickly be able and willing to buy or rent additional space, buy additional equipment, and hire more instructors if the demand could not be met with their present facilities. In fact, seven of the twelve trade schools and six of the eleven technical schools said they were planning expansion of either facilities or faculties, or both, at the time of the study.

The evidence seems rather clear, therefore, that the training capacity of the training schools was not a limiting factor for an adequate labor supply, nor was it likely to become so. This conclusion does not take account of the situation in the other major training institutions providing preparation for careers in the four occupations, namely the colleges (except that the sample did contain a couple of junior college programs). The capacity problem here is about the same as for all occupations that require college level education. College trained people are an important source of manpower for tool and die designer and engineering technician positions. In the long run, therefore, expansion of colleges is important for assuring adequately prepared people for these occupations. Although few of the sample practitioners had obtained their training at junior colleges, the expansion of the junior college program in Illinois and Missouri is potentially a very important resource for the training of these technical people. It is unlikely, in fact, with the expansion of junior colleges in the two states, together with the existing trade and technical schools, that a shortage of skilled or technical workers will develop in either state for want of adequate training capacity. Junior colleges, with sufficient emphasis on career training, would seem to be the ideal type of development for meeting the kind of manpower needs considered in this study.

Costs and Financing of Training

In considering the relationship between training costs and the supply of labor, the case of the tool and die maker can be distinguished from that of the other three occupations. The basis for the distinction is that ordinarily far less general or school education is required for the preparation of tool and die makers. As a consequence, the incidence of training costs tends to be different.

Although there is considerable variation from it, the standard preparation for a tool and die maker is a four or five year apprenticeship program. The classroom or related instruction in these programs is usually provided in a public high school or vocational school. The fee for this service is nominal and is often paid by the employer. The major part of this aspect of the training is therefore borne by the public. The cost of the on-the-job training is shared by the employer and the apprentice. The cost to the apprentice is in the form of opportunity costs; that is, the costs of foregoing the possibility for higher earnings in regular employment. The apprentice receives a wage during the period of his training that begins at a specified percentage, perhaps half, of the journeyman rate and is raised at specified intervals (usually every six months) to reach the journeyman level at the completion of the training. In the early years of the training period, the apprentice usually earns less than he would in comparable work as a regular employee. This sacrifice in earnings, however, does not appear to be an important deterrent to entry into the trade. As was indicated earlier, most employers were able to find plenty of candidates to fill their training spots. A minority of firms indicated, however, that they often lost apprentices to other firms before the training period was completed. One of the major reasons for this occurring is that apprentices sometimes receive offers of wages from other firms for tool and die maker or machinist positions that are above those they are receiving as apprentices. The opportunity costs borne by the apprentice, therefore, while not an important deterrent to attracting candidates, sometimes results in failure to complete the program. In firms where this is a problem it might be remedied, at least to some extent, by accelerating wage increments during the apprenticeship period. This solution, obviously, is not without cost, but it might be cheaper than losing apprentices before they complete their training. Presumably this solution would be most effective if the acceleration in wages occurred in the latter parts of the training program.

The employer's costs are of two types. One type arises from the differential between the apprentice's wages and the value of the product he produces. The other arises from the instructional costs of the on-the-job training. Costs of materials, scrap products, and machine and product damage can be treated as type one costs; that is, negative values for the output of the apprentice. No estimates were obtained of the magnitude of these costs. Employers seemed to differ as to their significance. On the one hand, some employers put great emphasis on them and were therefore very reluctant to conduct apprenticeship programs. On the other hand, some employers minimized the importance of the costs, as did the employer who felt the costs were repaid during the first year of the trainee's employment as a journeyman. The costs are undoubtedly much more burdensome for small employers, for whom, for example, one damaged jig is much more critical than for a large employer.

It has already been suggested that probably the most promising approach to encouraging an increase in apprenticeship training is to partially subsidize the employer's training costs. An example of this approach is the preapprenticeship program for tool and die makers that has been attempted under MDTA, in which the training cost for the employer is subsidized for at least the first year of the apprenticeship period.

An alternative approach would be that of subsidizing the costs of students taking course work at trade and technical schools. As noted earlier, substantial numbers of tool and die makers by-passed apprenticeship training, and some of these have obtained relevant skill training in trade or technical schools. This pattern of training could presumably be encouraged with some type of financial incentive to students similar to the MDTA preapprenticeship program. Persons completing one or two years of such training might then enter apprenticeship or on-the-job training programs in industry at a much higher level. Such an approach might be particularly helpful in encouraging entry to tool and die making by members of low-income and minority groups. The major difficulty with the approach is the wide variation in the quality of training institutions and, therefore, the problem of assuring that any subsidy would be usefully spent.

The suggestions discussed above assume that the primary reason for insufficient training of tool and die makers is the cost involved to the employer. The evidence for this is persuasive: There are sufficient numbers of interested candidates, but employers, to the extent that they engage in training at all, limit training to the number they feel will be necessary to meet their own manpower needs in the short run. Some train no tool and die makers at all, depending instead on their ability to buy workers trained elsewhere. Subsidization of the employers' training costs, particularly if they are willing to expand the number of people in their training program, would therefore appear to be an effective approach as well as wise public policy. A minority of employers indicated that the size of their training programs for tool and die makers was limited by minimum journeymen-apprenticeship ratios negotiated in collective bargaining agreements with unions. In these cases the obvious solution is to attempt to renegotiate the ratios and make them more liberal. Failing that, expansion would have to come in firms doing no training currently or training below the limits allowed in collective bargaining agreements.

The problems of training costs for tool and die designers and engineering technicians are different in that most of the training is not ordinarily done under employer auspices. In most cases the employers either hire workers, as they are needed, who already have gained substantial training and need only very specific training in the employer's own methods, products, and procedures, or current employees in lower level positions are urged to attend school on a part-time basis in preparation for promotion into designer and technician positions. For a majority of practitioners, the background training includes some college education. Except for the few cases in which employers offer tuition rebates to their own employees going to school, employers are not burdened with the training costs. These are borne primarily by the student himself.

The magnitude of the training costs for the students depends very much on the type and location of the school attended and whether they attend full time or part time. Costs are at a minimum when the student attends a public trade school or college in his own community on a part-time basis while he is employed. They are at a maximum if he attends a private trade or technical school or college away from his home on a full-time basis. In the latter case tuition is likely to be relatively high, likewise maintenance costs, and income foregone is at a maximum. Tuition costs at some of the larger and more popular trade and technical schools sampled in this study ran to $1,200 and more per year. On the other hand, junior college programs were available at free tuition for residents of the community. With the range of cost possibilities it is impossible to generalize what the costs of training amount to.

It can be said, however, that most of the practitioners in the three occupations seemed to be able to deal with the problem of training costs without undue difficulty. When asked to indicate whether they had overcome any difficult problems with respect to obtaining training, most (65 to 80 percent in the three occupations) said they had none. Less than 10 percent in each occupation indicated that finances were a problem. However, whether potential practitioners were barred from the field by high training costs is another matter.

An indication of how training costs are met is shown in Table 9-4, which shows the sources of funds used by those in the sample of recent Chicago trainees. These trainees, it will be recalled, had recently attended one of the sample trade or technical schools in the Chicago area. For all of the trainee groups, and especially for electronic technicians, part-time or full-time work played a very important part in financing training. Loans, company subsidies, and scholarships were relatively unimportant sources of support. The major exception to this is that most of the trainees in tool and die or machinist training were being subsidized under MDTA programs. It should be emphasized that this picture of how costs are met ignores college education. Were this added, it is likely that parents' help would be a much more significant part of the picture.

If the data from this sample were the only evidence available, it could be concluded that the costs of training for designer and technician positions, at least for those who were undergoing training, were not a significant barrier to an adequate supply of labor.[f] In general, employers did not lack for a supply of candidates for their own training programs and for the most part were not facing severe difficulties in hiring the labor they needed. Although the costs of training were rather substantial in many situations, trainees seemed to be able to meet them without much difficulty. Again, this fails to encompass those, especially minority group members, who might have been discouraged by costs. The high drop-out rates from training programs may also be related to training costs, especially as individuals discover they can ultimately enter the field without completing the formal program.

The main effect of training costs is to limit job opportunities primarily to persons who have the ability to pay. Entry is precluded to low-income groups. The low level of capacity utilization in training schools is another result of high training costs. Should, as seems to have been the case more recently, the demand for personnel in these fields accelerate, the pool of persons with ability to pay could prove insufficient to meet the expanded demand. Probably the strongest justification for intervention into the financing of education for these occupations is that it assists low-income persons who might otherwise be unable

[f]This conclusion, however, should be evaluated in light of the limitations in the recent trainee sample discussed in Appendix G.

Table 9-4

How Training Was Financed, Recent Trainees in Chicago (In Numbers)[1]

		Tool & Die Maker and Machinist	*Tool & Die Designer*	*Engineering Technician*	*Electronic Technician*	*Electronic Technician (Correspondence)*
	N =	110	24	11	64	139
Part-time or Full-time Work		36	9	5	30	112
Parents Help		10	6	3	18	8
Spouse Worked		5	1	0	4	5
Loan		0	1	1	6	6
Company Paid		0	1	0	7	4
Scholarship		5	2	0	0	1
M. D. T. A.		82	0	0	0	0
Self (Savings)		9	8	6	3	1
No Answer		0	0	0	0	4

[1] Figures in columns add to more than total N because some respondents cited more than one source of financing.

Source: Mail questionnaires, recent Chicago trainees.

to enter training. The tuition free junior or community college is perhaps the most promising institutional arrangement for making possible participation in training by youngsters from low-income families.

Evaluation of Training

Assessment of the training programs for the four occupations is complicated by the variety of training experiences the practitioners had. The discussion which follows will attempt a general evaluation.

The first point to note is that many start training programs, but few finish them. More than half of the sample training institutions (six of twelve trade schools, seven of eleven technical schools, and both of the correspondence schools for electronic technicians) said that completion rates in their various programs run less than 50 percent. Presumably an important reason for this is that entry to the four occupations requires no specified or prescribed preparation. Unlike the two medical occupations studied, there is no state control or professional standards set for the hiring of personnel. When an individual feels that he has learned enough to do a job, he can quit school and look for work.

Although the drop-out rate from training programs is high, it should be noted that a drop-out is not necessarily terminating his training forever. He may either interrupt his employment to return to school at a later date or pursue his schooling on a part-time basis. The fact that this occurs frequently is suggested in two ways by data in this study. First, the mail questionnaire follow-up of Chicago recent trainees showed that a large proportion of those who were identified by the training schools as drop-outs had returned to school by the time of the survey.[g] The proportions of drop-outs who were again attending school, either part time or full time, at the time of the mail follow-up were 64 percent of the former tool and die machinist trainees, 53 percent of the designers, 60 percent of the engineering technicians (nonelectronic) and 35 percent of the electronic technician trainees. Second, many of the practitioners, tool and die makers excepted, had plans for additional formal training, either on a full- or part-time basis (see Table 9-5). From 60 to 80 percent of the designers and technicians said they planned to take further training, suggesting the close correlation between continuing education and occupational progress in the three occupations. The likelihood that most of these plans will be followed through is suggested by the fact that a majority of practitioners had already taken some supplementary training since their first employment in the three occupations. This was the case for 57 percent of the designers, 64 percent of the electronic technicians, and 52 percent of the metal technicians. What is suggested is that the pattern of schooling and employment is not one of discrete chronology, but of interchange and coexistence. The fact that dropouts from training in any one class are high, therefore, is perhaps not as significant as it first appears.

The data in Table 9-5 summarize the responses of the practitioners to

[g]Drop-out respondents to the mail questionnaire included 22 in tool and die making or machinist training, 15 in designing, 20 in engineering technology or technician (nonelectronics) training, 65 in training as electronic technicians, and 29 taking correspondence course work in electronics.

questions regarding the formal occupational training they had received. The responses refer to specialized training other than that obtained in high school or college. In general, the responses indicate high satisfaction with both classroom and on-the-job or apprenticeship training for all four occupations. As would be expected in a situation where training experiences are so diverse, not everyone has the same high regard for the instruction he received. Nevertheless, at least two-thirds and generally more of the practitioners rated their training as excellent or good. Among the more dissatisfied, poor teachers were the most commonly criticized aspect of classroom instruction. With respect to on-the-job training, the tool and die tradesmen were most often critical of the inadequate number of instructors; electronic technicians found particular fault with the quality of equipment and limitations in facilities. The general picture, however, is one of satisfaction, and a majority, in most cases a large majority, found their training relevant to the jobs they were doing. That is, most felt they were making full use of their training in their jobs.

Not only were the practitioners generally pleased with their training, but many, as already noted, were eager to get more. The evidence is clear that this desire is related to the workers' perceptions that training is the key to progress in their fields. Most of them viewed prospects for advancement as good or excellent and saw training as the way to self-improvement and higher professional and financial status. The frequent seepage into higher status engineering classifications made this self-improvement a tenable position. Most of the minority who did not see advancement prospects in a positive light felt that the limits of their occupation had already been reached or that they lacked the requisite education and training. Presumably because of their favorable feelings about their work and their prospects, almost all of the practitioners anticipated remaining in their present occupation. Those who didn't had their sights on higher level positions.

On the basis of worker evaluations, then, there is little basis for criticizing the quality or relevance of the training available for the four occupations. Employers, however, were somewhat more cautious in their evaluations. In evaluating training programs outside those of their own companies, the percentages of employers giving various assessments were as follows.

	For Tool & Die Makers	*For Tool & Die Designers*	*For Electronic Technicians*	*For Metal Technicians*
Excellent or good	39%	35%	47%	39%
Varies	46	31	43	44
Fair or poor	15	34	10	17

Although employer ratings of training programs also tend to be favorable, the large proportions unwilling to lump all training institutions into the same rating category gives clearer evidence than the worker evaluations that there are

Table 9-5

Aspects of Workers. Training Programs, Four Occupations, Chicago and St. Louis Combined (In Percents)

		Tool & Die Maker	*Tool & Die Designer*	*Electronic Technician*	*Metal Technician*
Evaluation of Classroom Training	N =	118	66	76	21
Excellent–Good, Total		78%	75%	81%	66%
Excellent–Good, Recent Entrants		59	82	77	50
Excellent–Good, Veterans		82	74	84	70
Why Evaluate Less than Good	N =	25	16	15	8
Classes Too Large		12%	12%	13%	25%
Too Little Class & Theory Work		20	6	13	13
Not Enough Practical Work		12	6	13	--
Poor Teachers		36	38	20	63
Class Work Obsolete or Unrelated		12	6	20	--
Other		8	31	20	--
Evaluation of On-the-Job Training	N =	160	62	47	12
Excellent–Good, Total		79%	90%	70%	75%
Excellent–Good, Recent Entrants		83	88	75	100
Excellent–Good, Veterans		79	91	66	70
Why Evaluate On-the-Job Training Less than Good	N =	30	7	14	3
Too Few Instructors		30%	57%	21%	--
Not Enough Variety		30	--	7	--

Table 9-5 (*continued*)

		Tool & Die Maker	*Tool & Die Designer*	*Electronic Technician*	*Metal Technician*
Poor Equipment & Limited Facilities		7	--	36	--
Other		33	43	36	100%
Problems Had to Overcome	N =	174	89	85	26
None		87%	80%	65%	77%
Financial		4	8	9	8
Other		9	12	26	16
Whether Making Full Use of Training	N =	180	93	90	30
Yes		81%	77%	56%	87%
No--Training Too Specialized		1	2	2	--
No--Work Too Specialized		1	2	6	--
No--Other		17	19	36	13
Whether Took Supplementary Training	N =	177	95	92	31
Yes		42%	57%	64%	52%
Why Took Supplementary Training	N =	50	37	52	15
Required by Employer		20%	24%	13%	13%
Self-improvement		58	43	46	73
Advancement in Same Occupation		8	8	12	--
Advancement in Different Occupation		4	5	4	--

(continued)

Table 9-5 (*continued*)

		Tool & Die Maker	*Tool & Die Designer*	*Electronic Technician*	*Metal Technician*
Suggested by Employer for Advancement		2	11	8	7
Other		8	9	18	7
Whether Has Plans for Further Training	N =	177	92	91	31
Yes		28%	61%	82%	65%
What Can be Gained from Further Training	N =	42	47	72	31
Self-improvement or Better Background		42%	47%	28%	38%
Professional Status		26	21	40	13
Supervisory Status		5	- -	3	3
Improve Promotion Chances		12	13	7	10
Improve Status, Finances & Respons.		10	13	18	6
Personal Satisfaction		5	6	4	29
Chances for Advancement	N =	177	92	91	32
Excellent or Good		38%	60%	71%	60%
Why "Fair" or "Poor"	N =	82	28	26	9
Reached Limit		58%	54%	38%	33%
Age		24	7	12	- -
Lack of College Degree or Appropriate Education		9	29	27	56

Table 9-5 (*continued*)

		Tool & Die Maker	*Tool & Die Designer*	*Electronic Technician*	*Metal Technician*
Other		8	11	24	11
Why Good or Excellent	N =	45	40	48	15
Training and Experience		27%	22%	12%	33%
High Demand for Skills or Expanding Industry		31	38	14	27
If You're Good, can Advance		20	15	21	33
Other		22	25	53	7
Whether Will Stay in Occupation	N =	181	95	91	33
Yes		91%	89%	77%	85%
Uncertain		3	3	4	--
Why Won't Stay	N =	181	95	91	33
Wants to Get Professional Degree		--	28%	65%	100%
Other		11%	44	17	--
Wants Supervisory Work		11	28	12	--
Wants White Collar Job		56	--	6	--
Wants Design Work		22	--	--	--

Source: Worker interviews.

significant differences in quality among institutions. Employers were asked to name both good and poor training institutions in their geographic area. Many were reluctant to single out institutions for criticism, but the minority who did made it clear that some training places were presenting themselves as trainers for occupations for which they were not qualified to train. Some of those so identified were large establishments charging high fees for their services.

The study contained a number of other indicators of the variation in quality of training schools. One of these is that only a minority of persons in the worker samples had been trained at one of the schools in the training school sample (see Table 9-6).

Although there are a number of possible explanations for this, it is quite likely that a primary one is that the graduates of some of the training schools are unable to obtain employment with the major employers in the two labor markets because their schools have poor reputations among employers. This is supported to some extent by the particular schools represented among the practitioners. For example, all but seven of the thirty-four electronics technicians in Chicago trained at sample schools came from the same technical school. The other nine technical schools in the Chicago sample provided only seven electronics technicians in the sample of practitioners.

The other indicator of variation in quality of training programs is the evaluation of specialized training given by the practitioners who attended the sample training schools. Their evaluations of the training they had received were somewhat less favorable than those given by the practitioners generally, and their evaluations varied widely depending upon which school they had attended. The first point is illustrated in the following tabulation which shows the proportion of all practitioners and the proportion of those trained in the sample training schools giving fair and poor ratings to their classroom training.

Proportion of Fair and Poor Evaluations of Classroom Training

			Engineering Technicians	
	Tool & Die Makers	*Tool & Die Designers*	*Elec.*	*Metal*
Chicago				
All Practitioners	26%	32%	19%	37%
Practitioners Trained in Sample Schools	40%	37%	18%	44%

St. Louis				
All Practitioners	13%	0	20%	---
Practitioners Trained in Sample Schools	14%	0	25%	---

Although the differences are not large, except in the case of tool and die makers, the direction of the responses are generally less favorable for the practitioners from the sample training schools. Of more significance, however, was the variation in evaluations among practitioners from different schools. From some of the schools all practitioners gave excellent or good ratings; from others all gave fair or poor ratings.

Employers expressed the least satisfaction with the training available for tool and die designers. It is quite possible that the more specialized nature of the design needs for each employer made any general type of design training less than satisfactory. In general, trade and technical schools were favored by employers for training in tool and die making and electronics, and colleges were favored for engineering technology. Employers were about evenly split as to the best type of training for tool and die designers. As noted earlier, however, except for tool and die makers, a majority of practitioners in all the occupations had at least some college work.

One further note on evaluation of training needs to be made. It has to do with the adequacy and quality of students attracted into various training programs. As noted earlier, most employers were satisfied with the people they selected for their own company training programs. Training school administrators, however, were not so enthusiastic about all of the students who entered their programs. About half of the schools interviewed (six of the twelve trade schools and five of the eleven technical schools) expressed satisfaction with the quality of students obtained. The others experienced varying degrees of dissatisfaction, indicating such shortcomings among their students as lack of verbal skills, deficiencies in mathematics and science, and inadequate technical backgrounds. Since most of the schools had rather lenient entrance requirements, the phenomenon is not very surprising. The lenient standards are undoubtedly related to the inability of most of the schools to attract enough students to reach capacity.

In part, the difference in perception of the quality of students between the training schools and the employers can be attributed to the fact that they were talking about a somewhat different clientele. As noted earlier, most of the people in employer training programs, again with the exception of tool makers, had some college training. Many of those in the trade and technical schools had only high school or lower level educational preparation. Particularly among the large number of training school drop-outs, the student quality probably was lower than among those who entered company training programs.

Table 9-6

Proportion of Practitioners Trained in Sample Training Schools, Chicago and St. Louis

	Tool & Die Makers	Tool & Die Designers	Engineering Technicians Elec.	Engineering Technicians Metal
Chicago				
No. in Worker Sample	119	63	76	23
No. Trained in Sample Training Schools	30	27	34	9
Percent Trained in Sample Training Schools	25	43	45	39
St. Louis				
No. in Worker Sample	65	33	16	10
No. Trained in Sample Training Schools	28	10	4	3
Percent Trained in Sample Training Schools	43	30	25	30

Source: Worker sample.

Placement

The major placement question is whether or not the labor market mechanism effectively serves the transition from training to appropriate employment. Two questions are involved: Is the transition made quickly so that bottlenecks do not stand in the way of effective use of available labor? Do trainees find employment suitable to the training they have received? Both of these questions have been explored to some extent in previous chapters, and those discussions need only be referred to.

The time involved in the transition from training into employment was discussed in Chapter 7. It was noted that in all four occupations the time lapse between completion of training and finding a job was very brief (see, for example, Table 7-6 in Chapter 7). Both practitioners and recent trainees, for the most part, found their first job in a month or less.

The process by which the transition takes place was examined in Chapter 8. Emphasis was placed in the discussion on the influence of the operation of the internal labor market. The analysis showed, as has the examination of training programs in this chapter, that the training-employment relationship is a very close one. That is, large proportions of workers reported that they were already employed at the time they completed their training program. This reflects the fact that workers often enter training programs while they are employed and that often the training program they are in involves some on-the-job training with their present employer. The frequent closeness of the training-employment relationship assures an efficient placement process in many instances. In other cases, most trainees found employment shortly after leaving training.

On the question of the relevance of the training received to post-training employment, it has also been shown that a close relationship existed for the sample of employed practitioners. Most of the practitioners reported that they were making full use of their training on their current jobs. Additional evidence on the point is available, however, from an examination of the post-labor market experience of recent trainees.[h] The data are shown in Table 9-7.

With the exception of those trainees who had taken their training through correspondence schools, at the time of the survey a large majority of those who had completed training programs were employed on jobs that were in the same or related occupations for which they were trained. The closest fit between training and employment is shown for tool and die makers; in the other three occupations, numbers approximating one-third of the total were not employed in jobs that fit closely the training programs they had completed. Examination of the entire post-training occupational experience of the trainees reveals about the same picture. Again, tool and die makers show the closest relationship of their subsequent employment to their training experience. Among the other three occupations, the electronic technicians were somewhat less successful in obtaining training-related employment than the others.

Most of those who had completed training programs were employed at the time of the mail survey, although the percent employed among engineering technicians was substantially below that of the other occupations. The

[h]The practitioners, by definition, were employed in the relevant occupations. The trainees, a sample selected from the records of training institutions, may or may not be so employed.

Table 9-7

Post-Training Employment Experiences of Recent Chicago Trainees and Drop-Outs (In Percents)

	Tool & Die Maker and Machinist		Tool and Die Designer	
	Complete	*Dropout*	*Complete*	*Dropout*
N =	110	22	24	15
Time to First Job After Training				
Has Not Worked	2%	27%	12%	13%
Already on Job During Training	3	32	54	80
Less Than One Month	86	18	17	7
One Month or More	5	9	17	--
Unknown	4	14	--	--
Current Job				
Same as That Trained for	8	14	63	27
Related, but Lower Level	17	23	4	27
Unrelated to Training	5	18	17	7
Employed in Apprenticeship	65	5	--	7
Not Employed	5	32	17	13
Unknown	--	9	--	20
Where Employed				
Chicago Area	81	45	42	60
Illinois	5	5	17	13
Adjacent State	2	--	13	--

	Engineering Technician		Electronic Technician		Electronic Technician (correspondence)	
	Complete	*Dropout*	*Complete*	*Dropout*	*Complete*	*Dropout*
N =	11	20	64	28	139	59
	9%	35%	3%	11%	1%	2%
	45	30	31	32	64	56
	36	20	47	36	8	12
	1	5	16	11	11	2
	9	10	3	11	17	29
	55	20	42	7	7	--
	9	10	19	14	14	5
	--	20	23	50	51	81
	--	--	3	--	2	--
	36	45	3	21	9	3
	--	5	9	7	17	10
	36	35	62	54	1	2
	9	15	5	--	9	5
	--	--	6	14	24	31

(continued)

Table 9-7 *(continued)*

Where Employed (cont.)	Tool & Die Maker and Machinist *Complete*	Tool & Die Maker and Machinist *Dropout*	Tool & Die Designer *Complete*	Tool & Die Designer *Dropout*
Elsewhere	6	5	11	--
Military Service	1	--	--	--
Not Employed	5	32	17	13
Unknown	--	14	--	13
Industry of Employment				
Electronics	9	--	--	--
Metal Working	42	27	46	13
Job Shop (metal)	26	9	17	27
Other	12	23	17	20
Not Working	5	32	17	13
Unknown	5	9	4	27
Current Labor Market Activity				
Employed	94%	68%	83%	87%
Looking for Work (unemployed)	4	--	8	--
Training for Same Occupation	--	--	--	--
Attending Technical School	--	27	--	13
Attending College	--	--	--	--
Military	2	5	8	--
Other Training Program	1	--	--	--

Engineering Technician		Electronic Technician		Electronic Technician (correspondence)	
Complete	*Dropout*	*Complete*	*Dropout*	*Complete*	*Dropout*
19	--	16	4	43	42
--	--	5	4	3	--
36	45	3	18	5	3
--	5	3	7	14	17
9	5	58	11	19	10
9	25	2	4	2	--
--	--	--	--	2	2
18	20	27	54	61	71
36	45	3	21	4	3
27	5	11	11	12	14
64%	55%	88%	79%	90%	95%
--	10	2	--	--	--
9	5	--	11	--	--
--	25	--	1	--	--
9	5	5	4	--	3
18	--	6	--	2	--
--	--	--	1	--	--

(continued)

Table 9-7 *(continued)*

Current Labor Market Activity (cont.)	Tool & Die Maker and Machinist		Tool & Die Designer	
	Complete	*Dropout*	*Complete*	*Dropout*
Other out of Labor Force	--	--	--	--
Unknown	--	--	--	--
General Post-Training Occupational Experience				
No Employment	2	23	12	13
Entire Period in Occupation Trained for	73	18	67	47
Most in Occupation Trained for	1	4	4	--
Less Than ½ in Occupation Trained for	4	--	--	--
None in Occupation Trained for But in Labor Force	4	14	8	7
None in Occupation Trained for, Out of Labor Force	1	14	8	--
Most in Related Occupation	17	18	--	13
Relationship Not Clear	--	--	--	--
Unknown	--	9	--	20

Engineering Technician		Electronic Technician		Electronic Technician (correspondence)	
Complete	*Dropout*	*Complete*	*Dropout*	*Complete*	*Dropout*
--	--	--	7	4	2
--	--	--	--	1	--
9	30	2	11	1	2
64	25	41	7	6	--
--	--	3	--	2	--
--	--	2	--	6	2
--	30	25	50	52	86
--	--	2	7	3	--
18	10	17	14	14	3
9	--	9	4	6	--
--	5	--	7	9	7

(continued)

Table 9-7 (*continued*)

	Tool & Die Maker and Machinist		Tool and Die Designer	
	Complete	*Dropout*	*Complete*	*Dropout*
Evaluation of Training Received				
Excellent	45%	9%	17%	7%
Good	41	27	50	40
Fair	9	32	29	13
Poor	2	14	--	13
No Answer	4	18	4	27

Engineering Technician		Electronic Technician		Electronic Technician (correspondence)	
Complete	*Dropout*	*Complete*	*Dropout*	*Complete*	*Dropout*
27%	20%	25%	18%	29%	22%
45	35	59	43	45	41
18	25	12	25	22	30
--	15	2	7	4	5
9	5	2	7	1	2

Source: Mail questionnaire, recent Chicago trainees.

percentage unemployed in all trainee groups was very low, particularly considering the age group involved. Somewhat an exception to this generalization is the case of the tool and die designers, for whom the eight percent unemployment rate is at least double that of any of the other occupational groups. The higher rate probably reflects the fact mentioned earlier, that the demand for designers is particularly focused on experienced people. Also, those who have just finished schooling cannot properly be described as designers if they have had no experience. Most of those not employed, in all of the occupations, had returned to school or were in the military service.

As Table 9-7 shows, most of the trainees were well satisfied, as were the practitioners discussed earlier, with the quality of the training they had received.[i] There were, however, substantial numbers in all four occupations who gave only fair or even poor ratings to their training. The greatest degree of dissatisfaction occurred among the tool and die designers. As has been stated a number of times previously, the content and type of training programs appropriate for designers poses a greater problem than in the other occupations. And the post-training experience of designers appears to confirm this difficulty.

The electronic technicians trained in correspondence courses present a case apart from the other trainee groups. To begin with, nearly all of them were residents of places outside the Chicago area. They lived in all parts of the United States and, therefore, were not participants in the labor market here under study. A large majority of them were employed persons taking the correspondence course in their spare time. And the analysis of their post-training labor market experience shows that few of them were in jobs related to the training they had taken. It is not possible, on the basis of the mail questionnaire survey, to determine the reasons for this experience. On the one hand it is possible that the training they received did not adequately prepare them for related employment. It is also possible, however, that many, or even most, of them were not taking the courses with an occupational objective in mind. Their objective may have been avocational or it may have been to obtain a supplementary skill, in which cases they may not have sought related employment. The fact that three-quarters of them, for example, rated their training as excellent or good, in spite of their unrelated post-training experience, suggests that their interest in the training courses may not have been vocational.

Table 9-7 also summarizes the post-training labor market experiences of those trainees who dropped out of training before completing the program in which they registered. Like those who had completed a training program, most of the drop-outs were employed at the time of the survey. Substantially smaller proportions, however, had worked in the same or a related occupation as that for which they had begun training. It is notable, however, that substantial minorities did find employment in such positions, indicating again that entry to the four occupations is not limited to those who have completed prescribed training programs. Most of those not employed at the time of the survey were back in school again. In each of the trainee groups, the dropouts had less

[i] As noted in Appendix C, this could, in part, be the result of factors influencing the selection of persons for this sample.

favorable ratings of their training experience than did those who had completed training.

The responses of the recent trainees suggest three general conclusions regarding the effectiveness of the labor market in facilitating the adjustment from training to employment. First, the process appears to be a smooth one for trainees in all four occupations. In large part this is the case because of the many instances in which training and employment take place concurrently. For many there is no break between the two. And in cases where the trainee was not employed during the period of his training, the instances in which as much as a month was required to obtain employment were few. Second, nearly all of the trainees, unless they remain out of the labor force, find employment in the occupation, or in a related occupation, for which they were trained. The worst record in this respect was that of the electronic technicians, one-fourth of whom had no employment as electronic technician following the completion of training. Most of this latter group, interestingly, were trained at the same two schools in the area, which suggests that these two schools may not have come up to the standards of employers. The sample, however, was too small to be very positive about this conclusion. Third, those who dropped training before completion were much less likely to have had post-training employment in work related to the training they had begun. Even among drop-outs, however, only a small minority of those who were in the labor force most of the period following their dropping out failed to find related employment. Many of them returned to school again for further training.

The analysis of the post-training experience of recent trainees fails, therefore, to reveal any serious labor market barriers to the transition from training to work. In spite of great variation in the types, length, and content of training programs, most trainees find their way quickly into employment related to their training. Of the four occupations, tool and die designer poses the most difficult problem in this respect.

10 Factors Affecting Supply: Internal Adjustments and Employee Benefits

The manpower policies of the individual firm have an effect upon the adequacy of the supply of labor in the four occupations under consideration. Analysis of the extent and limits of adjusting to labor shortages through changes in manpower utilization practices by the firm and consideration of the relevance of employee benefits and certain labor relations matters to the shortages represents, therefore, an important element in identification and assessment of the shortages.

Manpower Utilization

Traditional economic analysis looks at the supply of labor to a particular occupation as a function of the wage rate. In a static model, the definition of the occupation is fixed and technology is given. Theoretically, however, the supply of labor to an occupation might be varied at a given wage rate by changing such variables as the minimum qualifications for membership in the occupation, the investment in training of workers, the distribution of duties among the occupation and related occupations (job redesign), the capital-labor ratio, and the quality of the product or service produced. The following discussion considers the extent to which these variables figure in the adjustment to labor shortage in the four occupations under study.

Hiring and Training

It has been noted in previous chapters that employer hiring practices for all four occupations tend to be flexible. That is, formal educational and training prerequisites for employment and for entry into training are of secondary importance. Of greater importance is the aptitude and ability of the individual to do the job required. The necessary ability can be acquired for any of the occupations through a variety of routes, ranging from on-the-job experience through trade and technical schools and colleges.

In all four occupations, minimum hiring qualifications have remained unchanged in recent years in most companies. The educational qualifications of entrants to the occupations, however, have risen, reflecting the general rise in the educational level of the population and labor force. It has been shown in previous chapters, in fact, that there has been no shortage of qualified candidates available for entry into company training programs. As a result, it has generally not been necessary for companies to lower entry or hiring requirements as an adjustment device in meeting the shortage. However, according to Table 10-1, a small minority of employers did say it had been necessary for them to hire tool and die tradesmen whose qualifications were below standards that had previously been applied. These were at least counterbalanced by employers who indicated they were able to apply higher standards.

An element in employer hiring practices related to the supply of labor is the fact that nonwhites have been utilized in only very small numbers in the four occupations. Whether or not this is the result of discriminatory hiring policies and/or practices (and to some degree it almost certainly is), it has not been a major cause of the labor shortage, since the problem has not been one of a shortage of qualified candidates for training. To the extent that discriminatory hiring practices have prevailed, however, the result has been a rationing of job opportunities among whites only. In the context of an analysis of labor shortages, the relevant interpretation of the racial distribution of practitioners of the four occupations is that limitations of manpower have not been so severe as to cause employers to turn their recruitment efforts toward minority groups as an alternative to larger than normal wage increases.

Company training programs are of great importance in determining the supply of tool and die tradesmen, particularly tool and die makers. For technicians the role of the employer is of less importance; training in the firm, where it occurs at all, is usually of short duration and focused on orienting the technician to company methods and products.

For tool and die makers and designers, companies do one of two things. Either they do no training at all and rely on their ability to hire workers who have been trained elsewhere, or they train at a level that will meet their own perceived needs for personnel, within the limits of their training capacity.[a] A major barrier to adjusting to shortages through the expansion of training programs is limitations in training capacity. Also, training costs are a factor keeping some firms from conducting training programs at all, as well as limiting the size of training programs of others. Very few firms without training programs had even tentative plans for establishing them at the time of this study. And most firms with programs had not expanded them in the past five years.

As alternatives to lowering hiring standards and expanding company training programs, most firms were able to meet their manpower needs by working their tradesmen overtime, contracting out some of their work (mainly tool and die

[a]In a minority of companies with training programs, the amount of training of tool and die makers is limited by journeymen-apprentice ratios established in collective bargaining agreements.

Table 10-1

Aspects of Internal Adjustments to Occupational Shortages by Firms, Four Occupations, Chicago and St. Louis Combined (In Percents)

	Tool & Die Maker	*Tool & Die Designer*	*Electronic Technician*	*Metal Technician*
N =	(57)	(31)	(26)	(24)
Have Duties in Occupation Changed in Past Few Years--Yes	(55) 42	(28) 39	(25) 84	(23) 48
How Duties Have Changed	(23)	(11)	(21)	(11)
Work More Complex	9	54	29	36
Work More Specialized	30	--	5	18
Requires More Precision	26	--	19	18
Taking Over Duties of Higher-Level Occupation	9	18	29	9
New Products & Techniques	22	27	19	18
Taking Over Duties of Lower-Level Occupation	4	--	--	--
Whether Former Duties Now Done by Other Workers or Machines	(54)	(27)	(25)	(23)
No	76	81	56	78
Yes, by Higher-Level People	--	11	20	13
Yes, by Lower-Level People	24	7	24	4
Yes, by Computer or Other Machine	--	--	--	--

Table 10-1 (*continued*)

	Tool & Die Maker	*Tool & Die Designer*	*Electronic Technician*	*Metal Technician*
Whether Significant Expansion of Other Occupational Groups to do Duties of Occupation	(53)	(27)	(25)	(23)
No	92	92	92	96
Yes, at Higher Level	--	--	4	--
Yes, at Lower Level	8	8	4	4
Effect of Shortage on Company Operations	(57)	(31)	(26)	(24)
No Significant Effect	56	68	73	67
More Overtime	9	10	4	12
Substitution of Lower Level People	2	--	4	--
Substitution of Higher Level People	--	--	4	4
Slowing of Work, Decreased Efficiency & Increased Costs	18	10	15	17
Contracting Out of Work	16	13	--	--
Have Minimum Hiring Requirements Changed	(50)	(27)	(21)	(22)
No	88	70	67	82
Yes, Raised	6	15	33	14
Yes, Lowered	6	15	--	--

(continued)

Table 10-1 (*continued*)

	Tool & Die Maker	*Tool & Die Designer*	*Electronic Technician*	*Metal Technician*
Have Minimum Hiring Requirements Changed (cont.)	(50)	(27)	(21)	(22)
Yes, Direction Not Specified	--	--	--	5
Any Adjustment of Hours or Salaries Because of Shortage	(46)	(25)	(20)	(22)
No	72	84	75	82
Yes, Increase in Wages or Salaries	2	--	20	--
Yes, More Overtime	20	8	--	14
Yes, Increase in Both Hours and Wages	2	4	--	--
Yes, Nature Not Specified	4	4	5	5
Whether Greater Supply of Engineers Would Affect Demand for Technicians	n.a.	n.a.	(21)	(22)
N. A.			5	18
No Effect			90	64
Would Increase Demand for Technicians			5	9
Would Decrease Demand for Technicians			--	9

Table 10-1 (*continued*)

	Tool & Die Maker	*Tool & Die Designer*	*Electronic Technician*	*Metal Technician*
Whether Greater Supply of Technicians Would Affect Demand for Engineers	n.a	n.a.	(21)	(22)
N. A.			--	14
No Effect			90	68
Would Increase Demand for Engineers			--	--
Would Decrease Demand for Engineers			10	14
Would Not Affect Demand, but Would Affect Use of Engineers			--	5
No. of Openings for Engineers				
None	2	--	--	4
One–Two	18	16	15	17
Three–Four	12	13	--	4
Five–Nine	26	16	15	33
Ten or More	42	55	70	42
Special Steps Taken to Meet Shortages	(53)	(33)	(26)	(24)
None	56	61	77	84
Contract Out	25	24	15	8

(*continued*)

Table 10-1 (*continued*)

	Tool & Die Maker	*Tool & Die Designer*	*Electronic Technician*	*Metal Technician*
Special Steps Taken to Meet Shortages (cont.)	(53)	(33)	(26)	(24)
New or Revitalized Training Program	--	--	--	--
Overtime Work	11	12	8	4
Contract Out and Add to Training	2	--	--	4
Contract Out and Overtime	4	3	--	--
Use of All-Purpose Utility Dies	2	--	--	--

Source: Employer interviews.

making),[b] and/or intensifying recruiting efforts. In the context of the relatively mild shortage situation, these methods of adjustment were apparently reasonably successful and more economical than hiring substandard workers or establishing or expanding company training programs. With the high age level of the tool and die maker work force, and the resultant high replacement needs anticipated for the future, it is likely that future shortages will grow more intense unless incentives are provided to encourage greater participation in training by industrial firms.

Job Redesign

Most of the evidence from the interviews with employers and workers indicates that job redesign played a minor role in adjustment to the shortage and, furthermore, that present utilization patterns offer little opportunity to adjust through this device.

Substantial numbers of employers (see Table 10-2) did indicate that the duties involved in the four occupations had changed during the past few years (in the case of employers of electronic technicians, a large majority so indicated). With the exception of the tool and die makers, however, employers said the changes were in the direction of increasing complexity; that is, members of the occupation were more likely to be taking over duties formerly performed by higher level personnel (e.g., engineers) than the reverse. These tendencies do not suggest great possibilities for job dilution or job simplification as an adjustment device. In fact, in a large majority of firms tasks were not being broken down so that workers with less training and skill could perform them. Tool and die making and the work of electronic technicians were the most susceptible to job dilution. About one-quarter of the employers of workers in these two occupations said lower level manpower was now doing some of the duties formerly performed by tool and die makers and electronic technicians. Over 90 percent of the employers for each occupation said, however, that there had been no significant expansion of employment in other occupational groups to do duties formerly performed by personnel in the occupations under consideration here. And virtually none of the firms indicated that company operations were adjusted in the face of manpower shortages by the use of greater numbers of lower level personnel. This suggests that to the extent substitution was occurring, it was being done independently of considerations of labor shortage. In the minds of employers, at least, the distinctions among various occupational groups are fairly firm, and duties cannot be shifted among them with any degree of facility. Interesting enough, given traditional assumptions about rationality, almost all employers felt that the relative availability of technicians and engineers had no effect on the extent to which either occupational group was utilized.

The interviews with the practitioners revealed a similar picture of relatively

[b] As was indicated in Chapter 7, the ability of some firms to contract out their tool and die work may reflect the higher wage rates paid by job shops and their consequent ability to attract more easily a tool and die work force.

Table 10-2

Worker Perceptions of Their Occupation, Four Occupations, Chicago and St. Louis Combined (In Percents)

	Tool & Die Maker	*Tool & Die Designer*	*Electronic Technician*	*Metal Technician*
N =	184	96	92	33
Any Major Change in Duties Since Began Job—Yes	(182) 29	(94) 28	(92) 38	(31) 55
Why Changes Occurred	(48)	(27)	(33)	(17)
Normal Advancement in Occupation	29	19	24	24
More Responsibility	35	74	54	65
Promotion, Transfer, Training, Experience	16	4	21	6
Less Responsibility, More Automation	17	--	--	6
New Materials (e.g., Plastic Dies)	2	4	--	--
Major Changes Since Began Type of Work—Yes	(174) 44	(91) 47	(88) 43	(26) 46
Why Changes Occurred	(67)	(43)	(32)	(12)
Normal Advancement and Changes in Technology	63	35	34	8
More Responsibility or Specialization	15	32	41	58
Promotion, Transfer, Training, Experience	7	14	12	33

Table 10-2 (*continued*)

	Tool & Die Maker	*Tool & Die Designer*	*Electronic Technician*	*Metal Technician*
Why Changes Occured (cont.)	(67)	(43)	(32)	(12)
Less Responsibility, More Automation	10	5	3	--
Wider Variety of Duties and Jobs	4	14	9	--
Whether Will Stay With Present Employer	(179)	(94)	(90)	(33)
Yes	86	78	79	79
Recent Entrants	70	58	71	62
Veterans	88	84	84	84
Under Age 25	40	45	73	40
Reasons Expects to Stay With Present Employer	(95)	(51)	(41)	(16)
Pay	1	2	15	--
Fringe Benefits	6	2	7	6
Job Security	24	20	10	12
Good Place to Work and/or Good Location	49	47	39	62
Other	19	29	29	19
Reasons Will Not Stay With Present Employer	(15)	(8)	(6)	(2)
Pay	13	--	--	--

(*continued*)

Table 10-2 (*continued*)

	Tool & Die Maker	*Tool & Die Designer*	*Electronic Technician*	*Metal Technician*
Reasons Will Not Stay With Present Employer (cont.)	(15)	(8)	(6)	(2)
Working Conditions	20	--	17	--
Poor Chance for Advancement	47	12	33	--
Usually Moves when Better Offer Available	13	50	--	50
Other	7	38	50	50
What Respondent Likes About Occupation—Percent Mentioning the Following	(183)	(96)	(92)	(33)
Job Content	90	92	91	94
Security	51	45	32	45
Pay	39	38	40	39
Fringe Benefits	42	37	32	48
Working Conditions	45	41	41	48
What Doesn't Like About Occupation—Percent Mentioning the Following				
Job Content	13	8	6	12
Security	3	4	7	3
Pay	35	20	23	18

Table 10-2 (*continued*)

	Tool & Die Maker	*Tool & Die Designer*	*Electronic Technician*	*Metal Technician*
What Doesn't Like About Occupation—Percent Mentioning the Following (cont.)				
Fringe Benefits	7	10	7	--
Working Conditions	14	10	10	18
Whether Making Full Use of Training—Yes	81	77	44	87

Source: Worker interviews.

little change in job design (see Table 10-2). Only a minority of practitioners in each occupation said the nature of their duties had changed since beginning their jobs or since beginning in the type of work. Those who indicated that change had occurred generally described the change as being related to normal advancement or progress in the occupation rather than fundamental change in the nature of the occupation.

Except for the electronic technicians, a large majority of the practitioners felt they were making full use of their training in their present positions. In the view of the electronic technicians, however, the possibilities for job redesign are greater in their occupation than in the others. And the employer interviews indicated that some substitution of lower level personnel had been occurring in this occupation.

The conclusion that the possibilities are not great for making better use of practitioners through job redesign can also be drawn from the responses of the practitioners to questions concerning their likes and dislikes about their work. Over 90 percent in each occupation were attracted to some aspect of the job content of their work. Very few found cause for dissatisfaction in the nature of any of their duties. It is unlikely that this pattern of responses would have emerged had they felt their talents and skills were being seriously underutilized or if major parts of their jobs had been diluted away. Nor would it be likely that such large proportions of them would indicate that they planned to remain with their present employer, particularly since alternative job opportunities were relatively plentiful. As would be anticipated, the younger workers expressed more inclination to change employers than the older workers. But the reasons they gave for their interest in moving did not, in general, seem to reflect dissatisfaction with the nature of the work they were doing.

In general, then, there is little evidence that job redesign was either an important aspect of adjustment to the shortage or that there is significant opportunity to adjust to shortages in these occupations by this method. The occupation of electronic technician appeared to offer the greatest opportunity for such adjustment, but apparently the shortage was not severe enough at the time of the study to have produced this result. On the other hand, the process of job redesign can proceed gradually and subtly, and it is possible that it has occurred to a greater extent than is shown in this study. In many small ways, changes in job assignment might occur without either supervisors or workers being particularly aware that they are occurring. Had the study been closely concentrated on this particular question, more change might have been shown to have taken place. To discover such change would require intensive observation over a long period of time.

Capital Substitution

The substitution of capital equipment for human resources has not been an important method for adjusting to shortages in the four occupations in recent years. Technological changes, in other words, have had little effect on the nature of the occupations under consideration or on the demand for workers in the occupations.

Employers were asked whether there were any duties formerly performed by workers in the four occupations that were now being done by workers in other occupational categories or by computers or machines. Almost none indicated that the introduction of new machines had had any significant effect on the nature of the work done by these workers in recent years (see Table 10-1). The practitioners were also asked to indicate whether their duties had changed in recent years and, if so, why. Again, only infrequently did their responses suggest that their work had been significantly affected by changes in technology. Only a few said that their jobs involved less responsibility or that more machine automation was involved (see Table 10-2). Only the tool and die makers among the four occupational groups included any number of workers at all who had experienced changes of this type, and even among them it was a very small minority.

A number of studies, mentioned in Chapter 2, indicates possibilities, however, for considerable change in technology in the future that could have very substantial effects on the nature of the four occupations, particularly for tool and die makers and tool and die designers. Computer programming of much of the work in both of these occupations is potentially in the future, and should it occur, the results could be substantial change in the nature of the occupations and in the demand for labor.[1] This potential, however, is developing largely independent of labor market conditions and cannot be viewed as a labor market response to labor shortage. Although it is possible to imagine circumstances in which labor shortages are so severe that they stimulate the development and introduction of capital equipment, none of the six occupations examined in this study, medical or industrial, elicited this type of labor market response in any significant way.

Quality of Service

It was noted in Chapter 8 that shortages in the four occupations were reflected mainly in the length of time required by employers to fill vacancies when they occurred. Two important ways of adjusting to the problem were to work extra hours and, in the case of tool and die making work, to contract work out to other firms. Another consequence of inability to fill vacancies quickly was that output and work flow were slowed for some firms. In answer to the question of how company operations were affected by the shortage, the most frequent response was that work was slowed and/or production was less efficient and more costly, although it was given by only a small minority of firms (see Table 10-1). A majority of firms said the shortage caused no significant change in company operations. Where it occurred, the slowing of operations often resulted in delay in filling orders. In this sense it can be said that one form of adjustment to the shortages was reduction in the quality of service offered to customers. However, this type of adjustment was not very frequent nor did it appear to have very serious consequences. The firms did not feel, for example, that their ability to compete was adversely affected.

The study did not show more serious forms of quality declines. It was not necessary, as it was in the case of medical technologists, for firms to hire workers who did not meet minimum qualifications for employment. Over time, in fact, the qualifications of workers engaged in the four occupations had been improving. And employers, as has been noted a number of times, were neither having difficulty finding qualified applicants for their training programs nor were they forced to upgrade personnel they regarded as marginal for the particular occupation. In fact, educational standards have been increasing steadily.

The analysis of this section makes clear that shortages in the four occupations were not so severe as to provoke employers into very extensive readjustment programs. Programs of hiring and training workers, the design of jobs, the use of capital equipment, and the quality of services provided were only minimally affected by the labor shortages, if at all. The moderate problem that labor shortages presented to employers was handled primarily by working overtime hours and, for tool and die making work, contracting out to firms which had the capacity for additional output. Although it can be said that there were shortages of workers in these skilled and technical occupations in the midst of general labor surplus in the market, the shortages were not serious enough to cause either significant problems for most employers or to result in substantial internal adjustments in the firm. The extent to which adjustment to labor shortages might take place through mechanisms discussed in this section under conditions of more severe labor shortage did not receive a genuine test in this study. It is likely, however, based on the information obtained in this study, that the primary methods would be additional overtime hours and some expansion of company training programs. There was not much evidence that other adjustment mechanisms would either be required or possible, except that more extreme shortage situations would be reflected in more frequent declines in services offered (e.g., longer delays in filling orders).

Employee Benefits and Employee Relations

The discussion above suggests that we are not likely to find much in the pattern of employee benefits in the four occupations that is of importance in explaining labor shortages. This, in fact, is the case.

It has already been noted that few employers adjusted to the shortage by increasing relative wages for workers in the four occupations (see Table 10-1). And the fact that adequate numbers of qualified candidates were available for company training programs indicates that wages were adequate for attracting sufficient numbers of qualified people to the fields.

Table 10-3 summarizes various nonwage benefits provided workers in the four occupations and compares them for firms indicating they were faced with a shortage of workers with benefits in those firms who said they were not. If benefits affect the decision of workers as to where they will accept employment, the no shortage firms would be expected to have more attractive benefit programs. The results are somewhat mixed, although there is some tendency for the results to be as expected. As a general caution it should be noted that the number of firms in the no shortage categories is very small and statistical comparisons are therefore hazardous. Also, for pension and medical plans the level of benefits provided are not compared because of the difficulty of comparing very complex provisions.

With reference to each of the benefit programs listed in Table 10-3, the following picture emerges.

Hospital and medical insurance plan financing is quite standard for all firms. Three-fourths or more of the firms paid the entire cost of the plan in each of the occupational categories. There was little difference between shortage and no shortage firms except for the case of electronic technicians, where financial arrangements for the plans were somewhat more liberal in no shortage firms. Almost all of the firms had provision for disability benefits, and the difference between the two categories of firms was small.

The norm for paid vacations does vary among the firms. For minimum vacations the firms divide on whether one week or two weeks are allowed. For maximum vacations, the norm is either three weeks or four weeks. Minimum vacations for designers and electronic technicians tend to be somewhat more liberal in no shortage firms, and maximum vacations are more generous for all occupational groups among the no shortage firms.

The number of paid holidays varies among all the firms only within the narrow range of six to eight days, and the norm is about the same for both groupings of firms.

The table shows considerable variation among the firms in the arrangements for financing pension plans, but the variation is not consistently related to whether or not the firm felt occupational shortages existed. Among employers of tool and die makers, the shortage firms had the more favorable arrangements for financing pensions. Possibly this is a reflection of the alleged phenomenon mentioned by some employers that tool and die makers are a special breed and that they are more interested in pay now than future security. However, employers of tool and die designers in the shortage category also had more favorable financing arrangements for pensions than did those in the no shortage category. Among employers of electronic technicians, on the other hand, the no shortage firms had the more attractive pension financing plans. The proportion of firms in this category with no pension plan at all was only one-third that of firms in the shortage category, and only one-half as many required the employee to pay the entire cost. Among employers of metal technicians, the difference between the two categories of firms was insignificant. The impact of shortages

Table 10-3

Fringe Benefits in Sample Firms, Four Occupations, Chicago and St. Louis Combined (In Percents)

	Tool & Die Maker			Tool & Die Designer		
	Total	*Shortage Firms*	*No Shortage*	*Total*	*Shortage Firms*	*No Shortage*
N =	57	43	10	31	23	5
Financing of Hospital and Medical Ins.						
All By Co.	80	81	79	87	87	80
All By Worker	4	2	3	--	--	--
Other	15	17	18	13	13	20
Have Disability Benefits	92	95	89	93	91	100
Minimum Vacation/Year						
One Week	88	88	89	60	64	40
Two Weeks	12	12	11	37	32	60
Other	--	--	--	3	5	--
Maximum Vacation/Year						
Two Weeks or Less	5	5	--	3	--	--
Three Weeks	40	47	20	35	39	20
Four Weeks	50	47	60	52	52	60
Over Four Weeks	5	2	20	10	9	20
Holidays Per Year						
Six Days	16	18	10	13	13	20

Electronic Technician			Metal Technician		
To-tal	*Short-age Firms*	*No Short-age*	*To-tal*	*Short-age Firms*	*No Short-age*
26	16	10	24	13	10
75	64	90	92	85	100
--	--	--	4	8	--
25	36	10	4	8	--
92	88	100	92	85	100
50	67	11	50	54	50
50	33	89	46	46	40
--	--	--	4	--	10
--	--	--	4	8	--
36	44	22	38	38	40
60	56	67	50	46	50
4	--	11	8	8	10
19	31	--	4	8	--

(continued)

Table 10-3 (*continued*)

	Tool & Die Maker			Tool & Die Designer		
	To-tal	*Short-age Firms*	*No Short-age*	*To-tal*	*Short-age Firms*	*No Short-age*
Holidays Per Year (cont.)						
Seven Days	42	37	60	51	43	--
Eight Days	42	44	30	35	43	--
Pension Plan Financing						
No Pension	24	15	56	19	13	40
All by Company	64	70	44	68	70	60
All by Worker	4	5	--	3	4	--
Other	8	10	--	9	13	--
Overtime Adjustment						
None	--	--	--	3	--	20
50%, 8 and 40 Only	44	42	50	52	57	--
100% Sun. and Holidays	33	33	40	29	26	60
Other, More Generous	23	25	10	16	17	20

		Tool & Die Maker	*Tool & Die Designer*
Do Unions Represent These Workers in the Company	N =	57	31
Yes		72	10
No		28	90

Electronic Technician			Metal Technician		
To-tal	*Short-age Firms*	*No Short-age*	*To-tal*	*Short-age Firms*	*No Short-age*
42	44	40	56	58	50
38	25	60	39	34	50
26	36	11	30	31	22
43	43	44	57	62	56
17	21	11	9	8	11
13	--	33	4	--	11
4	8	--	4	8	--
50	54	50	50	54	50
38	31	40	38	31	40
8	8	10	8	8	10

Electronic Technician	*Metal Technician*
26	24
23	25
77	75

(continued)

Table 10-3 *(continued)*

	Tool & Die Maker	*Tool & Die Designer*	*Electronic Technician*	*Metal Technician*
Effect Union Has Had on Company Recruitment Policy N =	39	3	5	4
None	77	100	40	75
Have Helped Co. Obtain Workers	15	--	40	--
Supposed to Obtain Workers Through Them	8	--	20	25
Effect Union Has Had on Company Training Program N =	37	2	4	3
None	38	50	100	67
Help Supervise Through Apprenticeship Committee	23	50	--	--
Limit the No. of Trainees Through Ratio Requirement in Contract	23	--	--	33
Encouraged Men to Take Training	8	--	--	--
Help Supervise and Limit No. of Trainees Through Ratios	5	--	--	--

Source: Employee interviews.

on the firm, then, was not consistently related to the important matter of how pension plans were financed, or even to the existence of a pension plan.

The last item on the table, the premium adjustment for overtime work, does not show a strong relationship to the incidence of the shortages on particular firms. For tool and die makers there was little difference in the types of overtime arrangements between shortage and no shortage firms. About the same proportion of firms of the two types made overtime payments of the type in the last two (most favorable) categories. In the three other occupations the no shortage firms had the more generous overtime provisions, although for the technicians the differences were not very great.

It can be concluded that there was a slight relationship between the employee benefits provided and the incidence of the shortage on the firm. Employee benefits of no shortage firms tend to be somewhat more generous than among the shortage firms. The relationship is weak, however, and there are probably other characteristics of no shortage firms, including size, that are equally, if not more, important. It was shown in Table 10-2, for example, that few workers in any of the firms mentioned fringe benefits as a factor in their intentions to remain with their present employers. The vague phrase that their present firm is a good place to work was a much more frequent expression in explanation of their satisfaction, and the expression probably covers a variety of factors as well as the level of pay and other benefits.

On the matter of employee relations, the study provided little evidence that labor-management relations were factors, either good or bad, in the labor supply situation. Most of the tool and die makers were employed by firms where they were represented by a trade union. In a small minority of the firms the employer said that the number of tool and die apprentices was limited by the journeyman-apprentice ratio negotiated in the collective bargaining agreement. On the other hand, there were also firms which indicated that the union was helpful through its role of assisting in the selection of apprentices, encouraging applications for apprentices, and emphasizing the value of apprenticeship training.

Unionization was not common in the other three occupations. Hiring, training, and utilization of the work force were largely at the discretion of the employer.

IV: Summary and Conclusions

11 Summary and Conclusions

Six skilled and technical occupations, for which there were apparent shortages of labor, were selected for their potential to yield generalizations concerning the extent to which labor market institutions respond to and facilitate adjustment to varying degrees of labor market tightness. The study was designed to examine labor market processes involved in the attraction, training, placement, and retention of workers in the selected occupations in two large labor markets. Each of the occupations could be described as at an intermediate level in the hierarchy of occupations, in that specialized training beyond a high school education was required.

The occupations are structured in a variety of institutional settings and, in general, are representative of a growing and important sector of the labor force. The particular selection of occupations provided an opportunity to examine the effects on the labor market adjustment process of such factors as the degree of product competition, trends in the demand for labor, entry routes to the occupation, the locus of responsibility for providing training, the type, extent, and standard of training required, as well as other variations in institutional arrangements.

In this concluding chapter we first consider the implications of the findings for general understanding of the labor market adjustment process and then turn to the more specific institutional problems that were observed and the types of policy questions that were raised.

General Conclusions on the Adjustment Process

We begin with a consideration of the question of whether or not shortages of labor in the six occupations did exist and, if so, how serious they were. One of the general questions raised in this analysis was whether serious and severe occupational shortages could coexist with moderate labor surpluses.

Extent of the Shortages

Judged by all evaluative criteria, both direct and indirect, it is evident that a shortage, which could be specified in terms of the Arrow-Capron model as a dynamic economic shortage, existed in both labor markets for the two medical occupations studied. These economic shortages prevailed despite the relatively loose character of each of the local labor market areas during the period in which the study was being conducted.

Although considerable evidence existed of attempts to restrain wage increases through administrative arrangements among the hospitals, relative wage and salary movements were in that upward direction which would be anticipated in a situation of labor scarcity. The concerns increasingly demonstrated by the majority of hospital administrators about the relationship between wage and salary scales and recruitment, and indications of accelerating rates of relative pay increases, furnish supplementary and perhaps conclusive evidence that both licensed practical nurses and medical technologists were in short supply. However, although the shortage of medical technologists was equally marked in the two labor markets, the extent of the LPN supply deficiency in Chicago was sufficiently limited to seemingly indicate that the labor market situation bordered between tightness and shortage. However, the relatively lower proportions of LPN's to nurse aides in Chicago would indicate that a much more serious shortage was hidden or concealed by the hiring of more nurse aides than the hospitals either wanted or found suitable in terms of maintaining the desired quality of nurse service. Conceivably, if these qualitative factors could be properly evaluated and weighed, the shortage of LPN's was equally prevalent in the two labor market areas.

If there were any surprises or unexpected results in this study, they were furnished by the four industrial occupations, one (tool and die maker) at a highly skilled level, and the other three (tool and die designer, electronic technician, and engineering technician) at the technician level. Despite some apparently conclusive national trend data and almost universal beliefs in the popular mind – virtually unanimously verbalized by employers – that serious shortages prevailed, no such situation could be inferred in these two major and highly diversified labor markets areas, which at the outset of this study were accepted as relatively typical ones. Wage trends, employer behavior, and the apparent movement of demand all are consistent indicators pointing to the absence of serious shortages, whether defined in popular terms or in economic context as dynamic. This situation existed notwithstanding the fact that alleged shortages in these occupations were almost unanimously cited by the structuralists as proof that a large number of such jobs were available.

The situation in the labor markets for the four industrial occupations studied could be described as one of tightness, causing a moderate degree of inconvenience to some employers. The inconvenience was manifested in the time necessary both to fill vacancies and to complete and deliver certain types of orders. This tightness meant (especially in the tool and die fields) that some functions, instead of being performed in a particular plant, had to be contracted out to specialized job shops which seemed to enjoy a comparative advantage in performance of these specialized functions and which, ostensibly, were able to recruit labor of the same type.

Wage changes and other evidences of employer behavior seem to belie the existence of a serious shortage. Wages in the four occupations advanced in the early 1960's at about the same rate as wages nationally. Had a serious shortage really existed it would have been difficult for employers to hire the appropriate personnel when business expanded. In such a situation it would have been rational for employers to keep these scarce, strategic, and irreplaceable personnel when business was somewhat slow. Such a policy was not evident and surprisingly substantial amounts of unemployment were experienced by workers in each of the four industrial occupations. Nor were the shortages sufficiently acute to induce employers (as has been the case in hospital occupations) to try to break the racial barriers or to urge unions to be willing to remove these same barriers. This would also apply in the nonunionized technical fields where the barriers adhere in the fears held by the practitioners about their occupational status were blacks to be recruited.

The picture is therefore a mixed one. In two of the occupations (licensed practical nurse and medical technologist) serious shortages did exist and had persisted over a long period of time. In another, that of tool and die maker, the situation was on the margin between a tight labor market and a shortage situation. In the others the market was tight but could not be characterized as in short supply in the sense that the term has been used in this study.

In general, the evidence is not impressive for support of the structuralist argument insofar as it relates to the question of a mismatch of worker skills and occupational demand. Exceptions were the cases of the licensed practical nurses in St. Louis; the medical technologists, generally; and to a more minor extent, the tool and die makers. Thus, there was evidence of structural problems in some of the occupational groups, but it was not a widespread phenomenon that pervaded the whole range of skilled and technical occupations surveyed.

General Factors in Market Adjustment

The adjustment process is influenced by the locus of the market and it is extremely important to note therefore that with the partial exception of the medical technologist case, the nexus of the labor market for the occupations studied was primarily a local one. Although the localization of market processes was common to most of the occupations, the institutional factors producing or ameliorating shortage tendencies varied greatly from occupation to occupation.

The Medical Occupations

Although characterized by a somewhat similar extent of shortage, each of the two medical occupations studied had unique and distinct labor market characteristics which should, over time, influence both the nature of the particular occupational shortage and its speed of adjustment.

The nexus of the LPN labor market is distinctly a local one. Almost entirely, new entrants into the field are recruited, trained, and find employment in the local labor market area. A small proportion, almost entirely female secondary labor force members, enter the local labor market area from outside with changes in their husband's residence, but it can be presumed that some, if not an equal, flow in the opposite direction exists.

The local labor market is characterized by a large pool of qualified potential entrants in the sense that age and education qualifications for training do not disqualify a large number of candidates. In addition, the comparatively short period of training, the low direct tuition costs, and the availability of MDTA training allowances which sharply reduce the opportunity costs of undergoing training all imply that the numbers disqualified by high training costs are minimal. These lower opportunity costs enable the recruitment of large numbers of low-income groups, especially blacks, who otherwise could not bear major income losses for training. Given the situation for LPN's in which age and educational requirements do not unduly limit supply, the much lower costs, including opportunity costs, and the consequent relatively much larger human resources pool from which occupational entrants can be drawn, it could be postulated that the speed of supply adjustments for LPN's would be substantially greater than for medical technologists. The seriousness of the LPN shortage should theoretically diminish over time, and this seemed to be occurring in actuality in the Chicago labor market.

The severe LPN shortage in St. Louis is thus related to the failure or inability of employing and training units to make the required adjustments. The two most significant retarding factors are the relatively lower wage levels for St. Louis LPN's compared to other local alternatives for whites which resulted from a more intensive effort of wage restraint in St. Louis hospitals and the failure to increase the number of training posts despite a relatively long waiting list of qualified applicants, virtually all black.[a] The long waiting list of blacks – slightly more qualified than whites, according to the available data for the St. Louis sample – would indicate that LPN wages are above the available alternatives for nonwhites in St. Louis. It should be pointed out that nearly all white applicants were admitted immediately to the next training class while blacks waited at least fifteen months.

The medical technology labor market is a regional one with some national linkages. Members of the profession are recruited into specialized medical

[a]If the number of training posts is regarded as fixed and not subject to alteration, and the labor force is geographically immobile, wage competition between hospitals will not increase the total supply, and the policy of cooperative wage administration is not irrational. Neither will the absence of wage competition reduce the total supply unless there is some movement out of the labor force or out of the occupation as a consequence of low wages.

technology training in hospitals from college and university pretechnologist curricula in which the candidates specialize in chemistry and biology. Although a specific hospital may normally recruit trainees – a large majority of whom stay either in the particular hospital or in the local labor market area – from any college and university in the country offering pretechnologist programs, most trainees in any particular hospital are drawn from a few regional college level educational institutions with which the hospital has established an on-going relationship.

The three to four year length of the pretechnologist program and the residential nature of many of the educational centers from which technologist trainees are drawn indicate a high cost of investment in the prospective technologist, generally borne by his family. This, plus the fact that, basically, recruitment into the field is not directly performed by the institutions experiencing the shortage, implies a slow speed of adjustment to a shortage situation, especially when contrasted with the LPN labor market. Thus, since in the short run the hospitals mainly recruit trainees from a given number, who in their educational institution elect to major in the field, the existence and attractiveness of a particular hospital training program can only affect the distribution of the shortage between different hospitals rather than affect the magnitude of the shortage itself.

Conceivably, hospitals in general could in the long run increase the number entering premedical technology programs out of the stock of students majoring in either biology or chemistry, either by larger wage increases or by making their own training programs more attractive through enhanced facilities and increased stipends. In this regard, however, each hospital feels that it is constrained to take a short-run view by assuming that its actions, albeit costly ones, are too limited to affect the total stock. The result is substantially reduced adjustment speed and an almost identical extent of shortage in each of the two labor market areas. Programs of shorter duration which offer lower opportunity costs to the prospective entrant could undoubtedly increase the number of potential recruits to the field and increase the speed of adjustment. However, in the case of the licensed technologist, the trend is to require a college degree for entry into a training program rather than three years of university training, a development that is contraproductive from the adjustment standpoint. The growth in the proportion of licensed black technologists among the new entrants is proof, however, that some adjustment is taking place. Unlike the case for St. Louis LPN's, the study yielded no evidence that an increase in the number of training positions, as the market is currently structured, would reduce the magnitude of the shortage.[b]

The Industrial Occupations

The labor markets for the four mechanical occupations were primarily local, despite some attempts by national aerospace and research-and-development

[b] As indicated above, there is considerable evidence to suggest that despite vacancies in training establishments for LPN's in Chicago, additional schools in dispersed neighborhoods could influence in a favorable direction the number of LPN trainees.

oriented firms to recruit members of these occupations on a national basis. But in the majority of cases the current job incumbents, especially in the tool and die makers field, were individuals who were recruited, trained, and found employment in the local labor market areas studied. This study uncovered no serious shortages in the four industrial occupations, with the possible exception of tool and die maker, where the situation most closely approached the shortage designation. This was the occupation in which the demand was increasing least in the two labor market areas, suggesting that the dynamic shortage model should be redefined to allow for cases such as this in which replacement needs are high although total demand is either stable or declining.[c]

The labor markets for the three technical occupations had characteristics akin to what Clark Kerr described as feudalized or Balkanized. Within any one broad occupational category (namely, electronics or metal technician) those who were so classified might be designated by varying job titles and specific duties, many of them related to the specific production processes of the particular firms and in some cases involving somewhat different patterns of on-the-job training. These more narrowly prescribed personnel could not easily transfer laterally to another firm in which a job in the same broad occupational category could have different duties and designations. Moreover, the actual jobs and functions of any given technician varied firm by firm, with some technicians in firms where engineers were relatively scarce fulfilling functions performed elsewhere by engineers while in others technicians were at best functioning as skilled laborers.

The labor markets studied differed significantly on the degree of competitiveness. Despite some degree of feudalization of the labor markets in the four technical fields, a much greater degree of competition seems to characterize these markets than those for the LPN's and MT's. The much larger number of employers, the far greater number and variety of channels of entry, the absence of licensing and accreditation provisions as well as specified lengths of education and training, and the lack of gentlemen's agreements or cartelization among the employers, all are factors making the technical labor markets more amenable to the conventional market adjustments.

In none of the four industrial occupations studied is there a single well-identified route to entry. Tool and die makers, however, come closest to pursuing a particular pattern in this regard. Slightly less than half (47 percent) came through the apprenticeship route, and nearly half had attended vocational or technical high schools. For the other occupations, varying combinations of junior college, university, technical and vocational school training, individual courses, company training programs, and informal on-the-job training were the routes through which people entered the occupation. Moreover, the education received had varying degrees of generality in terms of emphasis upon mathematics, science, English, and general engineering courses, as opposed to narrow technical how to training, oriented solely toward a particular field. In most cases the current job holders in the technical occupations did not pursue a given course at the college or technical school level leading to either a certificate or a degree in the field, and then subsequently employment, as did the personnel

[c]See Chapter 1 for an analysis of the Arrow-Capron shortage model.

in the medical fields studied. Instead, much of the education was in conjunction with employment and potential upgrading to technical positions. Thus, most of the practitioners in the technical fields were upgraded into their current posts after employment at a lower level.

It can be contended that a multi and diverse route system widens the possibility for entry and employment and by increasing flexibility enhances adjustment to a shortage situation. It can also be argued, however, that when the entry route is neither apparent nor certain the resultant vagueness increases the difficulty of attracting people into the appropriate programs and fields by removing the incentive to follow a given pre-employment program.

Although the data cannot be considered totally conclusive, the multichannel of entry and diverse education routes seem to be more flexible and responsive than those which require given qualifications for entry and, as in the case of the medical fields, have additional licensing and accreditation criteria. The supply of tool and die makers, for whom apprenticeship was the channel for entry in about half of the cases, seemed to be the least responsive, even though the demands in this field were almost entirely confined to replacement needs in the years covered by this study.

The flexible and relatively informal entry, education, and training routes seem to work because of the large number of persons in our society who, while employed in lower levels, have sufficient amounts of college level or technical education as well as mechanical knowledge and aptitudes to enable them to be easily trained for upgraded technical posts.

For all four industrial occupations, undue restrictions upon entry did not seem to explain the tightness of the labor market. However, cost factors which imposed limitations in the number of apprenticeship programs, the rigidity of the apprenticeship-journeyman ratio for the tool and die makers, as well as the failure of nonwhites to penetrate any of the four occupations, greatly qualify the above generalization. This failure of nonwhites to enter, or better, to be allowed to enter is undoubtedly due to a combination of discriminatory attitudes by workers – whether institutionalized through union pressures or maintained through the self-determined norms of the nonunionized technicians – and employers. It is intensified by economic inability to bear the cost of training, the inadequate educational preparation of the average nonwhite, and what might be termed the self-fulfilling prophecy complex which discourages attempts to enter by causing blacks to believe these fields are closed to them. Certainly breaking down these artificial barriers and restrictions would enable a potentially prime source of additional labor supply to be tapped at the current wage rates.

In addition to the lack of participation by nonwhites the potential supply in these fields appears to be hampered by an overemphasis upon the value of a college education. This overemphasis, which causes many who are marginal in terms of potential for higher education to shun types of training and employment which have less status, and which do not require higher education for entry, is a general over-all problem which will require both reorientation in educational publicity and in the typical counselor's attitude toward alternative types of employment. This reorientation must ultimately result in changing societal norms and status symbols towards certain jobs.

Training costs did not superficially seem to affect willingness to undergo training. This observation is based upon the ability of certain relatively high tuition specialized technical schools to attract recruits even in the face of competition from junior college programs. However, the large proportions of drop-outs from such programs, who found other avenues of entry into the field, indicate that such costs are important, especially if the training program precludes employment during training. While costs were not specifically mentioned as a deterrent to training tool and die designers, the loss of output through removing busy practitioners from production to teach students on the job does have a cost connotation which had an obvious effect upon the supply of training positions.

The costs associated with on-the-job training or more formalized company programs seemed to have deterred all but the larger firms with immediate demands for given types of personnel, which they could only obtain from upgrading, from undertaking training efforts. Companies that did undertake their own training programs generally restricted them to satisfying their own immediate needs rather than the over-all demands of the labor market. This resulted, especially in the tool and die maker field but also much more generally, in fewer people being trained by companies than would have been the case had an over-all approach, in which individual firms all bore their proportional share of the training costs, been taken by the firms jointly. The fear that workers would move after completing their training, thus removing any potential gain, deterred many firms, especially smaller ones, from training workers.

In general, there was no dramatic illustration of either job redesign or job dilution sufficient to generate the belief that such methods of economizing on technicians were either consciously resorted to or that significant opportunities for such types of adjustments were feasible. More than likely, the shortages were not intense enough during the period studied to have produced major pressure in this direction. The field of electronic technicians seemed to offer the most potential for change in the tasks and functions performed by the typical practitioner.

On the other hand, subtle changes in job assignments and in functions were observed in a significant number of situations. In all probability, these types of changes were much more significant and had greater total impact than indicated by the responses. Thus, important marginal adjustments to the shortages may have been taking place despite the absence of any dramatic or even large discrete changes.

However, it should be pointed out that job redesign could add as well as remove functions. Engineers in the same industries were also allegedly in short supply and some marginal transfers undoubtedly were taking place which added to the technician functions, thereby offsetting any loss of activity transferred to lower level personnel.

Technological changes, some already quite apparent, indicate possibilities for considerable substitution of capital for labor in the occupations, especially in the tool and die fields. Computer programming of much of the work in both tool and die occupations is feasible, and the future demand for these types of labor will undoubtedly be influenced by the rate at which such computer technology is introduced and spread. Although the potential for such substitution depends upon the generation of new knowledge and, thus, can be argued to be independent of particular labor market conditions, the rate and spread of such innovation could be affected by the magnitude of a shortage in the fields. However, up to the termination of this research, this process of substitution of capital for labor, with the possible exception of the medical technologists, has been of such insignificance as to render technological substitution relatively inconsequential as an adjustment mechanism to shortages.

Major Adjustment Considerations

A number of basic conclusions emerge from the general analysis of the labor market processes that are important in the adjustment to shortage situations.

1. The market for occupations at the level represented by those studied in this inquiry is largely a local one. Many, if not most, of the decisions that determine whether an adequate supply of labor will be available to meet the demand are made by individual workers, unions, employers, training institutions, and other agencies at the local level. Some of the implications of this generalization are explored further below when we consider the specific market institutions and their effects on the adjustment process.

2. In general, the market tends to work in the direction of bringing about adjustment in demand-supply relationships. In the type of situations we were exploring, in which general labor demand-supply relationships were in close balance, the market works pretty well. Although for some of the occupations studied serious shortages had developed and were persisting, market pressures were moving relative wages upward, albeit too slowly, and labor market decision-makers were making decisions which were generally in the right direction. In part, this was the case because particular policy instruments were available, such as MDTA training programs for LPN's, to meet a shortage problem.

The market, in moving toward balance, tends to work at the margin. Thus, while dramatic instances of innovations designed to deal with the shortage situations generally were not found, many modest changes in practices, which were difficult to pick up in the broad investigation conducted, were undoubtedly being made. The accumulation of these small changes, together with the fewer positive steps that were taken, kept the situations from becoming critical.

In fact the operations of the labor market for technicians seem to illustrate the point that adjustment is the sum total of different discrete small changes at the margin. When such marginal adjustments are through fixed, unvarying and limited ports of entry, when licensing and accreditation standards are rigid or when discontinuities exist in training and educational requirements between different components of the labor supply (as for practical nurses and technologists), the adjustment mechanism may not function with sufficient effectiveness to remove shortage.

3. The adjustment to labor shortage situations appears to work best in industries where the product market approaches the competitive model. The shortages were least severe in the industrial occupations where product competition made it important for employers to maintain high quality standards and, therefore, maintain a trained, quality work force. The shortages were most severe in the two medical occupations, where employing units tend not to be in direct competition with each other, and in which cases the adjustment tended to take place through sacrifices in quality of service. Such sacrifices were made, for example, by understaffing and by substitution of unskilled and untrained personnel for the unavailable skilled and trained. Quality seems to be better maintained by a more competitive labor and product market situation rather than through formal licensing or accreditation processes. A suggested implication is that particular attention needs to be given to the provision of labor supplies for noncompetitive industries.

4. While market pressures tended to push market institutions in directions which led to amelioration of shortages, the response was frequently delayed and sluggish. Thus, training capacity for LPN's in St. Louis did not expand in spite of a serious shortage of practitioners. Adjustment in the awkward and expensive training arrangements for medical technologists did not improve perceptibly; in fact, in the face of serious shortages the training period was lengthened and made more expensive. And, by and large, employers preferred to live with the shortages rather than to take aggressive steps to alleviate the situation. If any aggressive steps were taken, they were by the individual employing unit to improve its own relative position. Thus, as shortages developed, little change occurred in the traditional methods of recruitment, training, and utilization of worker supply.

5. The study suggests that broad options of educational preparation and training tend to facilitate adjustment to shortage situations. The shortage was most severe for the three occupations for which the entry routes were most prescribed and narrow – licensed practical nurse, medical technologist, and tool and die maker – although other factors were also important contributors to the shortage situation in these occupations. It was clear, nevertheless, that the absence of strict controls on entry facilitated adjustment. Thus, in the engineering technician occupations, upgrading of lower level personnel was the common route of entry to technician positions, and the possibilities for building on a variety of previous educational, training, and practical experiences provided valuable flexibility and increased the speed of supply adjustment.

6. Changes in relative wages played only a minor role in bringing about adjustment to the shortage situations. Wages for the two medical occupations, despite showing a slightly higher rate of increase in recent years than for wages

generally, have been unduly held down. In short, the rate of upward adjustment of wages for both occupations given that salaries are still lower than in fields requiring comparable ability and training, has been inadequate. Wage trends in the four industrial occupations have been comparable to wage changes in the economy generally. In these occupations, wages tend to be tied, by collective bargaining agreements or by practice, to wage rates in the industry generally, and it is difficult to single out occupations for particular attention. Over the years, wages of tool and die makers have suffered from the general tendency in manufacturing for occupational wage differentials to narrow. In general, however, wages in the four occupations seem to be commensurate with the duties of the jobs. It cannot be anticipated, however, that changes in wages can be used as a unitary instrument for dealing with a shortage situation.

7. The two medical occupations deviate from the four industrial occupations on the utilization of minority-group members. In the face of serious shortages and relatively unattractive terms of employment, particularly financial, the hospitals have turned to blacks and other minority-group members to staff their positions in practical nursing and to a lesser extent in medical technology. Thus, the utilization of members of these groups has been an important response to labor shortages.

In the four industrial occupations, on the other hand, virtually all of the practitioners are white. Blacks and other minority-group members are, therefore, an important untapped labor resource. The shortage problem in these occupations, however, is not primarily one of a shortage of potential candidates. In general, the supply of available majority-group members is adequate and they are generally better qualified and prepared to take advantage of employment opportunities. The shortages were thus not severe enough to confront employers with the alternative of either raising wages to increase the number of whites or of opening up opportunities for nonwhites in order to maintain the same wage rate. Special efforts by employers, unions, training institutions, and government will therefore be required to bring about representation of minorities in these occupations.

8. Without exception, the study of the six occupations revealed deficiencies in the availability and dissemination of relevant occupational information.

Policy Implications

The most general conclusion of the study is that the factors affecting adjustment in a particular labor market vary from occupation to occupation, and in a particular occupation can vary from labor market to labor market. Therefore, no one model or program is likely to be satisfactory as an approach to solving problems of occupational shortages. The implication of this is that manpower and educational programs should be tailored to particular types of occupational shortages and the localities in which they exist. General approaches, when used, should be constructed and administered as flexibly as possible, rather than assuming that a single solution will have applicability to all situations.

As an example of this point, the underlying assumption of MDTA training programs is that the supply of workers to an occupation can be increased by subsidizing the training costs of unemployed persons enrolled in training programs. For most of the six occupations studied here, however, training costs were moderate and by and large did not seem to be a hindrance to attracting an adequate supply of trainees. The occupation with the highest training costs for the trainee and for which training costs were a significant barrier to an adequate supply (medical technologist) is not an occupation in which it is likely that the supply can be increased by subsidizing the training costs of the unemployed. The point is not that MDTA programs are inappropriate, but that one approach is not sufficient for all problems.

Although the findings of this study suggest the need for multiple solutions to problems of occupational shortage, they do not tell us what the solution is for every type of problem. What follows, therefore, merely attempts to indicate the types of policies and practices, either public or private, that would fit the types of problems that were identified.

Entry into the Occupation

Relevant considerations concerning entry to occupations include wages, the availability and dissemination of occupational information, previous work experience, recruitment, and hiring standards. Two general findings of the study, namely that the markets for the occupations are mainly local ones and that solutions to shortage problems need to be particularized, are particularly relevant here and lead to the first point.

1. The study makes clear the need for the development of more adequate occupational information at the local level and its more effective dissemination to labor market decision-makers: employers, workers, the unemployed, vocational and other educational planners, and others. Included is the need for improved projections of occupational requirements to provide the base that could make possible effective planning and coordination of the development of training facilities and programs and effective counseling in the schools. The need for local labor market information has, of course, been recognized. The most recent analysis and specification of the need is in a recent report by the Advisory Committee on Research to the U. S. Employment Service.[1]

2. It would be helpful if improved labor market information (or even the present information) were tied in more closely with the secondary school system. Since occupational choice tends to be a process rather than a discrete action, informational inputs should be made at points where youngsters are making choices as to curricula. Should the U. S. Employment Service develop a strong staff of occupational and informational specialists in the local offices, such staff might be shared with the school system as a way of getting

occupational information into the classroom. Improved and intensified guidance and counseling efforts would also be helpful; most of the practitioners in the six occupations contended that they entered the field without benefit of systematic guidance, counseling, or efforts to recruit or interest them in the field.

3. Previous work experience proved important in the occupational choice of large numbers of the practitioners in the six occupations. Licensed practical nurses and medical technologists frequently had work experience in hospitals prior to deciding to enter the occupation. For technicians, the most frequent route into the occupation was upgrading from lower level jobs. Additional interest in the occupations might therefore be stimulated if firms that are experiencing labor shortage would attempt to develop part-time and summer employment opportunities for youngsters, and perhaps work with schools in filling the positions with youngsters who have exhibited interest or skills in areas where the firm offers employment opportunities. Not only would such arrangements give youngsters a first-hand view of employment and career opportunities, but they would also afford employers an opportunity to influence youngsters in making occupational choices.

4. Given that most of the training schools for the six occupations operated below capacity, enhanced recruitment efforts would be desirable. Particularly for the two medical occupations, for which the preparatory routes are definite and fixed, joint recruiting efforts by training schools and hospitals might be effective and economical. Contacts with schools and school counselors, including those at the college and university level, as well as more concerted, general publicity on opportunities and needs in the field would seem to be called for.

5. There were some indications that attraction of trainees into the industrial occupations, particularly the tool and die trades, is hampered by the heavy emphasis on the value of a college education, although this seemed to be quite a minor problem. Nevertheless, some reorientation in educational publicity and in counselors' attitudes toward manual work might be of some value.

6. In the cases of the two medical occupations, and especially for LPN's, a high proportion of the labor force consists of secondary workers. It is probable, therefore, that a considerable number of already trained but currently inactive practitioners are located in each of the local labor market areas. Undoubtedly some of these inactive practitioners, whose inactivity is the result of child care and home responsibilities, could be recruited on a part-time basis if hospitals would attempt to schedule their work in such a manner as not to compete with home responsibilities. In addition, as is already the case for LPN's, older women could be tapped as new recruits for training and then employment. The success of this recruitment device in the LPN situation would suggest that it could be employed for medical technologists. It seems likely that an untapped potential supply of undetermined but significant size exists from college educated older women, who for various reasons would desire to enter or reenter the labor force.

7. In general, formal standards for entry, either into training or into employment, were not unduly restrictive.

8. Wages as a factor in the shortage situations have been discussed previously.

As was indicated, it was concluded that wages in the two medical occupations had not advanced rapidly enough and adversely affected the recruitment of new entrants (at least whites) into training schools.

Training and Training Institutions

As has been previously indicated, a considerable variety of training institutions and arrangements are utilized for preparing workers for the six occupations studied. Also, varying amounts of institutional and on-the-job training are prerequisites for entry to full status in the occupations. Although it is difficult to generalize about the six occupations as a whole, the following points identify the main problem areas.

1. Costs of training for the student depend somewhat upon the type of institution the student chooses, but in general, vary from low for tool and die workers to high for medical technologists, with costs being moderate for the others. The MDTA approach is an ideal way of overcoming costs for the training of some persons as LPN's. The same programs should be useful for preapprenticeship training for tool and die makers and would serve the double purpose of encouraging entry to training by the unemployed and subsidizing some of the training costs for employers. Since training costs tend to be a barrier to the introduction of training programs by employers, the latter point is of some significance.

The most general development that should meet the problem of training costs for students is the junior or community college. With the possible exception of the tool and die maker occupation, all of the occupations studied here could be prepared for in the junior college, although arrangements would have to be made with hospitals and other institutions for necessary on-the-job training.

2. Substantial training costs are borne by the employer in the cases of licensed practical nurse (in the minority of cases when the hospital is the training unit), medical technologists, and the two tool and die trades. In the technician cases employers provide only the on-the-job training, and the training period is usually short and not a heavy financial burden.

In the LPN case most of the training is done in public facilities and financial burdens on the hospital are generally not a serious barrier to providing a sufficient number of training slots. As was indicated above, where additional training positions are needed the junior college would seem to be an ideal institution through which to provide them. The study did reveal the peculiar circumstance in St. Louis where the number of training positions for LPN's had not responded to the shortage, despite a waiting list or queue of considerable size. A fuller explanation of why the queue has not had an impact on the number of training posts would require further and more conclusive inquiry, although there was evidence that a reason for it was an attempt to retain racial balance (some proportion of whites) in the occupation. In the Chicago case for LPN's, better distribution of training facilities among neighborhoods would improve accessibility and undoubtedly increase the number of entrants into training.

The training arrangements for medical technologists are awkward and costly for both trainees and hospitals. One of two things would seem to be called for. One helpful change would be to bring together into one institution both the general academic and the specialized training in order to reduce the difficult problem of coordinating a university pretraining educational program with a hospital specialized training program. This would certainly ease the problem of attracting students into training. Again, the junior college offers the most likely opportunity to accomplish this. Some change in current requirements for entry into the specialized part of the training would be necessary. It might be accomplished by the creation of an intermediate occupational level between the certified laboratory assistant and the medical technologist (ASCP); that is, an Associate Medical Technology category. Or it might, alternatively, be accomplished by reducing some of the current requirements for entry into ASCP approved training for medical technologist and creating a higher level technologist position (e.g., graduate technologists) which is based on college or graduate education in the sciences. In any event, placing the bulk of medical technology training in the junior college would drastically reduce costs to the student and to the training hospitals. An alternative approach to the cost problem would be a subsidy program to larger training hospitals that would allow them to train numbers of students beyond their own needs, thus overcoming one of the present problems that the limited number of training hospitals cannot afford to train for the total needs of the market.

The case of the tool and die maker differs from the others in that nearly all of the training has to be provided by the employer in on-the-job experience. Two types of programs are helpful. One is the MDTA preapprenticeship training mentioned earlier. If this method covers some of the training ordinarily borne by the employer in the regular apprenticeship program, it could by reducing costs to the employer encourage the initiation of apprenticeship programs where they might not otherwise exist. Another is the cooperative program among employers represented by the Chicago Tool and Die Institute through which adequate training programs are assured and some of the costs of training are shared. Beyond these, a program similar to that suggested for the medical technologists, in which larger employers are subsidized for training apprentices for smaller firms, might be considered.

The tool and die designer case provides the most difficult of all. The general education required of the designer can be obtained at the junior college or in the university. The on-the-job portion is difficult to provide for in sufficient amounts because most firms have a small number of designers and are not in a position to utilize them extensively for training purposes. Direct subsidy of the costs of instruction is the only solution that suggests itself, and there is no current program through which this kind of arrangement is possible.

3. The type and quality of training for the six occupations appeared to be appropriate. Practitioners, trainees, and employers generally agreed that the

training received was good and appropriate. The technical and trade schools, however, did vary considerably in quality; some employers would not accept the graduates of certain schools.

Performance standards in LPN training did raise a question in that about one-third of the trainees failed. The standards, however, did not seem to be unduly severe or restrictive despite this obvious loss of potential members of the occupation. Since entrance requirements into LPN training are not at all restrictive, this rate of failure can be expected and it is likely that the imposition of much higher entrance requirements in an effort to minimize failure would sufficiently reduce the potential supply to result in, at best, no higher a supply. The subsequent labor market experience of the failures and drop-outs would indicate that, for the most part, the individuals could not have performed capably.

4. Training in each of the occupations seemed to have some peculiarity that had an affect on supply. For LPN's the training was not coordinated or integrated with the training for other nursing occupations. The result is that practical nurse is a dead-end occupation and this undoubtedly affects its attractiveness. Training in medical technology is characterized by the awkward splitting of university and specialized training. To some extent training of tool and die workers is hindered by apprentice-journeymen ratios. For tool and die designers instructor costs are a special problem. For all of the industrial occupations minority group members have been excluded but the technician occupations pose a particular problem in this respect. The road to technician positions is frequently up an occupational ladder, and potentially qualified blacks may be blocked at lower levels.

Placement

The study revealed no serious barriers in any of the six occupations in the transition from training to work. Most successful trainees obtained work of the type they were trained for in a very short period of time. The findings can be briefly summarized as follows.

1. For all of the occupations there was a very close training-employment relationship. In many instances the trainee stayed on at the establishment where he received his on-the-job training. In many other instances the trainee was already employed while he was engaged in training. Where the training-employment relationship was not this close the training institutions seemed generally to have close contact with employers and jobs were found quickly. Of the six occupations, tool and die designers had the most difficult transitional problems, mainly because the experience requirement was more likely to be lacking.

2. Completion of a training program provided clear labor market advantages to the successful trainees. Compared with the dropouts from training programs, those who completed the training had higher employment rates, lower

unemployment rates, higher labor force participation rates, speedier job-finding success, and more relevant employment with respect to their training.

3. It can be said, therefore, that the available labor market institutions were highly effective in facilitating the transition from training to work.

Occupational Retention

Occupational attachments to the six occupations were very strong. Nearly all of the practitioners expressed an intent to remain in their present line of work. Most of those who indicated they would not remain in their present type of work had their eyes on supervisory or other types of higher level positions and many of these indicated their intention to leave their employment for further schooling. Particularly among technicians there was interest in obtaining a professional degree. The following, therefore, may be concluded.

1. Little seepage or loss of supply resulted from movement out of the six occupations. Practitioners were generally satisfied with their type of employment and remained in it; there is, therefore, no serious problem of diseconomy resulting from poor utilization of training investments. The almost nonexistent opportunities for upward mobility of LPN's probably results in some limited loss of personnel over time and may represent somewhat of a departure from this generalization.

2. A much more serious problem of economizing the worker supply results from movement out of the labor force by members of the medical occupations. This problem is related to the high proportion of female members of the two occupations, especially among LPN's. The movements out of the labor force divert much of the new supply solely for replacement purposes and to the extent that either improved personnel practices, higher pay, or enhanced fringe benefits would prevent such movement, these personnel practices could have had some influence. The evidence indicated, however, that for those drawn into the two fields the influences of these personnel practices were of a very marginal incidence and the great bulk of the departures were for personal reasons. Undoubtedly, prevailing personnel practices, which determine the net advantages of the two occupations, were operative in affecting the potential number of new entrants, but the incurring of higher costs merely to keep the present personnel in the field does not seem to be warranted.

To the extent that turnover between employers, with some time taken out between successive jobs, caused some losses, improved personnel practices in some of the hospitals would result in economy of some personnel. However, factors other than personnel practices, especially in view of the ease of obtaining jobs elsewhere, were much more decisive in inducing turnover.

Manpower Utilization

A variety of mechanisms through which employers might adjust to shortages were explored, including job redesign, substitution of capital for labor, changes in quality of services offered, employee benefit programs, and various personnel practices. The following points summarize the main findings.

1. Job redesign had played some role in adjusting to shortage situations for the occupations at the technical level, particularly the two medical and the engineering technician occupations. The work of the licensed practical nurse and the engineering technician had been largely cut out of what had formerly been the duties of nurses and engineers. For the engineering technicians present utilization patterns appear to offer little opportunity for further extensive adjustment to shortages. Large differences in the utilization ratios of nurse aides, practical nurses, and registered nurses among hospitals suggest that additional personnel could be provided through further disintegration of function in some hospitals, such as through the separation from the LPN's work all activities which could be performed by the on-the-job trained nurse aides.[d] Some economy in the use of qualified medical technology personnel could be effectuated through job dilution and greater specialization of oft-performed routine tests which might be performed by lesser trained technicians who are in surplus rather than in short supply. The present unsatisfactory nature of most commercially trained technicians should not obscure the fact that the utilization of better trained one year technicians, partly generated through MDTA sponsored programs, could economize on the use of personnel currently in short supply.

2. Technological changes, which made possible the substitution of capital for labor, for the most part came about independent of labor market conditions. In none of the six occupations did labor supply factors appear to result in the development and introduction of capital equipment, although the timing of their introduction could have to a marginal extent been affected by the degree of labor shortages.

3. The quality of services offered by the industrial employers was not affected to an important degree by labor shortages. Increasing the length of time required to fill orders was the main consequence of short labor supplies, and this was a factor in only a small minority of cases. In the medical occupations, however, quality of services were lower than they would have been had an adequate quantity of qualified personnel been available. The latter point indicates that certification and licensing programs are not a guarantee of quality when the employer is free to assign duties and determine the ratios of types of personnel to be employed.

4. Shortages are not explained to any great extent by the pattern of employee benefits provided by employing units. A slight relationship was found between benefits provided and whether a particular firm was experiencing a shortage, but the relationship was weak. Wage levels did not correlate well with the degree of shortage experienced by firms.

In the case of hospitals, however, working conditions did appear to discourage participation in the work force. Understaffing of nursing personnel,

[d] It should be pointed out conversely that if all functions which are of sufficient complexity to require an LPN were removed from the nurse aides, the demand schedule for LPN's would probably, at least in Chicago, move to the right.

for example, particularly on the evening and night shifts, made it difficult to attract secondary workers into the labor force. Also, the nature of the work force for the medical occupations indicates that some additional personnel could be obtained through recruitment of part-time employees and older women college graduates whose home responsibilities, generally involving care of children, are declining. And experiments in the use of different shift arrangements (for example, six shifts rather than three) would be interesting to see whether better accommodation to the home duties of female secondary workers would produce an enlarged active labor force.

Appendixes

A

General Tables

Table A-1

Nonagricultural Employment in the United States, Chicago, and St. Louis, by Industry, 1960

Industry Group	United States *Number (Thousands)*	United States *Percent*
Total Nonagricultural Employment	54,234	100.0
Mining	712	1.3
Contract Construction	2,885	5.3
Manufacturing	16,796	31.0
Durable Goods	9,459	17.4
Fabricated Metal Products	1,135	2.1
Machinery, Except Electrical	1,479	2.7
Electrical Machinery	1,467	2.7
Transportation Equipment	1,569	2.9
All Other Durable Goods	3,809	7.0
Nondurable Goods	7,336	13.5
Transportation and Public Utilities	4,004	7.4
Wholesale and Retail Trade	11,391	21.0
Finance, Insurance, and Real Estate	2,669	4.9
Service and Miscellaneous	7,423	13.7
Government	8,353	15.4

[1] Includes Cook, DuPage, Kane, Lake, McHenry, and Will Counties.

[2] Includes St. Louis city and Jefferson, St. Charles, and St. Louis counties, Mo.; Madison and St. Clair counties, Ill. As of 1963 this area includes Franklin County, Mo.

Sources: Bureau of Labor Statistics, *Employ-*

Chicago[1] Number (Thousands)	Percent	St. Louis[2] Number (Thousands)	Percent
2,471	100.0	737	100.0
6	.2	3	.4
112	4.5	36	4.9
863	34.9	263	35.7
547	22.1	153	20.8
99	4.0	18	2.4
106	4.3	18	2.4
144	5.8	19	2.6
26	1.1	47	6.4
172	7.0	51	6.9
316	12.8	110	14.9
203	8.2	67	9.1
534	21.6	153	20.8
150	6.1	38	5.2
366	14.8	100	13.6
239	9.7	78	10.6

ment and Earnings Statistics for the United States, 1909–67, Bulletin No. 1312–5 (Washington, D. C.: U. S. Government Printing Office, October, 1967; and *Employment and Earnings Statistics for States and Areas, 1939–66*, Bulletin No. 1370–4 (Washington, D. C.: U. S. Government Printing Office, July, 1967).

Table A-2

Total Employment in the Service Industries in the United States, Chicago, and St. Louis, 1960

	United States		Chicago[1]		St. Louis[1]	
	Number (Thousands)	*Percent*	*Number (Thousands)*	*Percent*	*Number (Thousands)*	*Percent*
Total Employed[2]	60,289	100.0	2,494	100.0	754	100.0
Services	13,550	22.5	457	18.3	146	19.4
Business and Repair Services	1,611	2.7	72	2.9	18	2.4
Personal Services	3,858	6.4	108	4.3	39	5.2
Entertainment and Recreation Services	503	.8	19	.8	5	.7
Professional and Related Services	7,578	12.6	258	10.3	84	11.1
Medical and Other Health Services (Including Hospitals)	2,578	4.3	86	3.4	32	4.2

[1]Standard Metropolitan Statistical Areas. [2]Excludes agriculture, forestry, and fisheries.
Source: U. S. Census of Population, 1960, U. S. Summary, vol. 1, pt. 1, table 211; Illinois, vol. 1, pt. 15, table 125; Missouri, vol. 1, pt. 27, table 125.

B Occupations Selected for Study

The Choice of Occupations

Most previous studies that have been made of occupational shortages have dealt with such professional categories of workers as scientists, engineers, and economists. Seldom have specific subprofessional or technical occupations been the subject of systematic study. The objective of this study was to choose occupations below the professional level requiring fairly extensive education and/or training and whose relative importance and basic recruitment and training problems are sufficiently typical to render them valuable for study and subsequent generalization.

The general criteria established for selecting the occupations were: (a) substantial and continuing demand by area employers, (b) evidence of serious shortages of workers in the occupations, (c) the requirement of specialized trade or technical training of at least six months beyond completion of high school, and (d) that the baccalaureate degree was not generally required for qualifying for the occupation. In addition, it was decided to select pairs of occupations from the same industry, in order to simplify and economize in the collection of data. Thus, the occupations were selected from three industrial classifications.

The occupations were selected on the basis of preliminary interviews with representatives of public and private employment services, employer associations, training associations and training schools, and a few individual employers and union officials. On the basis of this preliminary survey, conducted in the summer of 1963, the decision was made to select occupations from three industry groups: medical services, metalworking industries, and the electrical machinery industry. The two occupations in medical services were chosen immediately so that the field work could commence; the other four occupations were chosen subsequently after additional investigation. The six occupations finally chosen were as follows:

Medical services:
- Licensed practical nurse
- Medical technologist

Metalworking and electrical machinery:
- Tool and die maker
- Tool and die designer
- Engineering technician – electronics
- Engineering technician – metalworking

C The Design for Data Gathering

Employer Interviews

For each occupation, the field work began with interviews with employer representatives. The research proposal had called for interviews with about 100 firms. For the two medical occupations a sample of 41 hospitals was selected from the Chicago and St. Louis metropolitan areas. The hospital samples, which were stratified by size, are summarized in Table C-1. The St. Louis sample comprises a larger proportion of total establishments in that city than does the Chicago sample. This is of little consequence except that it probably produces somewhat more reliable results for St. Louis than Chicago. The four largest hospitals in each city were included in the sample, and larger proportions of medium than of smaller hospitals were selected.[a] The main reason for sampling in this fashion was that employee samples were to be taken from the sampled hospitals later, and for reasons of efficiency hospitals with substantial numbers of employees in the two occupations were wanted. Also, some of the smaller hospitals do not have laboratories and therefore do not employ medical technologists. The sample design reduced the possibilities of selecting hospitals that would be unproductive of data concerning the two occupations under study. In the two cities combined over one-quarter of all area hospitals, employing nearly half of all hospital employees in the two areas, were represented in the sample.

In each hospital, interviews concerning both occupations were conducted with the hospital administrator and the personnel director. In addition, the director of nursing was interviewed regarding licensed practical nurses and the chief pathologist who headed the medical laboratory was interviewed for the medical technology occupation. The interviews were based on a topical agenda (see Appendix G), rather than a structured questionnaire. Where conflicting facts were given by the various hospital officials, an effort was made to reconcile them. Differences in viewpoint or interpretation, of course, were taken as given.

The interviews with hospital administrators were conducted between September, 1963, and February, 1964. All of the hospitals in the original sample agreed to submit to the interviews requested. Several, however, employed no practical nurses or medical technologists, in which cases only the relevant portion of the interview was used.

The design of the employer sample for the four industrial occupations was heavily influenced by the objective of using the same employers, to the extent possible, for the four occupations. Obviously this objective could not be met for the two technician occupations since they tend to be employed by different employers in different industries. The sample had to exclude small firms because

[a]The size categories used for sampling are arbitrary, but are based on points at which there were natural size breaks in the distribution of hospitals by size of employment. All of the hospitals in the "large" category were selected for the sample. Hospitals from the other two size groups were sampled randomly.

the smaller firms, although they might employ tool and die makers and designers, were unlikely to employ engineering technicians.

The decision was made, therefore, to define the relevant population as all firms in the electronics and metal industries with 400 or more employees. The electronics industry was defined as the electrical machinery industry [industry group 36 in the Standard Industrial Classification Manual (SIC) of the Budget Bureau], and the metal industries included primary metals (SIC group 33), fabricated metal products (SIC group 34), nonelectrical machinery (SIC group 35), and transportation equipment (SIC group 37).

The Illinois and Missouri state employment services provided us with lists of all firms covered by the state unemployment insurance laws in the two labor markets which employed 400 or more workers and which were classified in the above industrial categories. These firms formed the population of firms we considered relevant for the study. The lists included 49 electronics and 101 metal firms in the Chicago labor market and 10 electronics and 36 metal firms in St. Louis.

As in the case of the medical occupations, the sample was designed to assure representation of large firms, in order that the major employers in the area would be included and to maximize efficiency in obtaining worker interviews. Thus, for both industries all firms with 2,000 or more employees were included in the sample. The remaining firms were sampled randomly by a method which gave each firm a chance of selection for the sample proportionate to its contribution to employment in the total population being sampled. A firm with five percent of the total employment had a five percent chance of selection. An exception to this procedure was that all 10 electronics firms in St. Louis were included in the sample since the number was so small. Seventy-two firms were selected for the sample, 47 in Chicago and 25 in St. Louis.

The actual number of firms interviewed was 66, of which 45 were in Chicago and 21 in St. Louis. The sample characteristics are summarized in Table C-2. All but 6 of the firms selected for the Chicago sample were actually interviewed. Arrangements for interviewing could not be made with 1 large electronics firm and 1 metal firm. And 4 metal firms were ruled out of scope because they employed no one in the 4 occupations; 4 firms were selected randomly to replace them in the sample. The Chicago firms interviewed, therefore, conform very closely to the original sample selected.

The same is not true of the St. Louis sample. Only 4 of the 10 electronics firms would agree to participate in the study. Two smaller firms (under 400

Table C-1

Hospital Sample Design

	Establishments			Employees		
Size of Hospital	*No. of Hospitals in Universe*	*No. of Hospitals in Sample*	*Sample as Percent of Universe*	*Employees in Universe*	*Employees in Sample Hospitals*	*Sample as Percent of Universe*
Chicago						
Small (under 500)	79	11	14%	18,500	2,600	14%
Medium (500–1,999)	29	9	31%	25,300	7,700	30%
Large (2,000 & over)	4	4	100%	12,800	12,800	100%
Total	112	24	21%	56,600	23,100	41%
St. Louis						
Small (under 500)	24	6	25%	5,500	1,500	27%
Medium (500–999)	12	7	58%	8,500	5,300	62%
Large (1,000 & over)	4	4	100%	5,800	5,800	100%
Total	40	17	42%	19,800	12,600	64%
Total, Two Cities	152	41	27%	76,400	35,700	47%

employees) were added to the sample for a total of 6, but as Table C-2 shows, the sample is comprised mainly of small firms.[b] The metal industry sample suffered from the same problem. The original sample included 4 medium and large firms which were not able to participate in the study, and it was not possible to obtain substitutes for them in their size range. A total of 7 of the original 25 sample firms were dropped from the sample; 3 substitutes were selected among smaller firms to produce a final sample of 21 firms. The St. Louis samples in both industries, therefore, fall considerably short of ideal, particularly in their lack of representation of larger firms. This characteristic of the samples created further problems in the selection of worker samples.

For each firm in the sample, interviews were held with someone with a general staff responsibility in the company, such as the personnel director or the training director. In addition, interviews were conducted with a person in a supervisory capacity over each of the occupational groups being studied. Such a person could be a departmental supervisor or a foreman in the case of tool and die makers, a chief engineer or chief designer for tool and die designers, and chief designer or a department or section head in the case of engineering technician. Thus, four or more interviews were sometimes conducted in a single firm with respect to as many as three occupations. Unlike the case with the hospital administrator interview, these interviews were based on a structured interview form (see Appendix H).[c] All of the interviews were conducted between July, 1964, and March, 1965.

Because not all firms interviewed employed people in all of the occupations, the number of firms interviewed for the four occupations varied, as follows.

	Tool & Die Maker	*Tool & Die Designer*	Engineering Technicians *Electronic*	*Metalworking*
Chicago	39	24	20	16
St. Louis	18	7	6	8
Total	57	31	26	24

The distribution reflects a number of important characteristics of the samples. Most of the firms, both electronic and metalworking, employed tool and die makers, but some did not. Less than a majority, however, utilized tool and die designers. And the overrepresentation of small firms in the St. Louis sample is reflected in the small number of firms which could be interviewed about designers and technicians, because they employed none.

Worker Interviews

The general plan for obtaining a sample of workers in the six occupations was to select a subsample of employees in each occupation from each firm in the

[b] Since the entire universe of firms with over 400 employees was in the original sample, it was obviously not possible to substitute with larger sized firms.

[c] The hospital interviews had indicated that, with a number of people involved in the interviewing, it was difficult to obtain consistency among interviewers working from an unstructured agenda.

Table C-2

Employer Sample Design, Metalworking and Electrical Machinery Industries

Size of Firm	*No. of Firms in Universe*	Establishments *No. of Firms in Sample*	*Sample as Percent of Universe*
Chicago			
Electronics Industry	49	20	41%
Small--400-999	27	5	19%
Medium--1,000-1,999	12	5	42%
Large--2,000 & Over	10	10	100%
Metalworking Industries	101	25	25%
Small--400-999	68	14	21%
Medium--1,000-1,999	21	5	24%
Large--2,000 & Over	12	6	50%
St. Louis			
Electronics Industry	12	6	50%
Small--400-999	7	4	57%
Medium--1,000-1,999	2	1	50%
Large--2,000 & Over	3	1	33%
Metalworking Industries	36	15	42%
Small--400-999	28	13	46%
Medium--1,000-1,999	4	—	—
Large--2,000 & Over	4	2	50%

	Employment	
Employment in Universe	*Employment in Sample Firms*	*Sample as Percent of Universe*
89,363	67,072	75%
17,186	3,802	22%
15,799	6,892	44%
56,378	56,378	100%
113,704	46,303	41%
42,620	9,140	21%
27,054	5,519	20%
44,030	31,644	72%
16,053	7,465	47%
3,360	1,746	52%
2,536	1,493	59%
10,157	4,226	42%
59,077	35,468	60%
14,097	6,853	49%
5,591	--	--
39,389	28,615	73%

employer sample. Since many common topics were to be explored with both employers and workers, it seemed desirable to match the two samples in this way. At the time of the employer interviews, therefore, the interviewers were to make arrangements to obtain a sample of workers from each firm and discuss arrangements for conducting the worker interviews on the premises of the firm. The worker sample was designed before the employer interviews were conducted. The size of the subsample from each establishment was to be proportionate to the size of the firm with respect to total employment in all of the sample firms. Thus, a firm whose employment equaled five percent of total employment in the sample firms would contribute five percent of the worker interviews in the relevant occupations. Also, the worker sample was to be stratified in such a way that the sample would contain two recent entrants to the occupation for each veteran of the occupation. Recent entrants were arbitrarily designated as those who had been practitioners of the occupation for three years or less. The reason for attempting to weigh the sample in favor of new entrants was that the focus of the study was on the problem of current occupational shortages, and the experiences of recent entrants therefore seemed most relevant. Veterans, however, were to be included in the sample in order that any changes over time could be identified.

The method planned for obtaining the sample was as follows. At the time of the employer interviews, the interviewers were to ask permission to take from the personnel files of the firms the names and certain work history information of persons employed in the occupations under study. The interviewer was to identify whether the worker was a recent entrant or a veteran of the occupation, and then in accordance with the predetermined size of the subsample to be drawn from that firm, obtain the names of twice as many workers as were to be interviewed in that firm. To the extent that the organization of the personnel files allowed, the names were to be drawn randomly. The final sample, and alternates when required, were then to be drawn from the names obtained in this fashion.

The procedure worked fairly well for the medical occupations, although the personnel records were often inadequate for determining whether the worker was a recent entrant or a veteran. Few of the industrial firms, however, would allow this use of their personnel file, and the subsamples tended to be picked on an *ad hoc* basis at the time of the interview by the personnel manager or by a supervisor. Therefore, such factors as who happened to be working on the day of the interview and who the foreman was willing to release for an interview, and perhaps the judgment of a company official about who would be a good person to interview, all entered into the selection of the sample. Efforts were made in each case to influence the company to pick subjects at random, but the interviewers had little control over the selection. As a result of this and other factors, the original sample design had to be compromised very severely, particularly for the industrial occupations.

The sampling goals for the six occupations and the characteristics of the sample that was actually drawn are shown in Table C-3. As is obvious from the table, the actual sample departed considerably from the stated goals both in the number of interviews obtained in the six occupations and in the distribution between recent entrants and veterans.

Reaching the number of interviews planned for was hampered by two factors. First, not all establishments employed workers in the occupations that were the subject of the interviews. This was a problem only infrequently in the hospital interviews but was often the case in the industrial firms. As an example, in the twenty Chicago firms in the electronics industry sample, eleven employed no tool and die designers. And in the Chicago metal industry sample, five of the twenty-six firms employed no tool and die makers, nine employed no designers, and four employed no technicians. In addition, other firms employed only small numbers of workers in the occupations and were either unable or unwilling to provide the number of workers for interviewing that the sample called for. Thus, the number of interviews called for was at too ambitious a level for the number of firms in the employer sample.

A second factor limiting the size of the worker sample was that a number of the industrial firms refused to allow any interviewing of their workers at all, either on or off company premises. The reason usually given was that it was against company policy, and the blame was often shifted to a parent company. Others, however, were simply unwilling to take workers off the job, even for a 30-minute interview, and did not feel they should give out the names of employees for possible interviewing elsewhere.

An effort was made to offset this problem to some extent by increasing the size of the subsamples taken from firms who were willing to have their employees interviewed. The possibilities for this, however, were quite limited without exploiting those firms that were doing the most to be cooperative. Consideration was given to going to firms not in the employer sample to request permission to interview workers. In St. Louis, however, where the problem was most serious, most of the larger firms, from whom one might obtain a significant number of interviews, were already in the sample or had refused to participate in the study. In this connection, the sampling goals in St. Louis were damaged most severely by the inability of a very large industrial firm to allow its workers to be interviewed. The reasons given were intimately tied up with its status as an important defense contractor. Since this firm employed a large proportion of the workers in the labor market in three of the occupations we were studying, it seemed fruitless to try to improve the samples by going to other firms. In Chicago, interviews were obtained from employees of a number of firms not in the employer sample, particularly for tool and die makers and designers. Most of these were employees of relatively small job shops which were not included in the original employer sample because of their small size. Five large Chicago metal firms did not allow interviews with their employees, and this was the primary cause of the failure to reach the goal for interviews with engineering technicians in that city. Extended efforts were made to try to arrange worker interviews in these firms, but they did not succeed.

Table C-3

Worker Sample, Medical, Electronic, and Metalworking Industries

	Licensed Practical Nurse		Medical Tech-nologist		Tool & Die Maker	
	Goal	*Act.*	*Goal*	*Act.*	*Goal*	*Act.*
Chicago						
Recent Entrants	67	52	67	41	50	11
Veterans	33	33	33	47	25	108
Total	100	85	100	88	75	119
St. Louis						
Recent Entrants	67	50	67	46	50	12
Veterans	33	27	33	48	25	53
Total	100	77	100	94	75	65
Two Cities Combined						
Recent Entrants	134	102	134	87	100	22
Veterans	66	60	66	95	50	162
Total	200	162	200	182	150	184

Tool & Die Designer Goal	Tool & Die Designer Act.	Engineering Electronics Goal	Engineering Electronics Act.	Technicians Metalworking Goal	Technicians Metalworking Act.
50	16	50	30	50	5
25	47	25	46	25	18
75	63	75	76	75	23
50	8	50	7	50	3
25	25	25	9	25	7
75	33	75	16	75	10
100	26	100	37	100	8
50	70	50	55	50	25
150	96	150	92	150	33

The main reasons for failure to obtain samples with the desired ratio of recent entrants and veterans were two-fold. First, the objective appeared to be unrealistic for most of the occupations. New hires in the occupations were not occurring rapidly enough to provide the possibility of obtaining such a large proportion of new entrants. Secondly, either because of inadequacies in the personnel records or because of the method by which respondents were chosen, we did not have sufficient control over the selection of subjects to obtain the desired result. In any event, the goal was arbitrary and the failure to reach it was not of major consequence.

The worker samples obtained can be summarized as follows. The two medical occupation samples were obtained in accordance with the original sample design. The sizes of the samples were smaller than planned for and the proportion of recent entrants and veterans could not be controlled. Both of these objectives of the design, however, were arbitrary, and the sampling results were essentially as desired. The worker samples for the industrial occupations fell considerably short of goals, particularly for tool and die designers and engineering technicians in St. Louis and engineering technicians-metalworking in Chicago. The best that can be said is that we have a respectable, albeit not random, sample of tool and die makers in the two cities and tool and die designers and engineering technicians-electronic in Chicago. The inadequacy of the engineering technician-metalworking sample is not only the result of sampling problems, but also of sparse employment of such people in the two labor markets. Most firms who employed them at all employed them in small numbers. In any event, the limitations in the worker samples for the industrial occupations necessitate caution in utilizing the study results from this source.

The interviews with the licensed practical nurses and medical technologists took place between February and May of 1964. Those with members of the industrial occupations occurred between January and July of 1965 in Chicago and between June and September of 1965 in St. Louis. The interview form is shown in Appendix I.

Other Sources of Information

Three other sources of information for the study were tapped. First, administrators of specialized training schools which offered training leading to entry into the six occupations were interviewed (see Appendix J for the interview form used). In general, all schools in the two labor markets that could be identified as having relevant programs were interviewed. In the case of schools of medical technology, only a sample of the schools were contacted. Descriptions of the schools and their programs are given in the text in the chapters which analyze training programs (Chapters 5 and 9).

At the time of the training school interviews (mainly in the summer of 1965), school officials were asked to provide us a list of all enrollees in relevant programs who had either completed the prescribed training program or had dropped out of training during the previous year. Such lists were secured from twenty-eight schools, all of them in Chicago.[d] None of the St. Louis schools were able to respond to the request. Between September, 1965, and February, 1966, mail questionnaires were sent to both those who had completed training programs and those who had dropped out. The main purpose of the questionnaire was to obtain information that would provide a basis for assessing the relationship between training and post-training employment experience (see Appendixes K and L for the mail questionnaire forms used). Two mail follow-ups of nonrespondents were conducted. The returns to the survey are shown in Table C-4.

As the table indicates, there were substantial proportions of nonrespondents in each occupational group. In addition, we had no control at all over the selection of the names provided for the sample. We asked for the names of all enrollees, but we have no way of knowing whether the names were screened. For these two reasons, the results of the mail survey can be used only as gross indicators, not as precise measures of post-training experiences of recent trainees.

Finally, interviews were also conducted with about twenty-five high school counselors in the Chicago area. The subjects were not selected through any specific sampling design other than to get representation from different areas of the city and from various types of schools. No attempt was made to quantify the interview results and no formal interview guide was used. The results serve only to provide general impressions of counseling programs and the nature of problems involved. They are used only sparingly in this report.

Use of the Data

The methods of analysis used for the study are made clear throughout the report. Both because of limitations in the data themselves and because of the nature of the study, the data are not submitted to refined statistical analysis. Conclusions are not based on tests of statistical significance, but on the weight of evidence brought together from a variety of sources.

[d]The lists were obtained from four schools of practical nursing, twelve schools of medical technology, and twleve trade schools and technical institutes.

Table C-4

Result of Mail Survey of Chicago Recent Trainees

Nature of Training Program	*Number of Questionnaires Sent*	*Number of Returns*	*Percent Responding*	Returns for Those *Completing Training*	*Dropped*
Tool and Die Making or Machinist	191	132	69%	110	22
Tool and Die Designer	55	39	71%	24	15
Engineering Technology, Other than Electronic	51	31	61%	11	20
Medical Technology	105	72	69%	69	3
Licensed Practical Nursing	666	376	56%	307	69
Electronic Technology	546	308	56%	214	94
Total	1,614	958	59%	735	223

D Definition of Technician Occupations

Engineering Technician

The engineering technician may be employed in (1) research, design, or development; (2) production, operation, or control; or (3) installation or maintenance. Depending upon the functional area in which he works, the engineering technician may or may not work under the direct supervision of an engineer, his specialty may be directed toward creative engineering or toward production problems, and his duties may be related to the design, construction, installation, maintenance, or testing of products or equipment. In general, however, the technician's task is the application of scientific knowledge to workable and practical reality.

In executing his functions, the engineering technician is required to use a relatively high degree of rational thinking and to employ post-secondary school mathematics and principles of physical science. In so doing, he assumes the more routine engineering functions necessary in a technological-based economy.

Examples of duties of the technician include the preparation of engineering drawings; the construction and/or testing of components and equipment from engineering drawings, schematics, sketches, or verbal instructions; the rebuilding or repair of newly developed equipment; working with engineers in the modification of design, construction, or performance of prototypes, and the supervision of pilot-lot production.

In attempting to identify the range of occupations that fall in the engineering technician category, it might be helpful to note occupational groups that are excluded. Excluded from consideration in this study are the traditional skilled craftsman occupations (e.g., electrician), engineers with the baccalaureate degree, and workers engaged in essentially routine tasks of a semiskilled nature that require only relatively brief periods of on-the-job training to master. As a general rule, only occupations which require some formal training beyond the high school, such as in colleges, junior colleges, technical institutes or other specialized training schools, should be considered as in the technician group. However, a worker with long experience and self-study might also be able to fill some of the technician jobs.

Technicians employed in the manufacture of electronic products and equipment are designated *engineering technician – electronics;* those employed in the manufacture of nonelectrical metal products and equipment are designated *engineering technician – metalworking.*

E

Tables Supplementing the Chapter 2 Discussion of the Medical Occupations

Table E-1

Trends in the Number of Professional Nurse Graduates

	Year[1]	*Number of Graduates*
Calendar Year:	1900	3,456
	1905	5,795
	1910	8,140
	1915	11,118
	1920	14,980
	1927	18,623
	1929	23,810
	1931	25,971
	1932	25,312
	1935	19,600
	1936	18,600
	1937	20,400
	1938	20,655
	1939	22,485
	1940	23,600
	1941	24,899
	1942	25,613
	1943	26,816
	1944	28,276

(continued)

[1]Data from 1952 include Hawaii and Puerto Rico.

Source: U. S. Department of Health, Education, and Welfare, *Toward Quality in Nursing*, report of the Surgeon General's Consultant Group on Nursing (Washington, D. C.: U. S. Government Printing Office, February, 1963), Appendix Table 4, p. 62; for the year 1962-63, "Nurse Training Act

Table E-1 (*continued*)

	Year[1]	*Number of Graduates*
Calendar Year:	1945	31,721
	1946	36,195
	1947	40,744
	1948	34,268
	1949	21,379
	1950	25,790
	1951	28,794
	1952	29,016
	1953	29,308
	1954	28,539
	1955	28,729
Academic Year:	1955-56	30,236
	1956-57	29,933
	1957-58	30,410
	1958-59	30,312
	1959-60	30,113
	1960-61	30,267
	1962-63	32,400

of 1964," *H.E.W. Indicators* (October, 1964), p. xx.

Table E-2

Trend in the Number of Practical Nurse Graduates from Accredited Nursing Programs

	Year	*Number of Graduates*
Calendar Year:	1948	1,550
	1949	2,143
	1950	2,828
	1951	3,810
Academic Year:	1952–53	5,380
	1953–54	7,109
	1954–55	9,694
	1955–56	10,641
	1956–57	10,666
	1957–58	12,407
	1958–59	14,573
	1959–60	16,491
	1960–61	16,635
	1961–62	18,106
	1962–63	19,621
	1963–64	22,761

Source: U. S. Department of Health, Education, and Welfare, *Toward Quality in Nursing*, report of the Surgeon General's Consultant Group on Nursing (Washington, D. C.: U. S. Government Printing Office, February, 1963), Appendix Table 5, p. 63; U. S. Department of Health, Education and Welfare, Public Health Services, National Center for Health Statistics, *Health Resources Statistics, 1965*, Table 86, p. 115.

Table E-3

Sex Distribution of Employed Practical Nurses, 1950 and 1960

	1950			1960			Percent Change 1950–60	
	Male	*Female*	*Percent Male*	*Male*	*Female*	*Percent Male*	*Male*	*Female*
United States	5,640	130,901	4.3	8,859	197,115	4.1	57.1	50.6
Illinois:								
State	238	5,936	3.9	407	8,033	4.8	71.0	35.3
Chicago[1]	144	3,047	4.5	249	3,752	6.2	72.9	23.1
Missouri:								
State	154	3,741	4.0	216	5,646	3.7	40.3	50.9
St. Louis[1]	53	1,347	3.8	134	2,486	5.1	152.8	84.6

[1]Standard Metropolitan Statistical Area

Source: U. S. Census of Population Report, "Detailed Characteristics of the Population," (Washington, D. C.: U. S. Government Printing Office, 1960).

Table E-4

Age Distribution of Employed Female Practical Nurses in the United States, 1960

Age	*Number*[1]	*Percent*	*Numerical Change 1950–60*	*Percent Change 1950–60*
Total	197,824	100.0%		
Under 25 years	16,051	8.1	4,083	34.1%
25–29 years	12,050	6.1	4,357	56.6
30–34 years	14,034	7.1	5,476	64.0
35–44 years	38,861	19.6	14,284	58.1
45–54 years	51,326	25.9	19,247	60.0
55–59 years	24,691	12.5	7,723	45.5
60–64 years	19,855	10.0	4,870	32.5
65 years and over	20,956	10.6	6,089	41.0

[1] Includes 709 midwives.

Source: U. S. Census of Population Report, "Detailed Characteristics of the Population," (Washington, D. C.: U. S. Government Printing Office, 1960).

Table E-5

Average Monthly Starting Salaries and Monthly Going Salaries for Licensed Practical Nurses, Illinois Hospitals, 1955-1965, Metropolitan Chicago Hospitals, 1963 and 1965[1]

	Monthly Starting Salaries		Monthly Going Salaries[2]	
Year	*Illinois*	*Chicago*	*Illinois*	*Chicago*
1955	$178	--	$192	--
1956	181	--	198	--
1957	190	--	207	--
1958	200	--	219	--
1959	209	--	229	--
1960	221	--	239	--
1961	230	--	248	--
1962	237	--	256	--
1963	244	$289	265	$309
1964	251	--	273	--
1965	267	$309	289	$331

[1] State and federal hospitals excluded.

[2] Going salary is the mean salary of those employed in the occupational category.

Source: Illinois Hospital Association, *Hospital Salaries in Illinois*, Report Number 26 (September 1963) pp. 17–18; Report Number 33 (December 1965) pp. 17–18, 22–24.

Table E-6

Average Starting Salaries and Monthly Going Salaries for Medical Technologists (ASCP) Employed by Hospitals in the State of Illinois, 1955–1965, and in Metropolitan Chicago, 1963 and 1965[1]

	Monthly Starting Salary		Monthly Going Salary	
Year	*Illinois*	*Chicago*	*Illinois*	*Chicago*
1955	$304	--	$331	--
1956	321	--	347	--
1957	334	--	371	--
1958	350	--	389	--
1959	364	--	408	--
1960	382	--	424	--
1961	388	--	437	--
1962	405	--	450	--
1963	411	$419	456	$455
1964	421	--	466	--
1965	432	$432	485	$484
	Percentage Increase		Percentage Increase	
	Illinois	*Chicago*	*Illinois*	*Chicago*
1963–1964	2.4%	--	2.2%	--
1964–1965	2.6	--	3.9	--
1963–1965	5.1	3.1%	6.1	6.6%

[1]State and federal hospitals excluded.

Source: Illinois Hospital Association, *Hospital Salaries in Illinois*, Report no. 26, (September 1963) pp. 17–18; Report no. 33, (December 1965) pp. 17–18, 22–24.

Table E-7

Median Salaries of Medical Technologists (ASCP) by State, 1959

State	*Yearly*	*Monthly*
California	$5,108	$426
Michigan	5,013	418
Minnesota	4,828	402
Illinois	4,715	393
Indiana	4,714	393
District of Columbia	4,688	391
Arizona	4,636	386
Maryland	4,558	380
Alabama	4,517	376
Oregon	4,491	374
Washington	4,488	374
Wisconsin	4,459	372
Oklahoma	4,436	370
Connecticut	4,418	368
Texas	4,416	368
New York	4,353	363
New Jersey	4,350	363
Ohio	4,343	362
Colorado	4,329	361

Table E-7 (*continued*)

State	*Yearly*	*Monthly*
Missouri	$4,322	$360
Mississippi	4,286	357
Iowa	4,245	354
Florida	4,211	351
West Virginia	4,186	349
Nebraska	4,167	347
Louisiana	4,130	344
Kansas	4,120	343
Kentucky	4,107	342
Virginia	4,100	342
North Carolina	4,076	340
Georgia	4,047	337
Massachusetts	4,032	336
Tennessee	4,025	335
Pennsylvania	4,010	334
Arkansas	3,986	332

Source: National survey of full-time registered Medical Technologists (ASCP), January, 1959, by the Registry of Medical Technologists (ASCP) and the National Committee for Careers in Medical Technology.

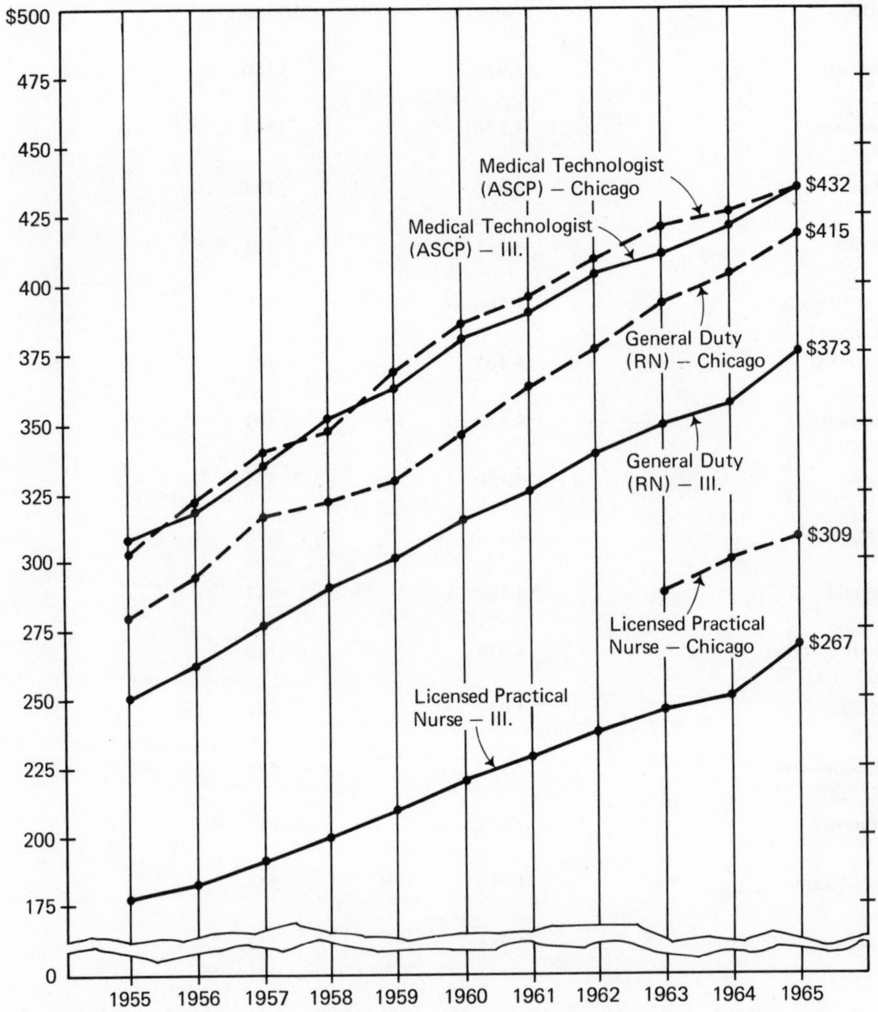

Figure E-1 Average monthly starting salaries for hospital personnel in the state of Illinois and Metropolitan Chicago, 1955-1965 (State and federal hospitals excluded). Source: Illinois Hospital Association, *Hospital Salaries in Illinois*, Report No. 26 (September, 1963); Report No. 33 (December, 1965).

F

Tables Supplementing the Chapter 2 Discussion of the Industrial Occupations

Table F-1

Significant Types of Education and Training Acquired by Engineering and Physical Science Technicians in the Experienced Civilian Labor Force, 1962

Primary Types of Education and Training	*Percent Distribution*[1]
Special training by employer	36.3
Course work without degree	29.6
Associate degree	5.6
Bachelor degree	7.3
Graduate or professional	2.8
Post-high school courses	9.1
Correspondence courses	13.7
Military training	23.6
Experience in present or related fields	55.1
Other	5.5

(continued

Table F-1 (*continued*)

Supplementary Education and Training	*Percent Distribution*
Apprenticeship	5.9
Other company training program	24.9
Military	17.2
On-the-job	22.6
High school extension courses	2.5
Homestudy correspondence courses	17.4
Agricultural training courses	.2
U. S. Armed Forces Institute courses	3.9
Work study programs	1.4
Workshops and seminars	3.9

[1]Since some persons indicated more than one type of experience and training, the percent distribution adds to more than 100.

Source: Howard V. Stambler and Annie Lefkowitz, "Education and Training of Technicians," *Monthly Labor Review*, vol. 87, no. 11 (November, 1964), pp. 1279, 1280.

Table F-2

Level of Education of Technicians by Occupation and Age, 1963 (Percent Distributions)

Age Distribution	All Levels of Education *Number*	*Percent*	*Less than High School*	*High School Grad-uates*	*Some Col-lege* [1]	*Bach-elor and Plus*
	All Technicians					
All Ages	844,800	100.0	12.2	24.6	53.1	10.0
Less Than 20 Years	14,200	100.0	7.6	29.7	62.6	--
20–24 Years	159,000	100.0	3.8	29.4	62.6	4.3
25–34 Years	296,900	100.0	6.7	22.4	58.6	12.3
35–44 Years	212,400	100.0	11.8	25.8	52.2	10.2
45–54 Years	107,500	100.0	21.8	26.5	41.7	9.9
55–64 Years	43,200	100.0	44.1	9.1	34.5	11.6
65 and Over	11,400	100.0	41.2	11.8	35.6	11.4
	Draftsmen					
All Ages	232,000	100.0	6.7	21.6	64.5	7.2
Less Than 20 Years	3,200	100.0	--	28.8	71.2	--
20–24 Years	51,300	100.0	2.3	30.7	65.4	1.6
25–34 Years	80,300	100.0	2.5	20.5	66.6	10.5
35–44 Years	57,100	100.0	4.6	19.5	69.0	6.9
45–54 Years	26,200	100.0	13.8	18.8	58.6	8.7

(continued)

Table F-2 (*continued*)

Age Distribution	All Levels of Education *Number*	*Percent*	*Less than High School*	*High School Graduates*	*Some College*[1]	*Bachelor and Plus*
			Draftsmen			
55-64 Years	9,300	100.0	43.0	5.0	42.5	9.5
65 and Over	4,600	100.0	45.4	9.5	35.9	9.2
			Engineering and Physical Science			
All Ages	439,000	100.0	14.5	25.8	51.0	8.7
Less Than 20 Years	6,100	100.0	12.6	49.5	37.9	--
20-24 Years	78,600	100.0	5.3	27.9	63.5	3.4
25-34 Years	164,600	100.0	9.3	21.6	58.7	10.5
35-44 Years	109,300	100.0	14.7	31.8	45.0	8.5
45-54 Years	57,900	100.0	28.2	27.4	33.8	10.5
55-64 Years	19,300	100.0	51.9	10.1	25.5	12.6
65 and Over	3,100	100.0	39.2	14.0	32.7	14.1

[1]Includes technicians without any degree and those with an associate degree but no bachelor's degree.

Source: Bureau of Labor Statistics, *Technician Manpower: Requirements, Resources and Training Needs*. Bulletin No. 1512 (Washington, D. C.: U. S. Government Printing Office, June, 1966), p. 27.

Table F-3

Technicians, by Industry, 1960 Employment and Projected 1970 Requirements

Industry	1960 Employment	
	Techni-cians	*Technicians per 100 Scientists and Engineers*
All industries	775,100	67
Mining	10,600	34
Construction	32,700	59
Manufacturing	420,200	68
Food and Kindred Products	8,100	82
Textile Mill Products and Apparel	4,700	81
Lumber and Furniture	3,700	123
Paper and Allied Products	6,500	62
Chemicals and Allied Products	39,500	44
Petroleum Refining and Products of Petroleum & Coal	11,700	42
Rubber Products	13,800	182
Stone, Clay, and Glass Industries	5,000	49
Primary Metal Industries	17,900	51
Fabricated Metal Products and Ordnance	37,800	99

Projected 1970 Requirements		
Techni-cians	*Technicians per 100 Scientists and Engineers*	*Percent Change Technicians (Projected) 1960–1970*
1,296,700	66	67%
14,000	34	32
63,300	59	94
749,300	70	78
12,200	81	51
5,400	82	15
4,200	120	14
11,800	62	82
70,600	46	79
17,300	42	48
16,700	180	21
7,600	49	52
29,100	51	63
94,100	99	149

(continued)

Table F-3 (*continued*)

Industry	1960 Employment *Techni-cians*	*Technicians per 100 Scientists and Engineers*
Machinery	72,100	101
Electrical Equipment	79,200	78
Aircraft, Missiles, and Spacecraft	49,000	46
Motor Vehicles and Equipment	24,500	69
Other Transportation Equipment	3,300	92
Professional and Scientific Instruments	21,300	81
Miscellaneous Manufacturing	22,200	73
Transportation, Communication, and Electric, Gas, and Sanitary Services	57,900	94
Transportation	10,700	91
Communication	30,400	125
Electric, Gas, and Sanitary Services	16,800	66
Government	138,100	81
Federal Government	61,400	62
State Governments	48,700	119
Local Governments	28,000	93

Projected 1970 Requirements		
Techni-cians	*Technicians per 100 Scientists and Engineers*	*Percent Change Technicians (Projected) 1960–1970*
99,000	101	37%
154,700	78	95
107,000	55	118
36,400	69	49
5,600	93	70
41,800	81	96
35,900	74	62
73,400	92	27
16,000	91	50
38,400	116	26
19,000	66	13
191,200	79	38
93,800	62	53
60,100	119	23
37,400	93	34

(continued)

Table F-3 (*continued*)

Industry	1960 Employment *Techni-cians*	*Technicians per 100 Scientists and Engineers*
Colleges and Universities	10,000	8
Other Industries	105,600	105
Miscellaneous Business Services	7,300	94
Medical and Dental Laboratories	7,400	463
Nonprofit Organizations	6,500	100
Engineering and Architectural Services	63,500	112
All Other Nonmanufacturing	21,000	76

Projected 1970 Requirements		
Techni-cians	*Technicians per 100 Scientists and Engineers*	*Percent Change Technicians (Projected) 1960–1970*
20,000	8	100%
185,600	104	76
20,300	93	178
12,700	454	72
10,600	100	63
102,300	12	61
39,700	76	89

Source: National Science Foundation, *Scientists, Engineers, and Technicians in the 1960's: Requirements and Supply* (NSF 63-34), p. 36.

Table F-4

Technicians, by Occupational Specialty, 1963 Employment and Projected 1975 Requirements[1]

Occupation	*1963 Employment*	*Projected 1975 Requirements*	*Percent Increase 1963–75*
Technicians, All Occupations	844,800	1,495,000	77
Draftsmen	232,000	375,000	62
Engineering and Physical Science Technicians	439,000	765,000	74
Engineering Technicians	308,500	533,000	73
Chemical Technicians	64,600	122,000	89
Physics Technicians	10,800	22,000	104
Mathematics Technicians	6,100	12,000	97
Other Physical Science Technicians	49,000	81,000	65
Life Science Technicians	58,100	139,000	139
Other Technicians	115,700	210,000	82

[1]Because of rounding the sum of individual items may not add to totals.

Source: Bureau of Labor Statistics, *Technician Manpower: Requirements, Resources, and Training Needs*, U. S. Department of Labor, (Washington, D. C.: U. S. Government Printing Office, 1966) p. 54.

Table F-5

High, Intermediate, and Low Projections of the Supply of Technicians from Pre-Employment and Technician-Related Training, 1963–1974

	High		Intermediate	
Source of Training	*Total*	*Annual Average*	*Total*	*Annual Average*
Postsecondary Preemployment Curriculum	522,800	43,600	434,000	36,200
MDTA Programs	61,100	5,600	40,700	3,700
College and University Graduates	74,100	6,200	60,500	5,000
College and University Drop Outs	104,200	8,700	47,600	4,000
Armed Forces Separations	60,600	5,100	15,800	1,300
Employer Training	436,900	36,400	232,800	19,400
Total--all sources	1,259,700	105,000	832,000	69,300

	Low	
	Total	*Annual Average*
Postsecondary Preemployment Curriculum	286,800	23,900
MDTA Programs	30,500	2,800
College and University Graduates	46,400	3,900
College and University Drop Outs	28,600	2,400
Armed Forces Separations	8,800	700
Employer Training	174,600	14,500
Total–all sources	575,700	48,000

It does not necessarily follow that all lows would occur together and all highs together as illustrated in this table. Any combination of high, low, or primary estimates among the six sources is possible. However, the totals shown illustrate the wide range of possible supply totals.

Because of rounding the sum of individual items may not add to totals.

Source: Bureau of Labor Statistics, *Technician Manpower: Requirements, Resources, and Training Needs*, U. S. Department of Labor, (Washington, D. C.: U. S. Government Printing Office, 1966) p. 76.

Table F-6

High, Intermediate, and Low Projections of Technician Requirements and Supply, 1963–1975

Level of Supply	*Total Manpower Needs 1963–1975*	*Supply with Preemployment or Technician-Related Training 1963–1975*	*Upgrading Needs 1963–1975*[1]
		High Requirements	
High supply	1,290,000	1,026,000	318,000
Intermediate supply	1,290,000	678,000	745,000
Low supply	1,290,000	469,000	1,002,000
		Intermediate Requirements	
High supply	1,025,000	1,026,000	---
Intermediate supply	1,025,000	678,000	426,000
Low supply	1,025,000	469,000	682,000
		Low Requirements	
High supply	887,000	1,026,000	---
Intermediate supply	887,000	678,000	251,000
Low supply	887,000	469,000	507,000

[1] Including estimated needs for those upgraded from 1963–1975 who would retire, die, or transfer to other occupations by 1975.

Source: Bureau of Labor Statistics, *Technician Manpower: Requirements, Resources, and Training Needs*, U. S. Department of Labor, (Washington, D. C.: U. S. Government Printing Office, 1966) p. 81.

G

Employer Interview Schedule: Topical Outline for Hospital Interviews

For Each Occupation

A. Demand

1. Present demand (number of unfilled job openings)
2. Trend in demand over past five years
3. Anticipated future demand

   a. How many

      1. Expansion needs
      2. Replacement needs

   b. How far in advance this can safely be predicted

B. Supply

1. Recruitment policies and evaluation
2. Selection policies and evaluation
3. Hiring policies and evaluation

C. Training

1. This hospital's involvement in training
2. Requirements for new hires
3. Who they take
4. Who they do not take
5. Evaluation of all training schools
6. Any use of commercial schools?

   a. Why or why not
   b. Evaluation of commerical school training
   c. Any tendency to hire more (or fewer) commercial school graduates

D. Pay and conditions of employment

1. Hospitalization and medical insurance
2. Meal allowance

(continued)

3. Annual vacation (weeks per year)
4. Sick leave (days per year)
5. Holidays (days per year)
6. Private pension plan

   a. __________% of salary contributed by hospital
   b. __________% of premium employee pays
   c. __________% of premium hospital pays

7. Laundry services
8. Starting salary (method of payment)
9. Salary range
10. Average hours of work
11. Any adjustments (salaries and/or hours) regarding shortages
12. Trends in pay (past five years)

E. Employee organizations

1. Any bargaining relationship?
2. Effect on training and recruitment

(Notification of possible return visit)

H

Employer Interview Schedule for Interviews with Industrial Firms

Note: Interviewer should begin by asking whether written job descriptions are available for the occupations we are interested in for this study. If so, ask for copies. If not, ask for the job titles used in the establishment for the occupations under study.

Ask for Each Occupation

A. Demand

1. a. How many _________s are employed in this establishment at the present time?
   b. How many were employed five years ago?
   c. (If the number of _________s has increased) What have been the major reasons for the expansion of the number of _________s you employ?
   d. Do you have any unfilled openings for _________s at the present time? How many? Are funds budgeted to fill all of these vacancies? If not, explain.
   e. How long on the average does it take to fill a vacancy for a _________? If this longer or shorter than the time required five years ago?

2. Would you say there is a shortage of qualified _________s? How serious is the shortage? If no, explain. If yes:
   a. In what ways have your operations been affected by this shortage?
   b. Has the shortage made it necessary for you to turn down any orders because you could not turn out the work on time? Explain.
   c. Has the shortage meant you have had to lengthen the time required for your company to turn out orders? Explain.
   d. Has the shortage in any way affected your ability to compete with other firms for business? Explain.

3. Have the duties of a _________ changed over the last few years? If so, in what ways?
   a. Are other workers now doing any of the work that _________s used to do? Explain.
   b. Have any other occupational groups expanded significantly to take over some of the work formerly done by _________s? Explain.

4. Have you taken any other steps to get the work done in the face of the shortage of ________s?

5. Have you laid off any ________s during the last few years? When? Explain why.

6. Do you expect your needs for ________s to increase or decrease during the next five years? By about how much? How much of the increase is for replacement? How much for expansion?
   a. How far in advance can you accurately predict your need for ________s?

B. Supply

1. What is this company's source of qualified ________s?
   a. Where do you recruit? (e.g., type of school, geographic location, etc.)
   b. What is this company's best source of recruits in this occupation?
   c. How do you recruit? (e.g., advertising, school visits, etc.)
   d. About what proportion of your ________s are obtained from other occupations within the company?

2. How would you evaluate the success of this company's recruitment practices for ________s? Excellent, good, fair, poor?
   a. Why?
   b. What improvements in present recruiting policies for qualified ________s would you recommend for your company?

3. Has it been necessary for this company to alter its recruitment policies or methods for obtaining qualified ________s in the past five years?
   a. If so, what were these changes?
   b. Why did the company find it necessary to make these changes?

4. Are any further alterations in recruiting policies and methods for obtaining qualified ________s anticipated within the next five years?
   a. If so, what changes?
   b. Why make these changes?

5. When applicants are interviewed for employment as ________s, what minimum qualifications does this company look for?
   a. Are you able to find sufficient ________s with these minimum qualifications?
   b. (If not), Why not?

6. Do you feel that your qualification requirements for ________s are:
   a. Too high? Explain.
   b. Too low? Explain.
   c. What changes, if any, would you recommend in these minimum qualifications?

7. Has your company either lowered or raised its minimum qualifications for ________s in the past five years?
   a. If so, why?
   b. What had the qualifications been?
   c. What effect did this change have on your ability to recruit sufficient numbers of qualified ________s?

8. What would you consider to be the optimum qualification requirements for ________s?
   a. Do you feel that people you are hiring now as ________s are far from these optimum qualifications?
   b. If so, in what respect?

C. Training

1. Is this company involved in formal (including on-the-job) training programs for ________s? If not, skip to question 4. If so:
   a. What are the minimum qualifications of workers accepted into this training program?
   b. Is entry into this training based on merit and experience of present employees, or are most trainees started in this program shortly after (or before) being hired?
   c. From what occupational groups are most trainees for ________s selected?
   d. How many ________s are now involved in this program?
      1) How does this figure compare with five years ago? Higher now? Lower? Same?

2. What is the nature of the training this company has for ________s?
   a. How long is the training period?
   b. After a person completes this training, is he automatically given a promotion and/or raise in salary?

c. Does the trainee receive a license or certificate upon completion of this training?
d. Is the control of the training program completely in the hands of management? (If not) Who else is involved in controlling the training, and what is their involvement?

3. What is your evaluation of this training program?
   a. Are enough qualified trainees attracted into the program? Explain.
   b. Would you like to be training more _________s? If so, why aren't more being trained?

4. Where are most of your qualified _________s trained (of those *not* trained by the company)?
   a. How would you evaluate this training? Excellent, good, fair, poor? Why?
   b. Do you think that the graduates of these training programs are adequately trained to be employed as _________s in this company?
      1. If not, why not?
      2. What additional training do they need?
   c. Do you think that this company is better qualified to train its own _________s?
      1. Does this company plan to initiate a training program (if has none now)?
      2. When?

5. What do you consider to be the *best* training schools for _________s in this city? Why?

6. What do you consider to be the least desirable training schools for _________s in this city?
   a. Why? (i.e., what qualities make them undesirable)
   b. Has it ever been necessary for this company to recruit graduates of this (undesirable) school? Why?
   c. Does your company now hire more (or fewer) graduates of this (undesirable) training school than before? More, fewer, same?

D. Pay and Conditions of Employment

Ask Only of Personnel Director

Would you please tell us what types of benefits are offered _________s in this company for each of the following items?

1. Hospitalization and medical insurance

2. Disability benefits

3. Annual vacation (weeks per year, per years of employment)

4. Sick leave (days per year)

5. Holidays (days per year)

6. Overtime–% adjustment in salary and average weekly overtime hours worked by _________s

7. Private pension plan
   a. Amount of pension
   b. _________% of salary contributed by employer
   c. _________% of salary employee contributes

8. Starting salary (method of payment)

9. Salary range for _________s

10. Average hours of work per week

11. Any adjustments (salaries and/or hours) regarding shortages

12. Trends in pay (obtain salary difference in past five years)

E. Employee Organizations

Ask Only of Personnel Director

1. What, if any, union(s) represent _________s in this company?

2. What effect has union(s) had on company's recruitment policies?

3. What effect has union(s) had on company's training program and policies?

(Next page is provided for interviewer to ask respondent whether his concept of technician is very different from ours, and how.)

(Notification of possible return visit)

I

Worker Interview

A. Personal Characteristics

1. Job title.

2. Name.

3. Marital status: Single, married, divorced, widowed, other.

4. Address and telephone number.

5. Date of birth.

6. Race: White, nonwhite.

7. Name of establishment.

   A. Department in which employed.
   B. Date started with company.
   C. Date started in department.
   D. Date started in position.

8. Usual hours of work per week.

   A. Hours at premium pay.
   B. Comments.

9. How long have you lived in this metropolitan area?

10. Did you move to this metropolitan area to seek employment? Explain.

11. Dependents:

    A. Number of children under age 18.
    B. Number of dependents 18 or over.

12. Are you the primary wage earner in your family? Primary, spouse primary, secondary earner? Is your wife (husband) also employed? If yes, explain.

13. Father's usual occupation. Mother's usual occupation.

B. Training

1. Education level (circle highest grade or year of school completed).

   A. 1. If attended high school, nature of high school education: academic, technical, commercial, general.
   2. If left high school, why did you leave?

   B. If attended college:
   1. Did you graduate? Number of years completed. Degree or certificate received.
   2. If not a graduate, why did you leave college?
   3. Special field.
   4. Name of school. Location of school.

2. Have you had any specialized vocational training (other than high school or college)? Was this training for your present occupation?

   A. If training for present occupation (Items 1–4 below):
   1. Type.
   2. When (months and years).
   3. Where trained.
   4. Length of training.

   B. If training for other occupation (Items 1–5 below):
   1. Type.
   2. When (months and years).
   3. Where trained.
   4. Length of training.
   5. Why are you not still in a job which utilizes this training?

3. How did you get into the training program for your present occupation? Were you counselled on the training available? If yes, by whom? SES, management, labor union, school counselor, other? Where? Do you think you received adequate counselling (information and advice) before you went into training? If not, explain why.

4. Did any of the training institutions actively try to recruit you into their training programs? *If yes:* What institutions? How did they go about trying to recruit you into training programs?

5. Do you think you knew enough about the occupation before training so that you could make an intelligent decision?

   A. What information would have made your choice easier?

6. What qualifications did you have to have to gain admittance into this training program?

7. Were you refused admittance to any training programs for your present occupation? If yes, explain the circumstances.

8. We would like your evaluation of the training you received.

   A. Classroom instruction: excellent, good, fair, poor? Why?

   B. Where taken.

   C. On-the-job and/or apprenticeship: excellent, good, fair, poor? Why?

   D. In which ways could the training be improved?

9. Did you have to overcome any problems in order to take or complete this training? If yes, what were these problems like?

10. After you completed this training, was it necessary for you to obtain a license or in some way be registered to practice this occupation?

    A. Licensing or registry agency and location.

    B. Licensing Process.

    C. Official title once licensed.

    D. Was a licensing examination required?

    E. Were you qualified to take this examination upon completion of the training program?

11. When you completed the training program, were you automatically in a job in the occupation? If not, why?

    A. How long did it take to obtain a job? Weeks.

    B. How did you obtain the job?

C. Did you know of any other job openings for ________s at the time? If so,
   1. What were they?
   2. Why did you take the job you did?
   3. Did you run across any jobs you would rather have had? Explain.

12. Have you had supplementary training since you started as a ________? *If yes:* Was this additional training required? If not, why did you take it?

13. Do you plan to take any further training? *If yes:*

   A. What will it be?

   B. When do you plan to start?

   C. What will you gain through further training?

   D. Do you have any specific jobs in mind?

14. (Note: APPLICABLE ONLY FOR VETERANS IN THE OCCUPATION)

   Have you ever had difficulty finding or keeping a job as a ________? If yes, why?

C. **Work History**

Note: Data on the following items were obtained from each respondent for all jobs held prior to the training received for his present occupation and for all jobs held after the training received for his present occupation:

1. When held the job: From (month and year) to (month and year).

2. Location of job (city and state).

3. Job title.

4. Industry in which job was held.

5. Brief job description.

6. Average pay.

7. Reason for leaving job.

D. Present Job

1. Was this your first job after training?

   A. If no, how did you obtain this job?

2. A. What do you think of your chances of finding a similar or better job as a _________ in other companies? Excellent, good, fair, poor? Explain.

   B. What do you think your chances are of advancing to a better job as a _________? Excellent, good, fair, poor? Explain.

3. Do you think you will stay in this occupation? Why?

4. Do you think you will stay with this establishment? Why?

5. How would you rate job security in this occupation? Excellent, good, fair, poor? Why?

6. What do you like about _________ as an occupation? Check one of the following mentioned by respondent: job content, security, pay, fringe benefits, working conditions, other.

7. What are some of the things you do not like about _________ as an occupation? Check any of the following mentioned by respondent: job content, security, pay, fringe benefits, working conditions, other.

8. Are you making full use of the training you have received? Explain.

9. Would additional training allow you to do more difficult and a greater variety of tasks than you do now? If so, what additional training would be required?

10. Have there been any major changes in your duties since you:

    A. Began on this job? Explain what they are and why they occurred.

    B. Began in this kind of work? Why?

11. We are studying this occupation because there are supposedly not enough people being trained for it.

    A. Do you think this is true? Not enough, enough?

B. (If person agrees that there is a shortage): What do you think can be done to persuade more people to enter the occupation?

Note to Interviewer: *Identify Free Response with an "S" and Prompted Responses With "P." Note Which Are Most Important*

(1) Information to potential entrants; (2) Quality of guidance and counselling; (3) Characteristics of the occupation itself; (4) Prevailing pay; (5) Prevailing working conditions; (6) Nature and extent of fringe benefits; (7) Other. In your opinion, which of these are the most important?

J Training School Administrator Questionnaire

Operations

1. How long has this school been in existence?

2. How are the operations of this school financed?

3. Who controls the operations and programs of this school?

4. How many faculty members are there here?

5. What is the average student–faculty ratio today?

   a. How does this compare with the past ratios?
   b. What is the optimum ratio?

6. [On this occupation (s)] would you give me a statistical breakdown on the numbers of people *starting* and *completing* training in this school in the past? (Get all years available.)

7. What kind of degree, license, or certificate is conferred to the graduates of this school?

   a. Is any testing required prior to conferment of this degree?
   b. (If so) Who controls the testing? Who confers the degree?

8. Does this school plan any expansion of training facilities in the near future?

   a. (If so) How much: Faculty, students, new and/or additional location(s).
   b. How soon?
   c. Why?

9. Could you give me a brochure describing the training course available for _________s at this school?

   a. Have there been any changes since this brochure was printed? (e.g., costs, training period, course load, minimum requirements, etc.)

10. Is this school now operating at full capacity? (i.e., as many students in training as possible with existing facilities)

a. (If not) Why not?
b. How many more students could you handle?

Recruitment

1. Where do you recruit your students? (Obtain all sources—high schools, the labor market in general, newspapers, etc.—and geographic locations of recruiting.)

    a. What agencies, schools, churches, etc., if any, assist you in recruiting? How?

2. How do you recruit? (Probe for all methods used.)

3. What is your best *source* of recruits?

4. What is your best recruitment method?

5. Have you changed your recruitment methods within the past ten years? (e.g., gone more to newspaper ads)

    a. Why?
    b. What results?

6. Do you anticipate or hope to change your recruitment methods in the near future?

    a. How?
    b. Why?

7. What are your minimum requirements for acceptance of new students?

    a. Have these requirements been raised (lowered) in the past ten years? Why?
    b. Do you anticipate raising (lowering) these minimum requirements in the near future?

8. Are you satisfied with the present qualities of entering students? (If not) Why not?

9. Is it becoming easier or more difficult to recruit students meeting your minimum qualifications?

   a. (If so) Why do you think this is true?
   b. If more difficult, what could be done about this?

10. Do you feel that high school counselors adequately counsel students on this occupation as a career opportunity?

11. Do you feel that there is adequate information about the occupation available to potential entrants?

12. Are any scholarships, loans, installment payment plans, or other forms of financial assistance available to students in this training school? (List types and amounts.)

13. From what age brackets are most of your students recruited?

14. Could you estimate for me the white, nonwhite ratio of your students?

15. We are studying this occupation because supposedly there are not enough qualified _________s being trained to fill the available openings in the industry.

   a. Do you agree that this is true?
   b. If not, why have we been led to believe this? (i.e., what is the error in available shortage statistics?)
   c. If so:

      1. What are the principal reasons for the shortage?
      2. What can be done to alleviate the shortage? [Probe all possibilities including: more government support (financial and otherwise), more thorough advertising campaigns, more money paid to people in occupation, better communication system between schools and employer, etc.]
      3. What does this school hope to do to help alleviate the shortage?
      4. Do you expect this shortage to become *more* or *less* chronic in the future? Why?
      5. (For LPN and/or Med. Tech. School) Do you feel that the services provided for patient care have in any way been affected as a direct result of the shortage? How?
      6. (For engineering tech., tool and die maker, and designer schools) Do you feel that production costs and/or rates of completing production goods have been affected as a direct result of the shortage? How?

K

Mail Questionnaire Survey of Recent Trainees for Those Completing Training Programs

I. Personal Data: Sex; Date of birth (month, day, year); Marital status.

II. When did you complete your training for (occupation)? Month, year.

III. List all jobs you have had since completing the training course: title, date started, date left, salary, name of company, city, state. At your present job, how many hours per week do you usually work?

IV. If you are not working now:

1. What are you doing at present? (Check one) I am looking for a job; I am participating in a training program or attending school (explain what type); Other (Please explain).

2. Have you worked at all since completing the training course? If "Yes" answer the following for the *longest job* you have had since completing the training course:

   a. When did you work on this job? From (month, year) to (month, year).
   b. What was the *title* of the job?
   c. For whom did you work? (name of company or organization) Location of the job: city, state.
   d. What was your salary when you left the job?
   e. How many hours per week did you usually work?
   f. What was the main reason for leaving the job?

V. How would you evaluate the training that you received? Excellent, good, fair, poor? What are your reasons?

VI. How would you evaluate the advice or counselling you received before entering training? Excellent, good, fair, poor? What are your reasons?

VII. How did you finance your training? Worked part time; Parents helped pay; Wife worked; Got loan; Company paid. Received stipend, scholarship, or other aid; Other.

L

Mail Questionnaire Survey of Recent Trainees for Those Who Dropped Out of Training Programs

I. Personal Data: Sex; Date of birth (month, day, year); Marital status

II. 1. When did you leave the training course for (occupation)? Month, year?

2. What was the main reason for leaving the training course?

III. List all jobs you have had since leaving the training course: title, date started, date left, salary, name of company, city, state. At your present job, how many hours per week do you usually work?

IV. If you are not working now:

1. What are you doing at present? (Check one) I am looking for a job; I am participating in a training program or attending school (explain what type); Other (Please explain).

2. Have you worked at all since leaving the training course? If "Yes," answer the following for the *longest job* you have had since leaving the training course:

   a. When did you work on this job? From (month, year) to (month, year).
   b. What was the *title* of the job?
   c. For whom did you work? (name of company or organization) Location of the job: city, state.
   d. What was your salary when you left the job?
   e. How many hours per week did you usually work?
   f. What was the main reason for leaving the job?

V. How would you evaluate the training that you received? Excellent, good, fair, poor? What are your reasons?

VI. How would you evaluate the advice or counselling you received before entering training? Excellent, good, fair, poor? What are your reasons?

VII. How did you finance your training? (Check those that apply) Worked part time; Parents helped pay; Wife worked; Got loan; Company paid; Received stipend, scholarship, or other aid; Other.

Notes

Notes

Chapter 1
Framework and Design of the Study

1. Hugh Folk, "Another Look at the Shortage of Engineers and Scientists" (Working Paper 6412, Department of Economics, Washington University, St. Louis, Mo., September 24, 1964).

2. David M. Blank and George J. Stigler, *The Demand and Supply of Scientific Personnel* (New York: National Bureau of Economic Research, 1957), p. 24.

3. Kenneth J. Arrow and William M. Capron, "Dynamic Shortages and Price Rises: The Engineering-Scientist Case," *Quarterly Journal of Economics,* vol. 73, no. 2 (May, 1959), pp. 292-308.

4. *Ibid.,* p. 308.

5. *Ibid.* (italics added), p. 293.

6. *Ibid.,* p. 302.

7. Blank and Stigler, *op. cit.,* p. 28.

Chapter 2
Occupational Characteristics and Trends

1. U. S. Department of Labor, *Dictionary of Occupational Titles, 1965,* 3rd ed., vol. 1 (Washington, D. C.: U. S. Government Printing Office, 1965), p. 494.

2. U. S. Department of Health, Education, and Welfare, Public Health Service, *Toward Quality in Nursing,* report of the Surgeon General's Consultant Group on Nursing (Washington, D. C.: U. S. Government Printing Office, February, 1963), pp. 9, 16; and *Education for the Allied Health Professions and Services* (Washington, D. C.: U. S. Government Printing Office, 1967), p. 7.

3. Figures for other years are in Margaret West and Beatrice Crowther, *Education for Practical Nursing, 1960* (New York: Department of Practical Nursing Programs, National League for Nursing, 1962), p. 14; and *Toward Quality in Nursing, Ibid.,* p. 11; see *Education for the Allied Health Professions and Services, Ibid.,* p. 14.

4. *Statistical Information on the Registration and Education of Professional and Practical Nurses, 1962,* report compiled by Freda Treptow and Margaret Seelye, Coordinators of Nursing Education (Illinois: Department of Registration and Education).

5. Mary M. Roberts, *American Nursing: History and Interpretation* (New York: Macmillan Co., 1955), p. 406.

6. *Toward Quality in Nursing, op. cit.,* p. 15.

7. *Ibid.,* p. 13.

8. "Nursing Training Act of 1964," *H. E. W. Indicators* (October, 1964), p. xx.

9. *Ibid.*

10. *Toward Quality in Nursing, op. cit.*, Appendix Table 5, p. 63.

11. National League for Nursing, "Practical Nursing Schools and Their Students," *Nursing Outlook*, vol. 1 (January, 1953), p. 51.

12. U. S. Census of Population Report, "Detailed Characteristics of the Population," vol. 1, pt. 1 (Washington, D. C.: U. S. Government Printing Office, 1960).

13. "Nursing Training Act of 1964," *op. cit.*, p. xiv.

14. *Toward Quality in Nursing, op. cit.*, p. 47.

15. U. S. Department of Labor, *Technology and Manpower in the Health Service Industry, 1965-75*, Manpower Research Bulletin No. 14 (Washington, D. C.: U. S. Government Printing Office, May, 1967), pp. 16-18.

16. American Nurses' Association, "Spot Check of Current Hospital Nursing Employment Conditions, June, 1961," mimeographed (New York: American Nurses' Association, 1961).

17. *Toward Quality in Nursing, op. cit.*, p. 18.

18. "Nursing Training Act of 1964," *op. cit.*, p. xvi.

19. U. S. Department of Labor, *Training in Service Occupations Under MDTA*, Manpower Research Bulletin No. 9 (Washington, D. C.: U. S. Government Printing Office, March, 1966).

20. U. S. Department of Labor, "Manpower Training Moves Forward," mimeographed (Washington, D. C., January, 1965).

21. *Technology and Manpower in the Health Service Industry, 1965-75, op. cit.*, pp. 73-74.

22. For a more detailed discussion of the duties of technicians and technologists see U. S. Department of Labor, *Health Careers Guidebook* (Washington, D. C.: U. S. Government Printing Office, 1965).

23. U. S. Department of Labor, "Definitions of Occupational Titles," *Dictionary of Occupational Titles, 1965*, vol. 2 (Washington, D. C.: U. S. Government Printing Office, 1965), p. 461.

24. *Technology and Manpower in the Health Service Industry, 1965-75, op. cit.*, p. 26.

25. Anna P. Fagelson, "Opportunities in Medical Technology," *Vocational Guidance Manuals* (New York: Vocational Guidance Manuals, Inc., 1961), p. 24.

26. Laura Street Jackson, "The Medical Technologist," *Vocational and Professional Monographs*, no. 100 (Cambridge, Mass., 1958) pp. 13-16.

27. Fagelson, *op. cit.*, p. 85.

28. *Ibid.*, p. 34.

29. *Health Careers Guidebook, op. cit.*, p. 165.

30. Fagelson, *op. cit.*, p. 35.

31. *Ibid.*, pp. 33-34.

32. *Ibid.*, pp. 33-39.

33. *Ibid.*, p. 39.

34. *Health Careers Guidebook, op. cit.*, p. 165.

35. *Technology and Manpower in the Health Service Industry, 1965-75, op. cit.*, p. 24.

36. *Ibid.*, pp. 73-74.

37. Walter M. Harting and George W. Brush, Jr., *How to Choose Your Technical Institute* (Cambridge, Mass.: Bellman Publishing Company, 1960), p. 5.

38. Ralph J. Smith, *Engineering as a Career,* (New York: McGraw-Hill, 1956), p. 118.

39. Social Research Associates, Inc., *Jobs in Technical Work* (Chicago: Social Research Associates, Inc.), p. 7.

40. Bureau of Labor Statistics, *Occupational Outlook Handbook,* 1966-67 ed., Bulletin No. 1450, U. S. Department of Labor (Washington, D. C.: U. S. Government Printing Office), p. 220.

41. *Ibid.*, p. 221.

42. See *Ibid.*, p. 223.

43. Social Research Associates, Inc., *op. cit.*, p. 25.

44. *Occupational Outlook Handbook, op. cit.*, p. 456.

45. Bureau of Labor Statistics, *Technician Manpower: Requirements, Resources, and Training Needs,* Bulletin No. 1512, U. S. Department of Labor (Washington, D. C.: U. S. Government Printing Office, June, 1966), p. 25.

46. *Ibid.*, pp. 36-37.

47. *Ibid.*, p. 41.

48. *Ibid.*, p. 38.

49. *Ibid.*, p. 35.

50. *Ibid.*

51. *Ibid.*, p. 42.

52. *Ibid.*, p. 34.

53. *Occupational Outlook Handbook, op. cit.*, p. 224.

54. Bureau of Labor Statistics, *National Survey of Professional, Administrative, Technical, and Clerical Pay, February-March, 1965,* Bulletin No. 1469, U. S. Department of Labor (Washington, D. C.: U. S. Government Printing Office, October, 1965); and *National Survey of Professional, Administrative, Technical, and Clerical Pay, February-March, 1966,* Bulletin No. 1535, U. S. Department of Labor (Washington, D. C.: U. S. Government Printing Office, October, 1966).

55. Quoted in John Brademas, "New Frontiers in Technical Education," *Technical Education News,* vol. 22, no. 1, Special Issue (1962), p. 4.

56. National Science Foundation, *Scientists, Engineers and Technicians in the 1960's: Requirements and Supply* (Washington, D. C.: U. S. Government Printing Office, 1964), p. 31.

57. "Technical Manpower in New York State," vol. 1, New York State Department of Labor, Division of Research and Statistics (December, 1964), p. 9.

58. *Technician Manpower: Requirements, Resources, and Training Needs, op. cit.*, see Appendix F, Tables 4-6 for details of the projections.

59. Herman P. Miller, "Education: An Advantage for a Lifetime," *Occupational Outlook Quarterly,* vol. 7, no. 4 (December, 1963).

60. *Occupational Outlook Handbook, op. cit.*, p. 457.

61. *Ibid.*, p. 458.

62. *Ibid.*, p. 456.

63. U. S. Department of Labor, *Career Guide for Demand Occupations*, 1964, p. 24 (cited in William Edward Tholke, "A Pre-Apprentice Program Under the Manpower Development and Training Act," M. A. thesis, University of Illinois, 1966), p. 54.

64. *Occupational Outlook Handbook, op. cit.*, pp. 456-457.

65. Bureau of Apprenticeship and Training, *Apprenticeship and Training in the Contract Tool and Die Industry*, Bulletin T-150, U. S. Department of Labor, (Washington, D. C.: U. S. Government Printing Office, November, 1959), pp. 1-3.

66. U. S. Department of Labor, *1966 Report of the Secretary of Labor on Manpower Research and Training Under the Manpower Development and Training Act of 1962* (Washington, D. C.: U. S. Government Printing Office), pp. 24-26; and "Machine Tool and Tool and Die Industries Expand," *Employment Service Review* (September, 1966), p. 63.

67. *American Machinist/Metalworking Manufacturing* (June 6, 1966), p. 131.

68. "Machine Tool and Tool and Die Industries Expand," *op. cit.*, p. 63.

69. *Ibid.*

70. *Ibid.*

71. *Apprenticeship and Training in the Contract Tool and Die Industry, op. cit.*, p. 1.

72. "More Jobs Than Skills," *Steel*, vol. 151 August 27, 1962, p. 26 (cited in Tholke, *op. cit.*), pp. 43-44.

73. *Ibid.*, p. 44.

74. *Occupational Outlook Handbook, op. cit.*, p. 457.

75. Corplan Associates, *Technological Change – Its Impact on Industry in Metropolitan Chicago – The Metalworking Industries* (Illinois Institute of Technology Research Institute, 1964), p. 49.

76. Bureau of Labor Statistics, *Outlook for Numerical Control of Machine Tools*, Bulletin No. 1437, U. S. Department of Labor (Washington, D. C.: U. S. Government Printing Office, March, 1965), p. 40.

Chapter 4
Factors Affecting Supply:
Information, Counseling, Guidance and Recruitment

1. See, for example, Eli Ginzberg, *The Development of Human Resources*, (New York: McGraw-Hill, 1966), p. 47.

Chapter 5
Factors Affecting Supply:
Training and Placement

1. See *Approved Schools of Medical Technology* of the Council on Medical Education, revised to June 30, 1964.

Chapter 6
Factors Affecting Supply:
Internal Adjustments and Employee Benefits

1. Reported in St. Louis Post-Dispatch, February 27, 1967.

Chapter 7
Extent of the Shortage

1. Bureau of Labor Statistics, *Industry Wage Survey, Machinery Manufacturing, April-June 1965,* Bulletin No. 1476, U. S. Department of Labor (Washington, D. C.: U. S. Government Printing Office, February, 1966), p. 10.
2. See William Tholke, *A Pre-Apprentice Program Under the Manpower Development and Training Act* (M. A. thesis, University of Illinois, 1966).

Chapter 8
Factors Affecting Supply:
Information, Counseling and Guidance

1. See F. Ray Marshall and Vernon M. Briggs, Jr., *The Negro and Apprenticeship* (Baltimore: The Johns Hopkins Press, 1967), esp. pp. 27-45.

Chapter 10
Factors Affecting Supply:
Internal Adjustments and Employee Benefits

1. See Corplan Associates, *op. cit.;* U. S. Department of Labor Statistics, *Outlook for Numerical Control of Machine Tools,* Bulletin No. 1437 (Washington, D. C.: U. S. Government Printing Office, March, 1965); also U. S. Department of Labor, *Technology and Manpower in Design and Drafting, 1965-75,* Manpower Research Bulletin No. 12 (Washington, D. C.: U. S. Government Printing Office, October, 1966).

Chapter 11
Summary and Conclusions

1. *Labor Market Information and the Federal-State Employment System*, report by the Advisory Committee on Research to the U. S. Employment Service (Washington, D. C.: U. S. Government Printing Office, February, 1968).

Index

Accreditation – licensed practical nursing schools, 15-16; medical technologists, 24-27; relation to quality and quantity of labor, 294, 298
Adjustments to shortages, 6-7, 69-71, 134-36, 176, 291-93; job redesign, 136-41, 264, 271, 276, 296, 306-7; technological change, 44-45, 276-77, 297, 306; hiring and training, 264-65, 271; and quality of service, 277-78, 298, 306; part-time work, 21, 28, 276, 307; overtime, 265, 277, 278, 285; contracting-out, 265, 277, 278 summary of, 297-99
Age, 16, 54-55, 97, 177, 200; *see also* Older workers
American Board of Pathology, 24
American Hospital Association, 27
American Medical Association, 24, 26, 28
American Nurses Association, 21; and right to strike, 22
American Society of Medical Technologists, 25
Apprenticeship (pre-apprenticeship) – qualifications, 41; for nonwhites, 177; as training, 244; formal programs, 235-36; earnings, 240; subsidization for, 240; MTDA program, 241, 302, 303; worker evaluation of, 245; as entry route, 294-95
Armed Forces training, 32, 33-35
Arrow, Kenneth, 4

Balkanization (Feudalization), 35, 294
Blacks; *see* Nonwhites
Blank, David, 3, 5
Board of Laboratory Assistants, 25

Capron, William, 4
Cartelization, 64, 294
Certification – licensed practical nurses, 15-16; medical technologists, 24-27; adjustment to shortage and, 298
Certified laboratory assistant (CLA), 25, 135
Chicago Tool and Die Institute (TDI), 41, 42
Collective bargaining agreements, 22, 145, 285, 299
College training – for medical technologists, 26-27, 87, 98, 111, 134, 293; for technicians, 32, 35, 187, 225, 238-39, 251; overemphasis on, 295, 301; coordination with hospital programs, 303
Computer technology, 277, 297
Counseling – on job opportunities, 72-73; in high schools, 82-83; need for improvement in, 84-86, 186-87; placement and, 194; conclusions about, 300-1
Crytotechnologist (CT), 25

Discrimination, 6 *see also* Nonwhites
Dropouts, 17, 122-23, 130, 217, 225, 242, 244, 262-63

Educational qualifications – for licensed practical nurses, 14; for medical technologists,26-27, 133-34; for tool and die trades, 40-41, 182, 251; minimum for LPN's, MT's, 86-87, 97-98, 264; of nonwhites, LPN's, MT's, 97; dropouts and, 122; employer views of, 133; of technicians, 238; relation to completion of industrial training, 244; upgrading of, 278; adjustment to shortages and, 294 298
Employee benefits, 21, 28, 144-45, 278-79, 285, 306
Employer views – on medical occupations market, 53-54, 64, 68, 102; on entry requirements, medical occupations, 133; on industrial occupations market, 151, 155, 161; on company training programs, 233-34, 245; on training schools, 250
Employment trends, 17, 21, 27, 36-37, 42, 43-45, 49-53, 150-51
Engineering technician, *defined* 29-30
Engineering technician – electronics, *defined* 30; working, *defined* 30
Entry to occupations – patterns of, 31-33; recruitment and, 98, 125; for technicians, 194; lack of single route for, 207, 213, 294; advantage of diverse routes, 295; for nonwhites, 6, 291-92; for medical occupations, 291-93; summary of, 300-2

Fair Labor Standards Act, 22

Hiring standards, 86-87, 97-98, 132, 196-201, 213, 264-66, 271, 292
Hours of work, 21, 22, 27-29, 40

Illinois Hospital Association, 22
Information on jobs, 72-73, 82-86, 128-29, 186-87, 194, 206, 207, 300

Job vacancies, 51-53, 155, 161, 182, 204
Junior colleges, 32, 35, 133, 215-16, 242, 244, 296, 302, 303

Kerr, Clark, 294

Labor-management relations, 285
Labor markets studied, 8-9
Labor shortage concepts – Arrow and Capron "dynamic shortage," 4-6, 7, 10, 289-90, 294; Blank and Stigler, 3-5
Licensed practical nurse (LPN), *defined* 14; occupational characteristics, 14-15, training and licensing, 15-17; employment trends, 17, 21; wages, hours, working conditions, 21-22; demand and supply, 22-24

Manpower Development Training Act, 3; training programs, 23, 35, 41, 135, 240-42, 297, 303
Medical technologist, *defined* 24-25; occupational characteristics, 24-26; education and training, 26-27; employment trends, 27; salaries, hours, working conditions, 27-29; demand and supply, 29
Metalworking industry, 45
Minority groups; *see* Nonwhites
Mobility, 58, 162-63, 305

National Association for Practical Nurse Education, 15
National Labor Relations Act, 22
National League for Nursing Education, 17
National Science Foundation, 39
Negroes; *see* Nonwhites
Nonwhites, 6, 17, 64, 71, 95, 112, 114, 177, 184, 204, 213, 246-47, 265, 291-92, 293, 295, 299, 302, 304
Nuclear Medical technologist (NMT), 25
Nurse supply, 15-17, 22-23

Occupational Outlook Handbook, 43
Occupations studied, *defined* 9-10
Older workers, 97, 177, 200; *see also* Women, Worker characteristics
On-the-job training, 32-33, 35, 41, 135, 204, 213, 225, 233, 234-35, 236-37, 238, 240, 253, 265, 271, 278, 294, 296, 302, 303

Placement, 127-28, 130-31, 162-63, 253, 262, 304-5

Recruitment – for hospitals, 99, 101-2; size of hospitals and, 99; techniques in, 103-4, 106-8; for training schools, 102, 161-62; employer views on, 101-2; worker views on, 104-6; employer efforts and, 201-6; by training schools, 206-7

Shortage *see also* Adjustments to shortages – *defined* 7-8, 49-51; severity of, 51-53, 70-71, 149-51, 155, 161, 289-97; employer views on, 53, 151; worker views on, 54, 59; and pay levels, 59, 64-65, 68-69, 163, 175-76; other evidence of, 69-71, 161-63; policy implications, 299-300
Skilled craftsman, 31
Steel, 42
Stigler, George, 3, 5
Straub, George, 42
Surveys on shortages – Illinois Hospital Association, 22; U. S. Employment Service, 23-24, 42; U. S. Department of Labor, 26, 29, 39-40; American Hospital Association, 27; American Medical Association, 28; New York State Department of Labor, 39; National National Science Foundation, 39; Bureau of Apprenticeship and Training, 41

Technical Education Bill, 39
Technicians – "technological team," 30-31; education, 31-36; patterns of entry, 31-36; wages, 36; employment trends, 36-37; demand and supply, 37, 39; employer views about shortages of, 151, 155; training school directors views about, 161-62
"Technological team," 29-31
Tool and Die Institute, 215, 234-35
Tool and die makers – *defined* 31; earnings, hours, working conditions, 39-40; training, 40-41; employment trends, 42; demand and supply, 42-45
Tool designers, defined, 31
Toward Quality in Nursing, 15
Training, 14-17, 26-27, 31-36, 40-41 (*see also* Training schools); cost and financing of, 239-41, 296, 300, 302-3; need for expansion of, 293; subsidization for, 240-42, 300, 302, 303
Training schools – recruitment for, 102, 301, 302-3; types of, 110-12, 214-17;

need for more, 112-15; cost and financing of, 115-19, 239-42; worker views on, 121-27; capacity of, 238-39; evaluation of, 244-51; skilled trade schools, 214-16, 242, 251; technical schools, 32, 33, 186-87, 216, 242, 251; correspondence schools, 216-17, 253, 262; standard programs, 224; background of trainees, 224-25
Turnover, 26, 53-54, 234, 305

Unemployment rates, 9
Unions, 40, 285
United States Bureau of Labor Statistics, 36, 39
United States Department of Labor, 26, 29, 40, 42
United States Employment Service, 23-24, 42, 300
United States Manpower Administration, 29
Upgrading, 32, 35, 141, 294-95, 301

Vocational-technical schools, 32, 33, 294

Wage rate adjustments, key role in shortage solutions, 5-6
Wages, 21-22, 27-29, 36, 39-40, 59, 64, 65, 68-69, 70, 84, 98, 144-47, 163, 175-76, 182-84, 278, 285, 290-91, 292, 298-99, 301-2
Wirtz, W. Willard, 39
Women workers, 16, 26, 36, 64, 65, 71, 95, 96-97, 98, 146, 182, 292, 301, 307
Worker characteristics, 177, 200-1
Worker views – access to jobs, mobility, 58; training, 58-59, 125-27; wages, 68-69; role of recruitment, 104; choice of employers, 105-6; placement, 128-30, 162-63; job redesign, 141, 271, 276; likes and dislikes on job, 145-46, 276; information and counseling, 186-87, 194; training schools, 206-7, 245
Working conditions, 21-22, 306-7 (*see also* Employee benefits)